FALCONRY
A GUIDE FOR BEGINNERS

Stuart Rossell and Black Musket

FALCONRY

A GUIDE FOR BEGINNERS

STUART E. ROSSELL

WESTERN SPORTING
SHERIDAN, WYOMING, USA

Text by
Stuart E. Rossell

Editing by
Brandy Collett
Abigail Duvall
Jessica Larson
Alistair McEwan
Alicia Pickett-Hale

Layout and Design by
David Frank
Western Sporting

Art Drawings
Nathan Birr
Western Sporting

Photographs
Stuart and Debbie Rossell
(Unless otherwise noted.)

© Text 2020 Stuart E. Rossell
1st Edition

Published by:
Western Sporting
Sheridan, Wyoming, U.S.A.
www.westernsporting.com
sales@westernsporting.com

All rights reserved. No part of this book may by reproduced
or transmitted in any form or by any means, electronic
or mechanical, including photocopying, recording or by any information
storage and retrieval system without written permission from the
publisher, except by a reviewer who may quote brief passages
or reproduce illustrations in a review.

Printed in the United States of America

ISBN 978-1-888357-04-2

Dedication

To my wife Debbie, for her support and encouragement while writing this book.

Contents

Acknowledgements 14

Preface 15

Author's Foreword 17

Chapter 1   Introduction to Falconry 23
                Language of Falconry
                Table 1: Hawks of Falconry
                Table 2: Nomenclature of Hawks
                Glossary

Chapter 2   The Hawks of Falconry 40
                Longwings
                Shortwings
                Broadwings
                Eagles

Chapter 3   Equipment and Housing for the Hawk 65
                The Mews and Weathering
                Equipment and Furniture
                      Jesses
                      Swivels
                      Leashes
                      Tethering
                      Bells

    Telemetry
    Hoods
    Perches
    Bath Pans
    Transport Box & Cadges
    Scales
    Gloves
    Lure and Lure Lines
    Creance
    Lure Machine
    Hawking Bags and Vests

Chapter 4 Trapping 120
    Types of Traps
     Bow Net
     Bal-chatri
     Pigeon Harness
     Noose Carpet
     Winding Up
     Cage Traps
     Dho-ghazza
     Phai Trap
    Bait
    Trapping Tactics
    Road Trapping

Chapter 5	The Basics of Training a Hawk 149
	Flying Weight
	Finding the Flying Weight
	Diet
Chapter 6	Training the Red-tailed Hawk 177
	Overall Goals
	From The Beginning
	As Training Progresses
	The Next Stage
	Using the Creance
	Summary of the Daily Routine
Chapter 7	Advanced Training 215
	Flying Free and Following On
	Dummy Lure
	Lure Machine
	Fitness Work
Chapter 8	Hawking 227
Chapter 9	The Harris' Hawk 243
Chapter 10	Wrapping Up 253
	Daily and Weekly Routines
	Field Etiquette
	Recovering Lost Hawks
	The Future
Apendices	Suggested Reading 264

Acknowledgements

To those who proof read the book and offered many suggestions, specifically, Alistair McEwan, Mark and Normajean Albright, Alicia Pickett-Hale, Chris Tocco, Steve Arndt, Rick and Judy West, Abigail Duvall, Brandy Collett, and Jessica Larson. To Debbie Rossell for help with the photographs. Thanks to Scott McNeff for a well-considered Preface. To David Frank of Western Sporting for his support and encouragement. To Nathan Birr for his drawings. To all these people and any others I may have inadvertently missed, my sincere thanks and appreciation are due.

Preface

Becoming a falconer in America requires undertaking a lengthy apprenticeship; a process that, on paper covers a minimum of two years, but in practice, is often a much lengthier commitment. In many arenas, a common philosophy is that "It takes a tribe…." In the falconry community, however, it is most often suggested that an apprentice tune out all outside influences and solely follow the advice of the sponsor. In all but the most unique sponsor/apprentice relationships it can be extremely beneficial to indulge in a secondary source of information, beyond the sponsor. Let Stuart Rossell be that secondary source of information.

With this book and video combination, Mr. Rossell has put together much more than an introductory guide to the hunting art and cultural heritage of falconry. This work represents a wealth of sage advice from an extremely fastidious author who has devoted a lifetime to mindful, daily management of multiple raptors of a variety of species. He has treated the practice of falconry as a lifelong adventure in learning. His perspective is unique in that way, and consequently, his advice is excellent and attention to detail—persnickety—in just the right way! Exacting, authentic instruction is just what the doctor ordered when you're taking on the responsibility of training your first hawk.

Stuart has an uncommon ability to point out nuances without getting lost in minutiae. For example, in the film portion of this compendium, his narration points out some of the finer details of interpreting the emotional landscape of a hawk while he takes us along with him for the very direct and uncomplicated manning and training process of a new passage Red-tailed Hawk. The process that he outlines in the training of "Mariah" (the hawk in question) is a very kind, gentle, and deliberate one, and seeing it play out on film is very tangible proof that if you adhere to Stuart's suggestions and follow the excellent goals that are outlined in the text, you will succeed in producing a successful hunting partner that is well mannered and in good health. What more could a falconer want from a relationship with a hawk?

In short, I wish I'd had access to this book back when I was training my first Red-tailed Hawk 25 years ago. I was lucky to have had a very good sponsor for my apprenticeship years, but I have no doubt that if I'd also had this book on my bedside table, I would have experienced an even greater margin of success at an earlier period of my development as a young falconer. I'll take this a step further, by stating that there are a great many practicing falconers who have been flying hawks for many years that will take away numerous lessons from what our author has presented in this fine work. Our community owes Mr. Rossell a debt of gratitude for investing the time that was required to create this delightful compilation. Many of us have wished for, or aspired to write, a guide such as this. On behalf of all of us, I'd like to thank him here.

With this combination book and video, Mr. Rossell has provided aspiring apprentices of the future a very valuable resource that will ensure success and greater enjoyment during their early years of practicing the art of falconry. This will be required reading for any apprentice that I take under my proverbial "wing" from this point on.

Scott McNeff - 2019
President, North American Falconers Association

Foreword

Falconry is the art of taking wild quarry in its natural state and habitat, using trained birds of prey. By its very nature, falconry involves the killing of other animals and I make no defense, for none is needed, for this fact. However, were the taking and killing of quarry, as the prey trained hawks catch is correctly called, the only reason for training and flying hawks I, and I think most of my colleagues, would never again fly a hawk. The taking of quarry is secondary to the simple pleasure of working with the raptors themselves.

Falconry is a very demanding hobby, not only of the falconer but also in many instances of his or her family. It requires dedication on the part of the falconer and often involves sacrificing time and resources that spouses especially would rather be spent on the family. Many falconers choose both their job and their location with falconry in mind. More so than any other sport, falconry is time consuming on a daily basis, for a trained hawk in flying condition, unlike other sporting implements such as bats, balls or even guns, cannot be left unattended or ignored for weeks or months on end and then be expected to perform up to the high standard that the falconer should expect. It is only the truly dedicated that continue in the sport for while many people will contemplate the idea and may even get to the point of getting a hawk of their own, to fly hawks at quarry year in and year out requires a degree of dedication that it is hard to imagine unless you have actually practiced the sport, or have come into contact with a practicing falconer. I am reminded while writing this, of a conversation between a concert pianist and an admirer who had just witnessed a top rate performance. The admirer said to the pianist "I'd give anything to be able to play like that," to which the pianist replied, "I gave 30 years of my life." Good falconers become such by dedication to their hawks and their sport and becoming a good falconer should at least be the aim of everyone coming into the sport for second rate falconry or glorified pet keeping is a travesty of what the sport can be.

Falconers hold the hawks they train in the highest regard. Not only that, but in most cases they also have very healthy respect for the quarry at which they fly their hawks. Few people who know anything about this sport can be ignorant of the efforts made by falconers to restore the Peregrine Falcon population of North America. Not so well known are the efforts by falconers to bring the Mauritius Kestrel back from the brink of extinction and ongoing work with other species of birds of prey around the world. Wherever efforts are made to help a species of bird of prey in the wild, you can be sure there are falconers in the mix and quite often at the forefront of those efforts. We are a caring breed with high standards and the practicing falconers of our time expect those coming into the sport to learn about and respect our history and ethics just as we should respect the history and ethics of those falconers that have gone before us. Be assured that we in the falconry community expect anyone coming into the sport to be willing to work to uphold our traditions, high ethics and standards and expect that you will not, knowingly, bring the sport into disrepute.

What then are the basic requirements from the new falconer looking to train his first hawk? The first requirement has nothing to do with hawks or falconry but rather is a requirement that anyone who hunts for a hobby must fulfill and that is having permission over land at which to fly the hawk at quarry. In many instances, while public land may be available, we rely on the goodwill of landowners for ground over which to fly our hawks. It is important that the falconer seeks and obtains permission to fly his hawk on private land. Uncaring falconers poaching on private land without permission have done much damage. Landowners are normally receptive to a polite approach to fly a trained hawk over their ground, even if they have posted it off limits to gun hunters, but where a falconer does not ask, he not only jeopardizes future access for himself but he taints the good name of other falconers in the area and those that come after him.

The two species of hawk most suitable for the beginner are the Red-tailed Hawk and the Harris' Hawk. Red-tailed Hawks are typically flown at rabbits, both jackrabbits and cottontails, and squirrels. Harris' Hawks will take, in addition to the above mentioned quarry, pheasants, ducks, coots and a variety of other birds. In addition to providing his hawk with regular opportunities to fly at the above-mentioned quarries, the falconer must provide his hawk with suitable accommodation to keep her healthy and in good condition. He must provide a suitable source of food, proper perches and other equipment for his hawks' comfort and well-being and to enable him to handle her. He must provide enough time on a daily and weekly basis to fly his hawk during the months of, at the outside, August through March. Falconry is primarily a fall and winter pastime. Ask yourself honestly, right now, "can I give a hawk sufficient time?" If the answer is "no," for the sake of your would-be hawk find some other way to enjoy falconry. I'm not saying don't participate, I'm just trying to discourage you from going down the road to disappointment for as one old falconer once said, "there is no finer sight than falconry properly done and nothing worse than the bad version."

To become a falconer in the United States, one needs to obtain a falconry permit. The Fish and Game department in your state will have the information needed to get started but at the minimum the beginner will need to pass a test and to have the place where he intends to keep his hawk, called the mews, and his basic falconry equipment inspected either by a representative of the Fish and Game department or, in some states, by the budding falconers' sponsor. A sponsor is a falconer who already has a falconry permit at the master or general level, and is the final requirement to obtaining an apprentice falconry permit. The new falconer will remain an apprentice for at least two years before being upgraded to general class as long as the sponsor approves. After five years as a general he may move up to a master class falconer. In some states this upgrade is automatic while in others it requires approval from the state agency that oversees falconry permits. Finding a good sponsor is possibly the most important step the beginner will take. Unfortunately, just because an individual has a general or master falconry permit, that does not automatically mean they will be a good sponsor, or even a good falconer. Take the time to attend local falconry meets, get to know other falconers in your area, talk to other apprentices and find out as much as you can before approaching a falconer to sponsor you. You will be entering into a fairly close relationship with this person and there has to be mutual trust from both sides. Many falconers are reluctant to sponsor someone until they know that the budding apprentice really is serious about taking up the sport and is not looking for just the next in a list of hobbies to spend a bit of time on before moving on to something else. In the ideal world you are looking for a sponsor with whom you get along, who has experience with Red-tailed Hawks and/or Harris' Hawks, and is a patient and good instructor. He or she will need to be willing to help you out as you design your mews, gather the equipment needed and hopefully, obtain your first hawk. If he or she lives close by and can supervise your efforts as you train your hawk so much the better. Such sponsors are few and far between but it is worth taking as much time in finding a decent sponsor as it is in finding a decent spouse.

 The best way to find a sponsor is to the make contact with the falconry club in your state, if such a club exists, and most states do now have their own clubs or associations. The new falconer should also make contact with, and join, the two national falconry clubs, the North American Falconers Association and the American Falconry Conservancy that have done so much to preserve and advance the sport. Not only will he help by adding to our numbers but he will also benefit by contact with other falconers through the clubs and by gleaning information from the journals and newsletters they publish.

 One might well wonder, with all the literature currently available, if another falconry book is really needed to which my reply would be, "probably not." But having flown hawks for over 40 years in both the United Kingdom and the United States of America and having taught falconry courses in both countries, I hope that I am not being overly arrogant in attempting to pass on some of what I have learned over the years, both from the hawks I've handled, the falconers it has been my privilege to know and the students

I've taught. While I have written this book with beginners in mind I have included things I've picked up along the way that I feel might also be of use to those who no longer consider themselves beginners.

While this book is intended primarily for the U.S. market, much of the information will be of use to falconers elsewhere. Readers in the U.S. may detect a slightly English feel to the book but having grown up in, and received my education in England before moving to the U.S. over 20 years ago, I hope that will not be an obstacle. Like most falconry books previously published I have referred to the falconer in the masculine throughout the book. This is merely for convenience sake and I trust will not offend the many fine female falconers already flying hawks as well as the increasingly large number taking up the sport. Likewise, when referring to a hawk I have used the time honored tradition of using the feminine and referring to her, out of respect, as 'she'.

Stuart E. Rossell - 2019
Palmyra, NY

Chapter One

An Introduction to Falconry

The Language of Falconry

Falconry is rich with unique terms, and each has its own specific meaning. It is important for the beginner to learn how to converse in the language of falconry so that confusion is avoided. The standard definition of "falconry" generally accepted by falconers around the World is "the taking of wild quarry in its natural state and habitat using trained birds of prey." Those who keep hawks, but do not take quarry with them, are not true falconers. "Quarry" is an animal we try to catch with a trained hawk. A person who practices falconry is a "falconer." There is no such thing as "falcontry," "falconing" or a "falconist," though all are terms I have heard. When we are trying to catch quarry with trained hawks, we are "hawking," not "hunting," which is something other folks do when they chase animals with dogs, guns, or bows and arrows. Falconers do not technically go hunting; we go hawking.

"Hawk" is a generic term given to all the birds of prey used in falconry. Thus, a Peregrine Falcon, American Kestrel, and even my African Hawk-Eagle pictured at the end of this chapter are all correctly referred to as "hawks" when they are used for falconry. We do not call them "birds" unless they are still in the wild. The hawks used for falconry are divided into three groups, the "longwings," "shortwings," and "broadwings."

It is customary in falconry books to provide a glossary of terms and one is included at the end of this chapter, but glossaries can be a bit dry to read. So here, we'll assume that you, the reader, and I have met for the first time and are having a discussion about falconry in general and about a particular hawk I am holding, my one time "intermewed, haggard, African Hawk-Eagle" whose name is Bella.

Falconry: A Guide for Beginners

To a knowledgeable falconer, this information I have just provided is enough to divulge Bella's sex, species, the age at which I got her, and how long I've had her.

The age at which any bird of prey begins its career as a trained hawk has a specific term given to it. This is the age when it is first captured or taken up for training. If the hawk is taken from the nest in the wild before it can fly, it is called an "eyass." The term will stay with it for the rest of its life as a trained hawk. If the same hawk is allowed to leave the nest, learn how to hunt for itself, and is then trapped while still in immature plumage, it is referred to as a "passager" or "passage hawk." Most passagers are trapped between the months of September and the following February, always in immature plumage. If the same hawk is allowed to remain in the wild, it will eventually molt into adult plumage, generally during the summer after it was born. The molt normally begins in April or May and ends in September or October depending on the species, and to some extent, the individual hawk. Were we to trap a hawk in adult plumage, as was the case with Bella, she would be referred to as a "haggard." It is illegal in the U.S. to possess haggards trapped here except in the case of the American Kestrel and the Great Horned Owl. In both these species, it is very difficult, if not impossible, to tell the age of a first-year bird by the plumage, the young and the adults both look the same. Because Bella was trapped in Africa, she does not fall foul of the law. Even though in the wild, a hawk naturally goes from being an eyass to a passager and then to a haggard, the moment a hawk comes into the hands of a falconer, its age determines the term by which it is known, either an eyass, a passager or a haggard, and the term will remain with the hawk all its life. Thus an eyass can be ten years old as a trained hawk, while the same bird in the wild would have become a haggard. When a hawk completes at least one molt in captivity, it is said to be "intermewed."

Prior to the 1960s, these descriptions were sufficient to describe the hawks of falconry, but about that time, falconers began breeding hawks in captivity in ever greater numbers. Today, the majority of hawks used in falconry are bred in captivity and are referred to as "captive bred." While most captive-bred hawks begin their training at roughly the same time an eyass would, there are differences significant enough that the term eyass does not apply, and so the distinction should always be made. Some falconers begin working with a hawk when it is very young, often only a day or so old. They raise the hawk around humans and expose it to lots of

Introduction to Falconry

activity so that the hawk grows up completely unafraid of humans and everything associated with them. Because they are denied access to their real parents, such hawks "imprint" on their human foster parent as a substitute. These hawks are correctly referred to as "imprints." Although the methods of raising them vary, the term "imprint" applies to any hawk raised by humans as opposed to being raised by either of its natural parents or another hawk acting as a foster parent.

It should now be clear that Bella was trapped from the wild in adult plumage and has molted at least once in captivity. But how would a knowledgeable falconer know she is a female? In birds of prey, the female of the species is always larger than the male, generally by about one third as much. As such, she is able to take larger quarry, thus historically the females have often been preferred for falconry. Although the males are perfectly capable of taking prey, they are often at a disadvantage where larger prey species are concerned. Thus, the female was preferred, and so when stating the species unqualified with the sex of any particular hawk, a falconer is confirming that the hawk in question is a female. So when I am referring to Bella as an "African Hawk-Eagle" I am implicitly stating, without mentioning the sex, that she is a female. Were I flying a male, I would refer to the hawk as a "male African Hawk-Eagle."

Several species of birds of prey most commonly flown throughout history have been given certain names to denote the males, and for one species, the female. Thus the term "tiercel" applies to the male Peregrine Falcon, while the term "falcon" applies to the female Peregrine Falcon. The term tiercel is used because tierce is a French term meaning one third, and the male Peregrine Falcon is one third smaller than the female. A "jerkin" is the male Gyrfalcon, a "lanneret" the male Lanner Falcon, a "sakret" the male Saker Falcon, a "jack" the male Merlin, and a "musket" the male Eurasian Sparrowhawk. Unfortunately, over the last thirty years or so, some of these classic terms for the different sexes have fallen into misuse as some falconers have started using the terms for the wrong applications. Some falconers wrongly apply the term "tiercel" to any male bird of prey. This is incorrect. The term "tiercel" on its own denotes a male Peregrine Falcon. Used with qualification, it can be applied to the male Northern Goshawk, the male Barbary Falcon, and the male Prairie Falcon (as in tiercel gos, tiercel barbary, tiercel prairie), but it should not be used for other species. Likewise, the term "falcon" is now commonly used to refer to all of the longwings. This is also incorrect. In the language of falconry, the term "falcon" only applies to a female Peregrine Falcon.

[25]

Falconry: A Guide for Beginners

Table 1

Species	Female Name	Male Name
Ferruginous Hawk	ferruginous	male ferruginous
Red-tailed Hawk	redtail	male redtail
Harris' Hawk	Harris'	male Harris'
Red-shoulder Hawk	red-shoulder	male red-shoulder
Northern Goshawk	gos	tiercel gos
Black Sparrowhawk	black spar	black musket
Cooper's Hawk	Cooper's	male Cooper's
Eurasian Sparrowhawk	spar	musket
Sharp-shinned Hawk	sharpie	male sharpie
Gyrfalcon	gyr	jerkin
Saker Falcon	saker	sakret
Peregrine Falcon	falcon	tiercel
Prairie Falcon	prairie	tiercel prairie
Lanner Falcon	lanner	lanneret
Barbary Falcon	barbary	tiercel barbary
Aplomado Falcon	alethe	terceleto
Merlin	merlin	jack
American Kestrel	kestrel	sparvette
Hobby	hobby	robin

Note: The hobby is a European species rarely used in falconry.
Non-indigenous species are becoming common in American Falconry.

Introduction to Falconry

Table 2

#	Species	Origin	Sex & Age	Correct Term
1	Merlin	captive bred	male, 4 years old	intermewed captive-bred jack
2	Merlin	captive bred	female, 4 years old	intermewed captive-bred merlin
3	Red-tailed Hawk	trapped from wild in immature plumage	male, first year	passage male redtail
4	Red-tailed Hawk	trapped from wild in immature plumage	female, first year	passage redtail
5	Saker Falcon	trapped from wild in adult plumage	male, age unknown, in captivity for 2 years	intermewed haggard sakret
6	Saker Falcon	trapped from wild in adult plumage	female, age unknown, in captivity for 2 years	intermewed haggard saker
7	Peregrine Falcon	taken from nest in the wild	male, 10 years old	intermewed eyass tiercel
8	Peregrine Falcon	taken from nest in the wild	female, 10 years old	intermewed eyass falcon

Note: It is not always necessary to refer to the number of times a hawk has been intermewed.

Falconry: A Guide for Beginners

On the previous page are listed eight hawks of different species obtained from different sources and at different ages. Hawks 1 and 2 are male and female captive bred Merlins, both four years old. Hawks 3 and 4 are male and female Red-tailed Hawks, both in immature plumage and trapped from the wild. Hawks 5 and 6 are male and female Saker Falcons trapped from the wild in adult plumage and have been in captivity for two years, and Hawks 7 and 8 are male and female Peregrine Falcons taken from the nest in the wild and have been flown for ten years. The chart shows the correct term that should be used for each of the eight hawks and shows how the age and sex of a particular hawk, where it came from and at what age it began its career as a trained hawk is easily disseminated between knowledgeable falconers.

By using the traditional terms in the same manner as they have been used for centuries, much confusion is avoided when discussing the hawks we train. It is unfortunate and to be regretted that the terms of falconry which were once so clearly understood, not only by falconers but also by many lay people have fallen into misuse. I make a plea here to everyone coming into the sport to learn the traditional meanings and stick to them.

You might now, in our hypothetical conversation, as is common practice for someone meeting a falconer for the first time, ask what the straps on Bella's legs are for. Falconers refer to these straps as "jesses." They are used to secure a hawk while it is on the gloved fist or a perch. There is one "jess" on each leg. We cannot use a leash around the hawk's neck as we would on a dog, for what are, hopefully, obvious reasons. When the hawk is not on the fist, it is normally tethered to a perch, not kept loose in an aviary or cage like finches or parrots. The hawk does not understand wire netting, and in excitement, might crash against it and break feathers. The falconer strives with every action to prevent feather damage to a hawk. Even though feathers can be repaired using a process called "imping," they are never as good as before they became damaged. Feathers are the tools a hawk uses to fly, and without a full set, it is not possible for a hawk to perform to its best. The two jesses are attached to a "swivel" to prevent them from twisting together. Through the other end of the swivel, a "leash," not a lead, is threaded. This leash is used as added security while the hawk is on the fist and is used to tie the hawk to the perch.

When a conscientious falconer ties a hawk to a perch, the hawk remains on the glove while the falconer ties a special knot called, not surprisingly, the falconer's knot. Only when the knot is tied will the hawk be placed on the perch and the hold on the jesses released. A falconer must take all precautions against a sudden "bate," the term

Introduction to Falconry

Bella, an intermewed, haggard African Hawk-Eagle.

given for the hawk's attempt to fly from the fist or perch. If a hawk were to escape with all its equipment trailing, it would soon get caught up, and if not retrieved, would die. There is often a leather "hood" hanging from the falconer's fist or from a vest or bag or perhaps the hawk itself is wearing it. This is the hawk's "hood," and it is placed on its head to calm it. In different periods of the hawk's life, the hood is worn for varying lengths of time. In the early stages, when the hawk is very afraid of its new surroundings, the hood helps keep it calm. Later on, as the hawk gets used to its new life, it will soon wear the hood less and less until, when fully trained, it is only worn to travel to and from the hawking grounds.

With this rudimentary introduction to the special language of falconry, we can move on, after a more complete glossary of terms, to the different types of hawks used in the sport.

Glossary

Note. These are terms as they should be used by falconers and not for bird watchers or other ornithologists.

Abba. An abba is a piece of cloth into which two pockets are sewn. The hawk's wings are put into the pockets, and the rest of the abba is wrapped around the hawk's body to safely secure it after trapping.

Accipiter. Any hawk of the genus *Accipiter*. Identified by their short rounded wings and proportionately long tail. This group is more generally and correctly known by falconers as shortwings.

Aspergillosis. Disease similar to miner's lung, in which fungal spores grow on the lungs and air sacs and often other areas. Most often the disease is fatal, but caught early, some of the new drugs have proven successful. Certain species, including Red-tailed Hawks, are susceptible to "Asper".

Austringer. Historically the name given to a falconer who flies only shortwings. It is not often used nowadays.

Aylmeris or Aylmeri jesses. Straps used to restrain raptors. Anklets are fitted around the hawk's tarsus and generally secured with a grommet. Through the grommet is fed a strap known as a mews jess for when the hawk has a swivel attached. For flying, a different strap called a flying jess or field jess is used. Alternatively, a hawk can be flown with only the anklets still on the legs and no jesses in the grommets. Traditionally made of leather, but in recent years nylon has been successfully used as a replacement for the jesses, while BioThane® has proved suitable for the anklets. The advantages of the latter two materials are strength and resistance to wear and stretch. This system replaces the older traditional jesses.

Bal-chatri or BC. A trap consisting of a wire cage. It is one of various shapes and is covered with nylon or plastic coated wire nooses. A bait animal is placed inside. When the hawk tries to get at the bait, one or more of its toes may become ensnared in one or more of the nooses. It is very suitable for trapping redtails.

Bate. When a tethered hawk tries to fly and is brought up short by its jesses and/or leash. A hawk can bate from either the fist or the perch.

Introduction to Falconry

Bechin. A small piece of food often referred to as a tidbit. Given as a reward to the hawk.

Bewit. A strap, normally made of leather but may also be made of BioThane®, used to secure the bell to the hawk's leg.

Bind. When a hawk catches and holds onto quarry.

Bird. From a falconer's perspective, raptors in the wild may be referred to as "birds," but once they are in the hands of a falconer, they correctly become "hawks."

Block perch. A perch with a circular flat top. Usually used for longwings though some other hawks also prefer them.

Bow perch. So called because it resembles an archer's bow stuck into the ground. Circular in cross section, it resembles the branch of a tree. Usually used for shortwings and broadwings, but many merlins and some other longwings seem to prefer them to the block perch.

Bow net. A trap consisting of one or two bows hinged at the end so that one bow moves through an arc of 180 degrees. Netting is attached to the bow(s). When set, the net lies under the bow that moves. Anything within the circumference of the bow will be caught when it is pulled over in an arc. Bow nets can be manually operated, released by remote control or fully automatic so that the hawk itself triggers the net when landing on the bait placed in the center of the net.

Braces. Straps, traditionally made of leather, but nowadays mostly of the nylon-type waterproof breathable fabrics which are used to open and close a hood.

Break in. The act of breaking through the flesh of a hawk's prey using the beak as the hawk first starts to eat.

Broadwing. A raptor that is neither a shortwing nor longwing. Generally belonging to one of the genera *Buteo, Parabuteo, Hieraaetus* or *Aquila*. A broadwing has broad, rounded wings, relatively short fan-shaped tails, and soaring flight.

Bumblefoot. Swelling in the foot or feet of a raptor caused by infection. It can be very serious if not treated in a timely manner by a competent vet.

Falconry: A Guide for Beginners

Cadge. Traditionally a square or rectangular frame on which several hawks, generally longwings, were transported in the field. A man, called a "cadger" stood in the center of the frame and the cadge was supported by straps going over his shoulders. In golf the term "caddie" is said to have come from this term. The term nowadays describes any perch used to transport a hawk in a vehicle.

Captive bred. A hawk that came from an egg laid by a female held in captivity. Captive breeding was first described hundreds of years ago, then apparently became a lost art. Renz Waller, a German falconer, bred Peregrine Falcons in captivity in Germany during the Second World War. Captive breeding was rediscovered in the 1960s in response to the decline of hawks in the wild and efforts by governments to restrict access to wild hawks. There are efforts by some to claim that because falconers can breed hawks in captivity, there is no need for them to take hawks from the wild. This philosophy should be challenged whenever it arises.

Carry. A hawk is said to carry when it tries to fly away with quarry it has caught or with the lure. Not a desirable trait and often the result of bad training by the falconer. A falconer is also said to "carry" a hawk when transporting it on the fist for taming purposes.

Cast. 1) The act of a hawk regurgitating a ball of fur or feathers, being the indigestible parts of the last meal. 2) The act of launching a hawk off the fist. 3) To hold or restrain a hawk by placing the hands around its shoulders and wings for putting on equipment, imping, or coping. 4) Two longwings being flown together.

Cere. The skin, often waxy looking, at the base of a hawk's upper mandible.

Cope. Trimming a hawk's beak and/or talons to reduce the length or sharpen them or reshape them for any other reason.

Crabbing. When two hawks try to grab each other out of aggression.

Creance. A light line, generally fifty yards in length, used to secure a hawk during training.

Deck feathers. The two center tail feathers of a hawk.

Introduction to Falconry

Dho-Ghazza. A trap consisting of a fine net suspended between two poles. The hawk gets entangled in the net as it tries to catch the bait animal placed behind the net.

Draw. To draw a hood is to close it.

Entering. Introducing a hawk to quarry. A hawk is only entered once to any particular type of quarry. Generally the falconer looks for a very easy opportunity for the hawk when entering it to ensure its success.

Eyass. 1) A young bird of prey in the nest. 2) A hawk taken from the nest for training. A trained hawk, originally taken from the nest for training, retains this title for its whole life.

Falcon. A female Peregrine Falcon. Often incorrectly used to describe any of the longwings or the female of any of the longwings.

Falconry. The art of taking wild quarry in its natural state and habitat using trained birds of prey.

Feed up. Feeding the hawk all of its daily rations at once, generally done at the end of the training session or when the hawk has made a kill.

Flying weight. The weight at which a hawk is in the correct condition to be flown at quarry. If flown overweight, it may refuse quarry or refuse to come back to the falconer. If flown underweight, it will be more susceptible to disease and may lack enthusiasm and energy for flying.

Flush. Not really a falconry term, but falconers use it a lot. To flush quarry is to make it fly or run so that the trained hawk has a chance of catching it.

Foot. When a hawk uses its foot to catch hold of something, it is said to "foot" its catch.

Free lofted. A recent term used to describe the action of allowing a hawk to remain loose in the mews, as opposed to being tethered to a perch.

Fully summed. A hawk is said to be "fully summed" when all the feathers have finished growing following the molt.

Falconry: A Guide for Beginners

Game. An English term, which technically refers only to game birds such as grouse, pheasant, partridge and quail. Often nowadays misused when the term quarry is more appropriate. See Quarry.

Game hawk. A longwinged hawk trained to wait on and flown at game birds such as grouse, pheasants, partridges or ducks.

Game hawking. Flying a longwing at game birds. The term is often incorrectly used to describe the flying of any type of hawk at quarry when the correct term for such a practice is "hawking."

Hack. A period of liberty for a young hawk to learn how to fly, use the wind, and practice other skills. Eyass hawks and chamber-raised or parent-raised hawks may be "hacked" whereas imprints are "tame hacked." The term "wild hack" has recently been coined to describe the former, but this is incorrect as the term "hack" already applies to the situation.

Haggard. A hawk trapped from the wild in adult plumage. Native raptors, with the exception of the American Kestrel and the Great Horned Owl may not be used for falconry in the United States when taken as haggards.

Hard penned. A young hawk is said to be "hard penned" when all its feathers have finished growing. The term only applies to first-year feather growth.

Hawk. A generic term covering all the species of birds of prey when used in falconry. When talking generically of trained birds of prey, a falconer should correctly refer to them as "hawks," not birds. For instance, even if referring to a female Peregrine Falcon, which individually is correctly called a "falcon," a falconer can say "I'm going to check on the hawk." It is not correct to say "I'm going to check on the bird." If a falconer has more than one hawk, even if all of them are raptors to which other names such as "falcons" or "tiercels" apply, it is still correct to say "I am going to check on the hawks."

Hawking. To go hawking is to take a trained bird of prey out to fly it at quarry.

Hood. A leather cap, which covers the hawk's head including its eyes so that it cannot see, thus having a calming effect.

Introduction to Falconry

Hood shy. A hawk is said to be hood shy when, generally because of bad training, it refuses to take the hood either by dodging the head repeatedly or bating off the fist to prevent being hooded. A hood shy hawk is an embarrassment to any falconer.

Imping. Repairing broken feathers.

Imprint. A hawk raised away from its parents. As it grows up, it does not recognize others of the same species. It may treat the falconer as its parent.

Intermewed. A hawk is said to be intermewed when it has completed at least one molt in captivity.

Jack. A male Merlin. The term 'jack merlin' is incorrect.

Jerkin. A male Gyrfalcon.

Jesses. Straps placed around the hawk's legs to restrain it.

Leash. A long strap up to four feet or more, usually made of strong synthetic material, but traditionally of leather, used to secure the hawk to its perch. The leash runs through the swivel which is attached to the jesses.

Longwing. Any raptor of the genus *Falco*, which is characterized by long pointed wings and a relatively short tail, dark eyes, malar (or moustachial) stripe and a tooth on either side of the upper mandible.

Lure. 1) A "recall lure" may be any object that the hawk has been taught to associate with food. 2) A "dummy lure" is an object made to resemble a type of quarry that the falconer wishes the hawk to chase.

Made. A hawk is said to be "made" when there is no doubt that it will fly a particular quarry. It generally requires at least ten kills. For instance, a hawk is said to be "made" to rabbits when it will chase them without hesitation.

Make in. A falconer makes in to a hawk when he carefully approaches her on the lure or quarry.

Manning. The act, or process, of taming a hawk as opposed to training it. A well-manned hawk fears nothing associated with its life as a trained hawk.

Falconry: A Guide for Beginners

Mews. A name traditionally applied to the building where hawks were kept when molting. Now applied to any building used to house a trained hawk at any period of its life.

Molt. The process whereby a hawk replaces its feathers. Generally the molt occurs once each year beginning in the spring and lasting an average of six months.

Musket. A male Eurasian Sparrowhawk. Used with qualification, as in a "black musket" to refer to the male Black Sparrowhawk. Sometimes incorrectly used for the male Sharp-shinned Hawk.

Mutes. The droppings of a hawk. In a singular form it is used to describe the action of producing them. When it defecates, a longwing mutes, whereas a shortwing or broadwing slices.

Passager, Passage Hawk. A raptor trapped from the wild after it has left the nest and become independent of its parents, but has not yet molted.

Pigeon Harness. A trap consisting of a jacket, generally of leather, covered by nooses and worn by a pigeon. When the hawk attacks the pigeon, more often than not, it will get one or more of its toes caught in the nooses.

Pitch. The height at which a hawk, generally a longwing, waits on.

Plumage. The feathers of a hawk. A hawk kept in perfect plumage throughout its life should be the goal of every falconer. A hawk in bad plumage, perhaps with broken or worn feathers, might mean a falconer's equipment, housing or handling of the hawk need attention.

Quarry. The animals that trained birds of prey are taught to chase. Sometimes incorrectly called "game" when the latter term correctly applies only to game birds such as grouse, pheasant, partridges or quail.

Raptor. Another term for a bird of prey. A typical raptor is characterized by excellent eyesight, strong feet and talons for killing prey, and a strong beak for dismantling the prey.

Introduction to Falconry

Ring perch. A perch circular in circumference and shaped in a ring, used for shortwings and broadwings. Not as useful as the bow perch and not recommended by the author.

Ringing up. A hawk's flight that circles ever higher.

Rouse. The act of a hawk puffing out all its feathers and shaking them.

Screen perch. A long piece of wood under which hangs carpet or some other material. The hawk is tethered to the top of the perch so that it can only move the length of its jesses. If the hawk bates off, it uses the carpet to climb back up to the top of the perch.

Screamer. A hawk is said to be a screamer when it gives the same cry that was used to beg food from its parents. In the wild, after becoming independent, hawks give up this practice, but a badly trained hawk can develop into a screamer if it learns to treat the falconer as its parent.

Sharp set. A hawk is said to be sharp set when she is hungry and in good flying condition. Falconers also use the term 'keen' to describe the same thing.

Shortwing. Any raptor of the genus *Accipiter*, typically characterized by short rounded wings and long tail.

Slip. A chance for a hawk to chase quarry. It is the falconer's responsibility to provide the hawk with regular slips at quarry. A good slip will result in a decent opportunity to take quarry, while a bad slip is the opposite and may result in a miss or even a lost hawk. A hawk is "slipped" at quarry when released to chase it.

Stoop. The headfirst downward plunge of a bird of prey from high in the air.

Strike. To strike a hood is to open it.

Take up. To begin the training process of a bird of prey.

Tiercel. A male Peregrine Falcon. With qualification, the term may be used with the male Northern Goshawk, male Barbary Falcon or the male Prairie Falcon as in tiercel gos, tiercel barbary or tiercel prairie. Often incorrectly used to refer to any male bird of prey.

Falconry: A Guide for Beginners

Tidbit. A small piece of food offered to a hawk. See Bechin.

Tiring. A tough piece of food used to prolong the hawk's meal, thus facilitating manning.

Train. A hawk's tail. The train on a bride's wedding dress is said to be named after this.

Waiting on. A hawk, generally a longwing but sometimes a broadwing, is said to "wait on" when it climbs above the falconer and waits, high in the air, for the falconer to flush quarry for it.

Weather. A hawk is said to weather when placed on a perch outside to enjoy the weather.

Weathering Area. A weathering area is any area of ground where hawks are put out to weather and which may or may not be enclosed. A weathering enclosure is an area where a hawk may sit outside protected from other animals and the elements by an enclosure.

Wind up. The term given to circling a hawk with the creance or other length of line, thereby entrapping its legs.

Yarak. A state of physical and mental preparedness that a shortwing is said to be in when it is ready to fly keenly at quarry.

Introduction to Falconry

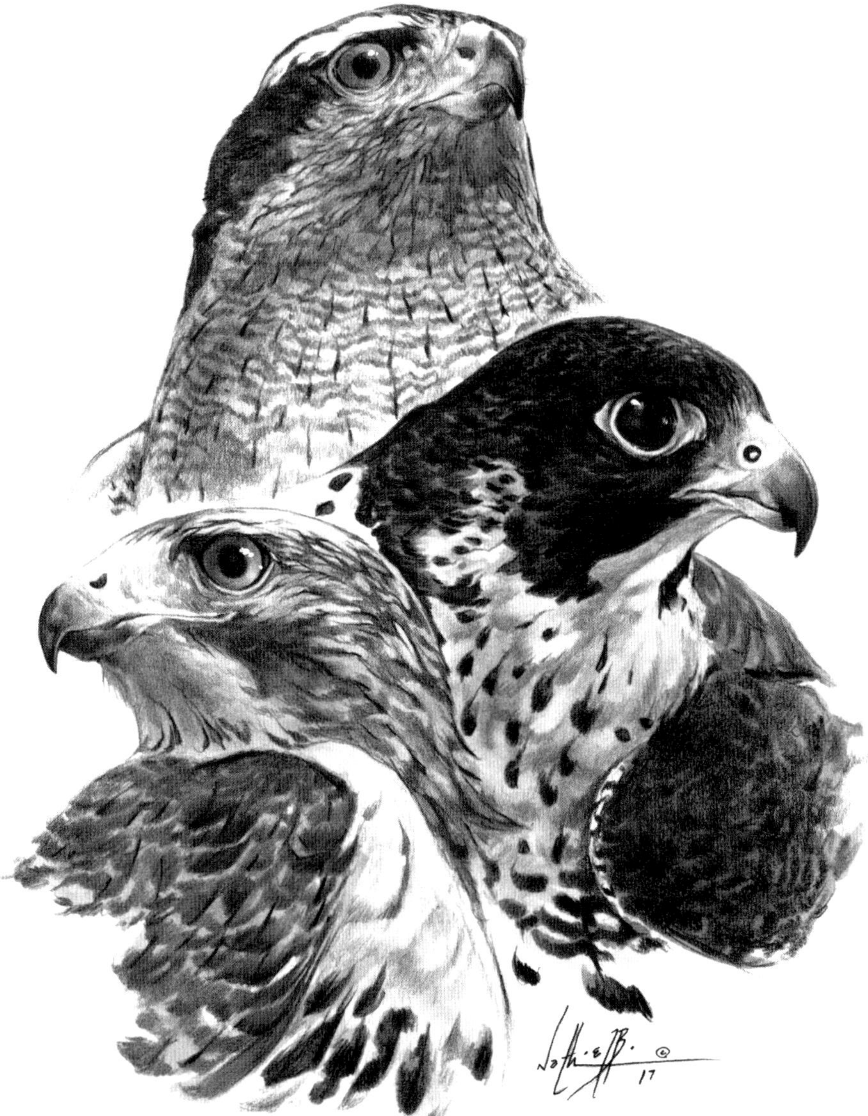

Chapter Two

The Hawks of Falconry

The birds of prey commonly used for falconry are divided into three groups: longwings, shortwings, and broadwings. All are correctly called hawks, it being a generic term. The three groups have evolved to occupy different niches in the wild. They hunt in different ways and in different habitats, and they pursue different prey. While there is much overlap among the three groups, it is important for the budding falconer to realize it is not possible to make a particular species of hawk do things that it has not evolved to do in the wild.

> Hawk. A generic term covering all the birds of prey used in falconry. When still in the wild, it is permissible to refer to hawks as birds, but once training has started they should only be referred to as hawks.

For a falconer's first hawk, I recommend one of two broadwings; my first choice would be a passage Red-tailed Hawk and only if that is not available, a Harris' Hawk that is either a passager or captive bred. The Red-tailed Hawk is a fairly common, relatively easily obtained and trained hawk. As such, it is a good choice for the newcomer with no experience. Passage hawks are trapped from the wild in immature plumage, generally between the months of September and February. They have learned how to hunt for themselves and are independent of their parents. For someone new to the sport of falconry, having a hawk that already knows how to kill for itself is a distinct advantage; it is at this stage in training a bird of prey that many beginners run into trouble, especially those who have no other experience in hunting of any kind. As a cautionary note however, I do not advise a beginner to try his or her hand at either eyass or captive-bred redtails. Such hawks require a degree of skill in training and handling that most beginners don't have. If not trained and entered correctly, eyass or captive-bred redtails can rapidly become vocal or aggressive to the trainer. Once these traits manifest themselves, they are extremely difficult to cure.

Falconry: A Guide for Beginners

Where passage redtails are not available, the Harris' Hawk is the most suitable species for a beginner.

The Harris' Hawk is one of the most popular species flown in falconry. Because of their gregarious nature in the wild, they quickly learn to appreciate the efforts of the falconer in helping them obtain food and because of this, and their relatively easy going nature, their willingness and ability to take a wide variety of quarry and the ease with which they may be flown in groups, they are very popular with falconers. Being a broadwing they are fairly easy to train and manage. The downside however, is that they can be so easy to work with many falconers, beginners in particularly, have trouble getting them into correct flying condition. What I mean by that is they may have a hawk that is obedient to the fist and lure but not very successful at catching quarry. Even though Harris' Hawks are easy to fly, they still require discipline on the part of the falconer to bring the best out of them. Whereas a redtail will show the falconer it is over or underweight by the way it acts, the Harris' Hawk will often mask such a condition. It is a sad fact that many Harris' Hawks are not flown properly and are almost flown in a rather lackadaisical manner by indifferent falconers. It has been said by more than one experienced falconer that but for the Harris' Hawk, many modern day falconers would not continue in the sport because they lack the skill and discipline to fly the more challenging species. This is not the fault of the Harris' Hawk however, but rather those that fly it in an undisciplined way.

> Slip. A chance to chase quarry. It is the falconer's responsibility to provide the hawk with regular slips at quarry. A good slip will result in a good opportunity to take quarry, while a bad slip is the opposite and may result in a miss or even a lost hawk. A hawk is "slipped" at quarry when released to chase it.

Shortwings, though trained using methods similar to the broadwings, are far more difficult to work with, and their training should only be attempted by falconers who have had success in the field with at least one of the broadwings. The same applies to the longwings, though for different reasons. Even many falconers experienced in flying both broadwings and shortwings severely underestimate the difficulty of providing top quality slips that are required on a regular basis for a longwing to perform well.

When it comes to selecting a hawk for a beginner a key component is the size of the hawk. There is a narrow margin for error for making mistakes when dealing with a smaller hawk. This applies not just to feeding the hawk but also in terms of equipment including housing. For these reasons I do not recommend the beginner try his hand on small hawks such as kestrels until he has some experience with the larger species already mentioned.

The Hawks of Falconry

Longwings

The longwings are characterized by their long pointed wings, dark eyes, moustachial stripe called a "malar stripe" that are below the eyes on the sides of the head, and their rapid mode of flight. On each side of the upper mandible, longwings have a tooth used for killing their prey. Like all hawks, longwings catch prey with their feet, but they generally kill it by dislocating the vertebrae with a couple of powerful bites whereas the broad and shortwings kill using the power of their feet alone and rarely use their beak to kill their prey. The longwings typically catch their prey by superior speed. To achieve this, they are inherently the most persistent of all the hawks in level flight. In addition, many of them use height by converting it into speed. They thus deliberately position themselves above their intended prey and dive down onto it in a stoop. For species such as the Merlin, these stoops are relatively short, while larger longwings such as the Peregrine Falcon often position themselves hundreds of feet above the intended victim. Estimated speeds in such a stoop vary from 120 to 250 mph. While no one has yet conclusively determined their top speed, suffice to say they are very quick while in a stoop.

A male gyr-saker hybrid, showing the dark eye, malar stripe, and tooth on the upper mandible. All characteristics of the longwings.

Falconry: A Guide for Beginners

Trained longwings are flown in one of two ways. The first is called "out of the hood" or "off the fist." In this type of hawking, the longwing is slipped directly from the falconer's fist at birds either on the ground or airborne, but always at quarry that can be seen. The intended quarry must be found in very open country for the hawk will have to catch up to it and climb above it before it can begin stooping at the quarry. If slipped in country that has enough cover for the quarry to escape, the hawk will have no chance to get on terms with it, let alone put in a decisive stoop. If this happens too often, it will become disappointed and likely either refuse to chase or go off looking for quarry on its own, soon becoming lost to view. Historically, birds that are not as fast as a longwing in level flight such as rooks, crows and gulls were chosen as quarry for this style of flight. The hawk is slipped directly into the wind, forcing the prey to also fly into the wind. Because of a longwing's superior speed, it will, if it persists, eventually overtake the prey. The selected quarry, as soon as it knows it is being pursued, will start to plan escape routes. By choice, the prey will dive into any available cover, relying on the fact that if the cover is heavy enough, the hawk will break off the pursuit. Longwings, while fast, are not as maneuverable as most of their prey species and are thus reluctant to follow prey into thick cover such as woods or trees. The falconer helps to avoid this situation by only slipping the hawk when such cover is so far away that the hawk will have enough time to catch up to the prey and commence stooping at it. Some species such as herons and kites and some individuals of other species flown this way will, when pursued, attempt to outfly the hawk by "ringing up," climbing ever higher in an attempt to tire out the hawk, causing it to give up. The stage is then set for a classic ringing flight of the type that has thrilled some of the greatest rulers in history as well as many falconers, for if the hawk is persistent, it will go to immense heights to reach the quarry. I have seen flights at gulls go up so high as to be out of sight of binoculars, and the hawk, if successful at catching the prey, is then only found by the use of radio telemetry.

Longwings can also be flown at ground quarry such as rabbits as long as they can be found in areas where they can be persuaded to run across relatively open landscape. In the U.S. the jackrabbit lends itself to this flight using the large longwings such as gyr-saker hybrids and others of similar size. In the U.K. rabbits, if found in open areas, brown hares and blue hares can all be taken with large longwings if the falconer sets the flight up correctly. In other parts of the World, particularly in the Middle East, rabbits have long been considered a worthy quarry for longwings.

> Cover. Cover is any type of brush or trees into which quarry can escape a pursuing hawk.

The Hawks of Falconry

A gyr-saker hybrid stooping at a gull. Historically gulls were flown with large longwings as they tested their powers of flight and provided a good aerial battle. In some European countries gulls are still flown at while in the U.S. only those operating under a depredation permit are able to fly at gulls.

The second way of flying longwings is from the waiting-on position. A longwing waits on by flying above the falconer and holding position there in anticipation of quarry being flushed. To flush the quarry is to force it to fly or, in the case of a mammal, to run so the hawk has a chance of catching it. The hawk is thus acting on faith that the falconer will "serve" it, ("serve" being the term for the falconer's flushing of the quarry) whereas in an out of the hood flight, the quarry is there right in front of the hawk. While waiting on, a hawk may circle above the falconer or may, if the wind is at all strong, simply fly into the wind as fast as it is being blown back or it may course to and fro across the sky. Position in waiting-on flights is critical, for the falconer needs to serve the hawk only when it is overhead and not flying too wide. The hawk can thus stoop almost vertically down onto the prey when the falconer flushes it. The height at which a hawk waits on is determined by the hawk's age, experience, the type of quarry, and to some extent,

Falconry: A Guide for Beginners

the falconer. In general though, the higher the hawk flies, the more stylish will be the ensuing stoop. Most falconers entice their longwings to wait on as high as possible, and heights of over 1,000 feet are not at all unusual. At such a height, a falcon with a wingspan of over three feet looks not much larger than a swallow.

Peregrine Falcon waiting on.

Duck, grouse, pheasant, partridge, quail, and a few other species of birds are all flown at in this way, and this type of hawking is correctly called "game hawking." This term has fallen into misuse in the last 30 years by falconers who use it for any form of taking quarry with trained hawks. The correct term for the latter is simply hawking. To clarify, game hawking is when longwings are trained to wait on above the falconer. Hawking applies to all other forms of taking quarry with a trained hawk. While it is possible to take ducks, pheasant, quail and even grouse with longwings flown directly out of the hood, the flights go a long distance from the falconer and are lacking in style. Waiting on is natural to some species, particularly Peregrine Falcons, and they adapt fairly easily to it.

> Hawking. To go hawking is to take a trained bird of prey to the field to fly it at quarry.

The Hawks of Falconry

Peregrine Falcon stooping.

Falconry: A Guide for Beginners

For falconry purposes, the large longwings need to be flown over fairly open country. This is not necessarily because they cannot fly in enclosed country, but because the falconer must slip them at, or serve them quarry, in an area where the hawk has enough time to put in at least one decent stoop before the prey reaches cover. In addition, because of their aerial nature, it is not unusual for longwings to take on prey they happen to see flying up to a mile or more away. If the horizon is only 100 yards away, the falconer will very quickly lose sight of the hawk, for once airborne, a hawk's horizon will rapidly increase. For waiting-on flights, the type of quarry at which the hawk is flown decides the openness of the country. Ducks will normally put into water to escape from the stoop of a longwing; they will not dive into trees or bushes as, for example, a crow would. Because of this, the falconer has to flush the ducks away from the water they are on and across open ground, and they must stay in the air for a sufficient length of time to allow the hawk to complete a stoop. If at a nice high pitch, the height at which a longwing waits on, it may take the hawk ten or more seconds to come down, and so the next piece of water needs to be at quite a distance. If the ducks are on a river or a large piece of water, it will be difficult to get them to fly out over dry land at all. So it is clear that knowledge of a hawk is not enough to catch quarry. The falconer needs to know what the selected quarry is going to do. Just as one cannot make a hawk do something it has not evolved for, neither can one consistently make quarry behave in a way that will quickly get it killed, at least not if the goal is to have a sporting flight. This is summed up in the "life/dinner" principle. To a hawk, the quarry is merely its dinner. To the quarry, the hawk is its life, therefore the quarry tends to have a greater incentive for winning than the hawk.

> Put in. Quarry puts in to cover when it goes into something such as trees (for crows) or water (for ducks) where it is safe from the hawk.

The longwings commonly flown in the United States are the Gyrfalcon, Saker Falcon, Peregrine Falcon, Prairie Falcon, Merlin and American Kestrel. Recently a number of Lanner Falcons, Aplomado Falcons and a very few Red-necked Falcons have also been flown, and their use will likely increase. In addition there are a number of hybrids available, most often between two species but occasionally among three or more. The most successful hybrids are the gyr-peregrine hybrid, peregrine-saker hybrid, gyr-merlin hybrid and peregrine-merlin hybrid. When discussing a hybrid, the father is named first, thus a gyr-peregrine hybrid is produced from a male

The Hawks of Falconry

Steve Chindgren's tiercel gyr-peregrine hybrid moments after striking a sage grouse.

Gyrfalcon (jerkin) and a female Peregrine Falcon (falcon). The differences among the various species and hybrids are numerous, and many are not included here because the purpose of this text is to provide the beginner a basic overview.

Falconry: A Guide for Beginners

Intermewed "falcon," or female Peregrine Falcon.

Immature Barbary Falcon.

The Hawks of Falconry

Intermewed Jerkin.

Falconry: A Guide for Beginners

Female American Kestrel

Merlin.

The Hawks of Falconry

Intermewed male gyr-saker hybrid.

Immature gyr-saker hybrid.

Falconry: A Guide for Beginners

Immature peregrine-saker hybrid.

The Hawks of Falconry

Aplomado Falcon.

Prairie Falcon.

Falconry: A Guide for Beginners

Shortwings

The shortwings, also known as accipiters because of their scientific name, typically live in wooded or even forested areas. Shortwings catch their prey in the wild by a combination of stealth and acceleration. They try to get as close to their intended victim as possible using any available cover, and when the prey has spotted them, they quickly accelerate and try to overtake it. Shortwings, whether instinctively or from previous experience, know by the way a particular species flies whether it is the type of bird they can outfly, that will land after flying a while, or that can outfly them and they react accordingly. Thus a pheasant may be chased by a wild goshawk right across an open field whereas the same goshawk chasing a pigeon in the same field will give up once the flight speeds of the two birds match and it has lost the element of surprise. The difference is that with the pheasant, the gos knows that pretty soon it will have to seek cover and land and in doing so will slow down and so it keeps up the pursuit whereas the pigeon can easily fly for miles and outdistance the hawk. I have, on a number of occasions, been hawking with students who point excitedly to a gull flying a quarter mile away and wonder why my Black Sparrowhawk doesn't go catch it like some gull seeking missile! Shortwings simply do not behave in such a way. To catch that gull would require us being within fifty yards of the gull just as it rises from the ground when slipping the hawk. In this case, the superior acceleration of the shortwing could come into play. But where the gull is already in flight some distance away and without any element of surprise, a Black Sparrowhawk will not be able to succeed. Gulls know that, Black Sparrowhawks know that, and new falconers learn fairly quickly that they cannot change nature. Now if it were a pheasant in the air a quarter of a mile away, the hawk would know from previous experience and to a certain extent through instinct that a bird such as a pheasant would soon look for somewhere to land. In such a scenario, the hawk would go straight for it. If cover is far enough away the hawk might be able to overtake it in the open and pull it out of the air. If cover were closer the pheasant would dive in and, if the hawk were a wild one, it would probably be safe. However a trained hawk, with a falconer and preferably a dog to assist it, can catch that pheasant on the reflush.

The Hawks of Falconry

Marc Preston's intermewed goshawk takes a rabbit.

Bingo, an intermewed black musket on a pheasant.

[57]

Falconry: A Guide for Beginners

Because they are quicker off the mark and faster in flight than the broadwings, shortwings are more capable at taking birds as they rise such as ducks, pheasants, partridges etc. The goshawk, formerly known as the 'cooks hawk' because of the amount and variety of quarry it could provide for the table, will take a wide variety of quarry including rabbits, hares, jackrabbits, quail, partridge, pheasant, ducks and other quarry besides. The temperament of shortwings means they need to be flown by a falconer with some experience. They are normally flown directly off the fist, whereas the broadwings are often allowed to follow the falconer from tree to tree. If this is tried with the shortwings, most of them, though by no means all, will begin to self-hunt and when that happens they quickly become difficult to control in the field and difficult for the falconer to keep up with. The shortwings commonly flown in the United States are the Northern Goshawk, both American and European subspecies, the Cooper's Hawk, and the Sharp-shinned Hawk. A few Eurasian Sparrowhawks have been flown, with numbers likely to increase. Two or three Black Sparrowhawks have also been flown. While it is possible to take all three American species from the wild in various states, both as eyasses from the nest and as passagers, some species including the native species are now being bred in captivity. Because of captive breeding U.S. falconers also now have access to European Goshawks, including the large Finnish and Russian hawks, and Eurasian Sparrowhawks. While no Black Sparrowhawks have been bred yet in the U.S. hopefully this will change soon and falconers will also have access to this species for flying.

Alec May's goshawk closing in on a brown hare.

The Hawks of Falconry

Alistair McEwan's intermewed goshawk about to take a blue hare.

Alistair McEwan slips his male goshawk at a rising pheasant.

[59]

Falconry: A Guide for Beginners

Goshawks are fast enough to take ducks, pheasants and other birds on the rise if given a close enough slip. Here Alec May's goshawk closes in on a mallard.

Broadwings

The broadwings make up the final group of hawks used in falconry. In the wild, their broad, rounded wings and short broad tails distinguish them from the long and shortwings. They habitually hunt from perches or while soaring in warm air or up currents from hills. They typically prey on mammals of various sizes and birds that are caught before they achieve top speed. Broadwings lack the acceleration of the accipiters and do not have the stamina or speed to overtake birds in full flight as do the longwings.

While broadwings may not be able to take as wide a variety of quarry in the trained state as a shortwing, or provide the dramatic high flights of the longwings, they compensate by their placid nature and ease of training. They are the ideal hawk for a beginner or those without the temperament, patience, or experience to bring out the best of a shortwing or longwing. Partly because of their easy going nature, broadwings do not require being flown or handled as often as other species and are therefore a favorite of falconers for whom time is a major concern. What they lack in fire they make up for by their willingness to be agreeable to the falconer.

The broadwings commonly flown in the United States are the Red-tailed, Harris', and Ferruginous Hawk. The Red-shouldered Hawk, while it is allowed by some states, is not generally thought to be suitable for falconry.

A redtail-ferruginous hawk hybrid belonging to Keith Talbot.

Photograph by Keith Talbot.

Falconry: A Guide for Beginners

Al Jordan's Harris' Hawk.

John Kellerman's intermewed passage male Red-tailed Hawk preparing to be cast off.

The Hawks of Falconry

Eagles

The various species of eagles can also be classed broadly, as broadwings, though their handling and flying should not be attempted by anyone with less than several years' experience with other species of hawks, and in particular with other broadwings such as the Red-tailed Hawk and Ferruginous Hawk. The eagle most commonly used throughout the U.S. and Europe is the Golden Eagle.

Dexter, a passage male Golden Eagle belonging to Chase Delles, closes on a jackrabbit.

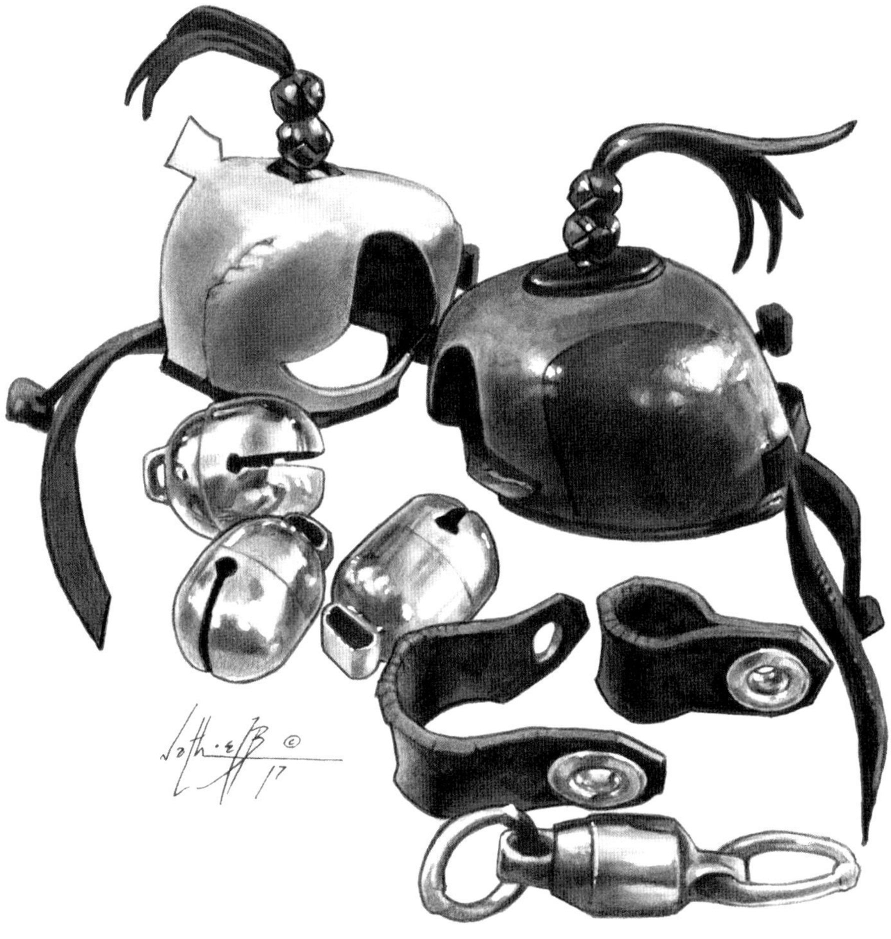

Chapter Three

Equipment & Housing for the Hawk

The Mews and Weathering Area

The place where the hawk is housed is called a "mew" or "the mews." This began in reference to the housing traditionally used for molting hawks during the summer months, but the term has been adopted for any shed, outbuilding or specially built structure where a trained hawk is kept.

The housing of a trained hawk offers a dilemma in that the needs of the hawk vary depending on how long it has been in training, and to some extent, the time of year and even the hawk's personality. A newly trapped hawk or one recently taken up for training will need to be tethered to a perch and probably hooded for the majority of the time during the first few days to prevent too much bating. Were the hawk to throw its hood and be left tethered to any kind of perch, it would likely bate quite a lot, possibly damaging feathers and certainly damaging its frame of mind in the process. For this reason, it is beneficial if the mews can be made completely dark when necessary. In practice, this means any windows should be able to be temporarily covered, either with a hinged shutter that can be closed at will or by boards temporarily screwed onto the outside of the window. However, this can make the building dangerously hot for the hawk, so adequate airflow must be provided by means of blind ventilation, vents that let in air but not light. This can all be avoided by keeping a good selection of hoods on hand so the hawk can be properly hooded with a hood it cannot remove.

> Bate. When a tethered hawk tries to fly and is brought up short by its jesses and/or leash. A hawk can bate from either the fist or the perch.

> Hood. A leather cap that covers the hawk's head including its eyes so that it cannot see, thus having a calming effect.

[65]

Falconry: A Guide for Beginners

Once the hawk is trained, many falconers prefer to leave it free in the mews to fly around a little and choose which perch to sit on. This is called free lofting. However, caution should be used when free lofting a hawk because many hawks spend too much time bouncing around the mews, resulting in damage to feathers and blunting of talons. Other hawks constantly flutter up against the barred window trying to escape. I have seen hawks with cuts on their wing butts caused by such activity as well as broken tail and primary feathers. If a hawk does jump around a lot, it will be better for it to be tethered to a perch while in the mews, and if it still spends a lot of time bating, it should remain hooded while inside as it did earlier in training. The actions of each individual hawk should determine whether free lofting is suitable and whether the hawk needs to be hooded while in the mews. I do not like to see hawks constantly bating or flying around the mews; they are signaling that something is wrong, and they should be hooded until they have grown more accustomed to life as a trained hawk.

If a falconer intends to always tether a hawk in the mews or learns that it will not settle while free lofted, then it is necessary to select a perch for tethering. For a broadwing or shortwing, once it is trained, I would use a table-mounted loop perch or bow perch rather than a perch on the floor. Being higher up, a hawk is less likely to bate than if tethered to a perch low to the ground, and it can also see out the window where there is something to focus on, preventing boredom that can lead to bating. The table is the width of the mews and four feet deep. It is placed at waist height and has a lip four inches high that runs around the perimeter. This is filled with corn cob litter, sand, or gravel, depending on preference and weather conditions. For instance, gravel may blunt a hawk's talons if contact is made with it, whereas sand can get inside an anklet and cause abrasion to a hawk's leg. Corn cob litter, which is my preference, will become moldy in really humid weather and should not be used in such climates unless cleaned out every day.

If a hawk is to be free lofted, a couple of different perches can be provided in the mews, but these should not be put in place while the hawk is still tethered to a lower perch. If there are higher, desirable perches in sight, the hawk will bate towards them.

When a hawk is free lofted, one of the perches should be placed by the window a few inches higher than the bottom of the window and at least 12 inches away from it. Another perch can be placed high up across one corner. The hawk will often use this one to roost on at night. Another perch can be located across the far end wall. A hawk does not need more than three perches in the mews, but it is useful

Equipment and Housing for the Hawk

to have them made from varying materials, perhaps one from natural wood, another covered in longleaf Astroturf, and another in shortleaf Astroturf. Some hawks, including redtails, are fond of a ledge to lie on. This need be nothing more than a shelf measuring 18 by 24 inches that is covered in coco mat and secured high up against one wall. It is here that a larger mews allowing a bit more room to fly is an advantage and offers more comfort. A bath should also be placed where the hawk cannot mute into it. While an 8 foot square is the minimum, a hawk will spend a lot of time in the mews. This makes it wise to build something bigger if possible. A good mews will last 20 years or more if constructed properly, so time and money spent to build it right are investments that repay themselves in the comfort of the hawk.

My own routine, once the hawk is trained, is to turn it loose into the mews as darkness is beginning, then put it out on the weathering lawn tethered to a perch fairly early in the morning. If my hawk is calm enough to be free lofted during the day, I leave it inside if there is a forecast for inclement weather. But on all other days, I still put my hawk outside on its perch rather than leave it free lofted. This is because even those hawks who do adapt well to being kept loose will generally start to bounce around the mews when flying time approaches. Damage can be done to feathers in the space of a few short minutes. Even tethered to a perch, many hawks become active as flying time approaches. Bingo, my black musket, had to be hooded two hours before flying time to keep him from bating incessantly. Once hooded, he would sit patiently resting on one foot until picked up and taken out hawking.

The first thing to consider when building a new mews is size. The minimum recommended for a Red-tailed Hawk is 8 feet by 8 feet square with a roof as high as possible, one that is at least 6 feet. Because plywood comes in 4 foot by 8 foot sheets, it is not too difficult to construct a building this size with a roof that slopes from 8 feet high in the back to 7 feet in the front. Personally, I prefer a larger building, and the one pictured on the following page is 14 feet long by 8 feet wide by 8 feet high. The window should be covered with vertical metal bars such as electrical conduit, spaced 1½ inches apart. This will prevent the hawk flying out, and just as important, keep predators such as raccoons from getting in. It is worthwhile to put up a screen of wire mesh at least 6 inches beyond the metal bars to decrease chances of the hawk's fighting a raccoon through the bars. If the enclosed weathering ground is immediately outside the mews, then this latter precaution is not necessary because the wire surrounding the area will keep predators from getting to the window. Wire netting must never

Falconry: A Guide for Beginners

be used to cover the window. Any type of wire allows a hawk to hang onto the front of the window, wrecking tail feathers in no time at all. It is only vertical bars that prevent talons from getting a hold. The mews should be fitted with a double door to prevent the hawk's accidentally flying out when a human steps in. If the weathering ground is directly outside, this will achieve the same result as a double door.

I prefer to line the inside of the mews with fiberglass reinforced plastic (FRP), which comes in 8 foot by 4 foot sheets, because it can easily be cleaned and disinfected by hosing it down. Plastic walls are much easier to clean than wood, and being white in color, they add a lot of light to the mews. Ideally, the floor of the mews should be concrete to prevent any animals from digging in. I use pea gravel on the floor of the mews to a depth of about 4 inches, and the hawk's droppings are cleaned out each week by putting the soiled

A typical mews with enclosed weathering area attached. The mews is 14 feet wide by 8 feet deep by 7 feet high at the front. The weathering area is 16 feet by 14 feet by 8 feet high. The wire folds out at the bottom for 3 feet and is covered by the gravel path, thus preventing any predator from digging in. Having a large weathering area allows the perch to be periodically moved so the area around it does not become soiled.

Equipment and Housing for the Hawk

gravel into a bucket, taking it out, and dumping it. The droppings will be accumulated and collected from under the hawk's favorite perches, and the amount of gravel removed won't amount to much more than a quarter of a bucket. Once a season, or more often if it proves necessary, I replenish the gravel. The entire mews is hosed down at least twice a year and more often if necessary. For disinfectant, a product called F10® can be obtained. During the hawking season, much of the hawk's time is spent outside in the weathering area so the mews is only occupied at night. Even during the molt, I normally handle my trained hawks so the mews does not get unduly dirty.

While tethered outside to a bow or block perch, a trained hawk is said to be weathering. A weathering area is a caged area inside which the hawk sits on a perch. Many falconers do not use an enclosed weathering area, and many hawks have been killed or lost because of this omission. To tether a hawk on a lawn unattended and therefore unprotected is to invite disaster. Cats, stray dogs,

> Weather. A hawk is said to weather when placed on a perch outside to enjoy the weather.

escaped ferrets, raccoons, and a whole host of other mammals including man himself have been known to attack trained hawks, or, in the case of misguided human beings, to release them. From the air, Great Horned Owls, Red-tailed Hawks, Cooper's Hawks, goshawks, eagles, ravens, crows, turkeys, domestic geese and peacocks have all been known to attack tethered, trained hawks, sometimes fatally. Equipment failures include broken jesses, swivels and leashes, rings on perches, tops that come off block perches, and even perches being pulled out of the ground because the spikes are too short or the ground not firm enough. All of these have led to lost hawks. A hawk that escapes because of a broken swivel, leash, or ring is trailing a death sentence as it flies away and will, sooner rather than later, get caught up somewhere and die. It is vital therefore that budding falconers not only build a suitable mews but also an enclosed weathering area. The interpretation of state or federal regulations is unimportant; it is not the government's responsibility to care for the hawk, it is the falconer's.

The weathering area can be either a permanent structure or a large cage that can be moved, probably with a bit of effort, around a larger lawn. A moveable cage must be large enough that the hawk cannot touch the netting with any part of its body, especially the wings. In practice, if on a bow perch, this requires an area at

Falconry: A Guide for Beginners

least 8 feet square and preferably 10 feet square. If the structure is permanent, it must be large enough to allow moving of the bow perch inside it every couple of days, otherwise the grass beneath the perch and the area where the hawk tends to bate will quickly become ruined. I do not like low roofs in weathering areas. If my hawk bates while on the fist inside the weathering area, its wings may well come into contact with the netting over the roof and cause feather damage. It is imperative that no part of the hawk's body is able to touch the wire that surrounds the weathering area, or there will be damage to feathers.

The only safe place to land for a hawk that bates from its perch is soft grass. I have used several different materials around perches over the years for hawks to bate onto including sand,

A captive-bred male Harris' Hawk, weathering while protected in an enclosed area. Many hawks have been killed when put out to weather without the protection of a weathering area that is enclosed.

Equipment and Housing for the Hawk

gravel, indoor/outdoor carpet, rubber mats and both longleaf and shortleaf Astroturf, but all cause wear to the talons, and some cause other problems as well. I knew a musket that got one grain of sand lodged up inside his anklet, and the wear it caused put him out of action as a falconry hawk for the rest of his life; one grain of sand did that! The only safe material for a hawk to bate onto regularly is grass, preferably at least an inch or two in length. If a hawk is still at the stage of frequent bating and cannot, for whatever reason, be placed on soft grass, it should be kept hooded.

The advantage of a moveable weathering area is that, if the grass does become soiled, the cage can be moved to a new area. It is also useful to perch the hawk in areas where, as it becomes tamer, there is increasingly more activity to watch. Thus, in the early stages, a hawk may be set out to weather in a quiet area of the garden, but with time and tameness, can be placed near greater activity. This helps in manning, and more importantly, if the hawk does bate, it is less likely to blame the falconer than if the bate took place while being carried on the fist. It's a small psychological difference, but an important one. The placing of the perch and weathering area is therefore a really useful tool in getting the hawk manned.

The netting surrounding the weathering area should be plastic-coated wire or plastic-coated chain link. It serves both to protect the hawk from predators and to prevent feather and cere damage should there be an equipment breakage causing the hawk to bounce off the mesh in an effort to escape. Use of chicken wire must be avoided because it will cut the cere badly and might not contain the hawk or protect it from predators. I once converted a spare breeding chamber into a pigeon loft by taking down part of one wall so the pigeons had

> Cere. This is the skin, often waxy looking, at the base of a hawk's upper mandible.

access to the outside, putting in an entrance for the pigeons to come and go, and covering up the remaining part with chicken wire. One morning I opened the door to be greeted by a rather large, very contented looking Great Horned Owl. He was content because he'd killed all my pigeons! When he saw me, he panicked and flew to the other end of the chamber, and proceeded to fly straight through the chicken wire as though it wasn't even there, and carried on his way, presumably with a bit of a headache, or at least so I hoped. The moral of the story is that if chicken wire is not strong enough to keep a Great Horned Owl in, it's not strong enough to keep one out either!

Falconry: A Guide for Beginners

Equipment or Furniture
Jesses

A pair of jesses is the first item of equipment the hawk needs. The falconer uses these to hold onto the hawk or to tether it to the perch when not on the fist. A hawk wears one jess on each leg, fixed around the tarsus, the part of the leg between the foot and the knee. For a hawk the size of a redtail, jesses need to be about 8 inches in length. To prevent them from twisting together, both jesses are attached to a swivel that is in turn attached to a leash. In the past there was a choice between one-piece traditional jesses that are about 8 inches long or the Aylmeri jess system invented by the late Major Guy Aylmer and the late William Rutledge in the 1930s. The disadvantage of traditional jesses is a slit, used to attach the swivel, at the end of each jess. When the hawk is flying free, the leash and swivel are first removed, and the hawk is flown with only the jesses in place. There is a real danger of the slit getting caught in branches or other obstacles. If the hawk is ever lost, the danger becomes even greater because the hawk will soon get caught up, and not having the falconer to come to the rescue, it will remain trapped until starving to death or being eaten by a predator. Traditional jesses have no place in falconry because there are better options available.

> Jesses. Straps attached to the hawk's legs to restrain it.

Aylmeri jesses consist of three parts. The first part, the anklet, is sometimes also called a cuff or bracelet, and is fixed around the tarsus. The anklet has a hole punched in it that will accommodate either a mews jess or a flying jess. In the standard Aylmeri anklet, this hole is used to place a brass grommet that also serves to secure the anklet in place.

The size of the hole and associated grommet depend on how wide the mews jesses need to be. My size preference for redtails and Harris' Hawks is a grommet that is $5/16$ of an inch in diameter. The second part of the Aylmeri system is the mews jess. Some 8 inches in length for a redtail, it has a button at one end that stops it from being pulled through the hole in the anklet. At the other end is a slit where the swivel is attached when the hawk is to be tethered. When the hawk is free flown, the mews jesses are removed and replaced with field jesses. A field jess, the third part of the system, is similar to a mews jess but does not contain the slit for the swivel and is therefore less likely to catch up when the hawk is free flown. Field jesses can also be permanently fixed to the anklets and in fact should be when the hawk is free lofted to provide for safe handling while in the mews. When the time comes to fly the hawk, the falconer secures the field jesses

Equipment and Housing for the Hawk

between ring and middle fingers, removes the mews jesses, and the hawk is ready to be flown. This method is also useful for hawks that tend to foot the falconer when the jesses are being changed.

While it may seem safe to leave mews jesses in place when the hawk is free lofted, it is uncanny how the slits on these jesses can get a hawk caught up, even in an apparently safe mews. I was looking after a collection of hawks for a falconer many years ago, one of which was an imprint sakret free lofted inside a mews. Early one morning, I went out to find he had put a foot through the bars and caught the slit of a jess on the small protruding head of a screw that held the key to the mews. He was hanging upside down by one leg. He had a swollen foot for a couple of days, but fortunately no long term harm resulted.

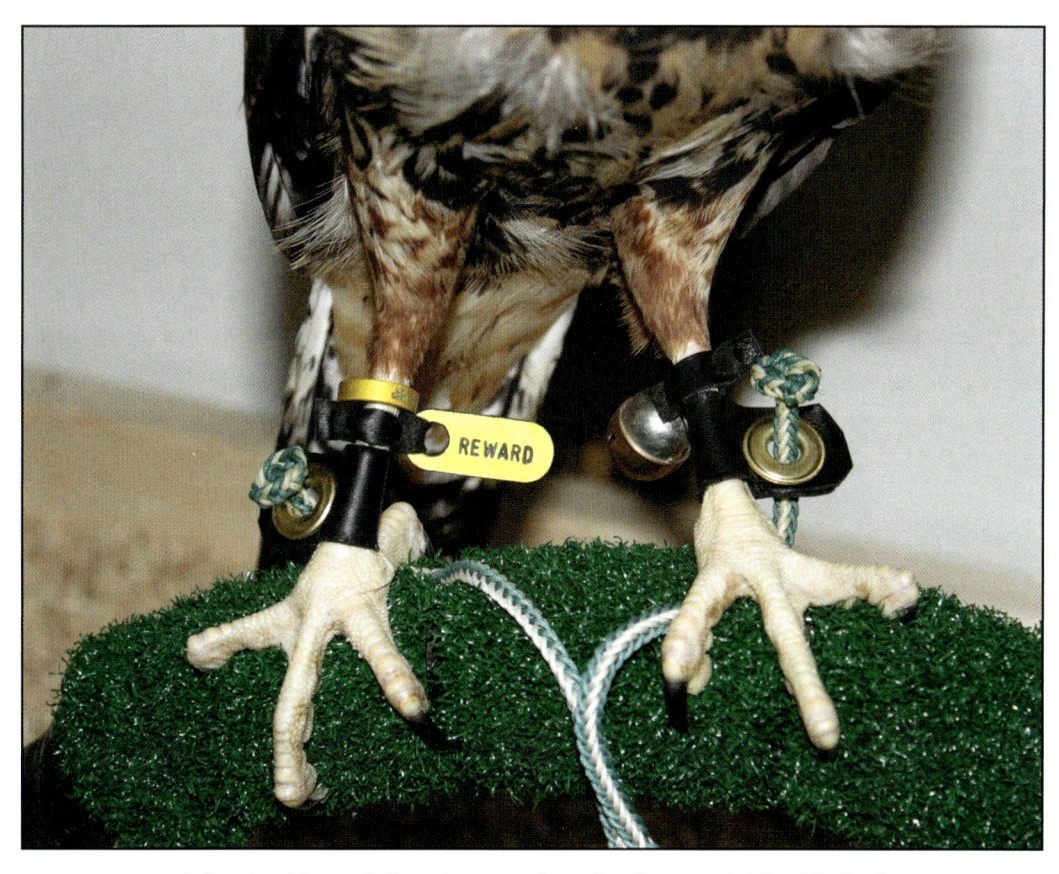

Aylmeri anklets, a bell, and a reward tag fitted to a male Harris' Hawk. When secured to a perch, mews jesses, here the braided nylon type, are threaded through the anklets so that a swivel and leash can be attached. When the hawk is flying free or free lofted in the mews, flying jesses made of leather and without any slits in them are used, or alternatively no jesses are threaded through the anklets.

Falconry: A Guide for Beginners

Another alternative when flying the hawk free is having no jesses at all in the anklets. This is the method I prefer when working with any hawk that is hood trained. The hawk thus flies with only the anklets, and if lost, there is no fear of getting caught up in a tree. I use what is called a loop jess, first described by Phillip Glasier in his book *Falconry and Hawking*. It is made from a length of braided Dacron about 18 inches long that has one end permanently secured to the glove. I do this by tying a slip knot and placing the loop formed over the gloved little finger and pulling it tight, but it can also be attached to the D-ring if the glove has one. The other end is left hanging when not in use. Preparatory to a flight and while the hawk is still hooded on the fist, the first mews jess is removed, and the free end of the loop jess is put through the empty grommet, then wrapped around the ring and little finger. The other jess is then removed. When the time comes to slip the hawk, the hood is removed and the gloved hand is opened as the hawk flies away so that the loop jess pulls free of the anklet and remains attached to the glove.

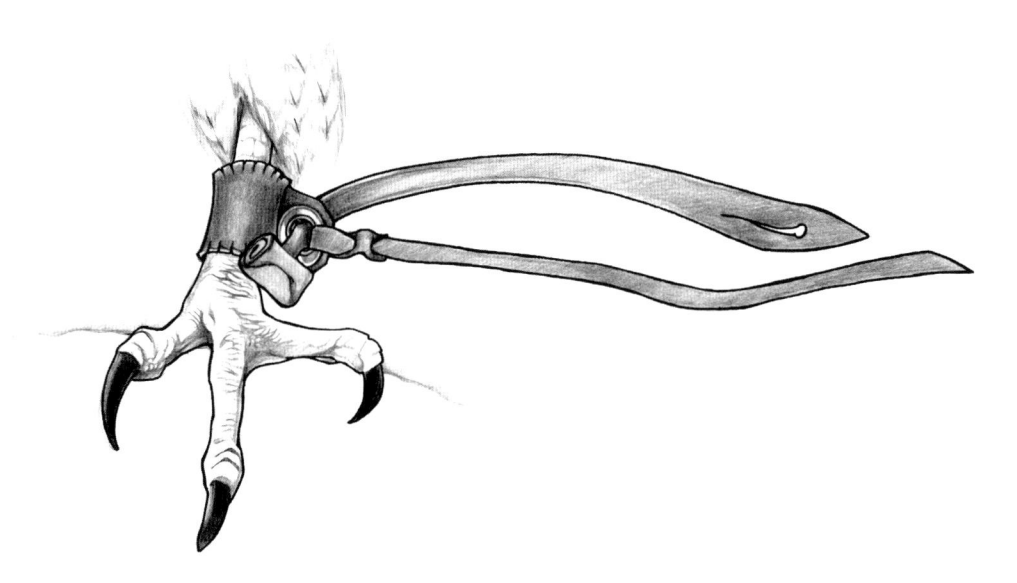

A mews jess with a permanently attached flying jess. When the hawk is flown free or is put into the mews to be free lofted, the mews jess is removed, leaving only the flying jess in place. The advantage of this system is that the hawk cannot remove the flying jess as many hawks do while loose in the mews. Also, if the hawk is a bit free with its feet and tries to foot while the mews jesses are being changed for flying jesses, the method allows the falconer to keep hold of the foot while taking the mews jess out or replacing it, thereby preventing the hawk from footing.

Equipment and Housing for the Hawk

Lost hawks have later been found breeding with anklets (and sometimes even bells, as was the case with the author's second kestrel) still attached to them. I have seen trained hawks caught up wearing non-slitted flying jesses and have also seen an annoyingly large number of falconers who use the Aylmeri jess system, but who don't remove the mews jesses when flying their hawks free. Such a practice shows a complete lack of regard for the welfare of the hawk and an even greater lack of understanding of the advantages of the Aylmeri jess system.

While this passage Red-tailed Hawk correctly has flying jesses in place when flown, they are much longer than they need to be, thereby increasing the risk that they may wrap around a branch and trap the hawk high in a tree. Furthermore, when taking dangerous quarry such as squirrels, the hawk may inadvertently trap one of the jesses with its own foot rendering it unable to move. When taking a squirrel, the hawk needs to be able to use both feet freely so that it can get a secure hold on the squirrel's head to avoid being bitten. For these reasons, I prefer to fly hawks without any flying jesses in place.

[75]

Falconry: A Guide for Beginners

The making and fitting of Aylmeri anklets is shown in the photographs below.

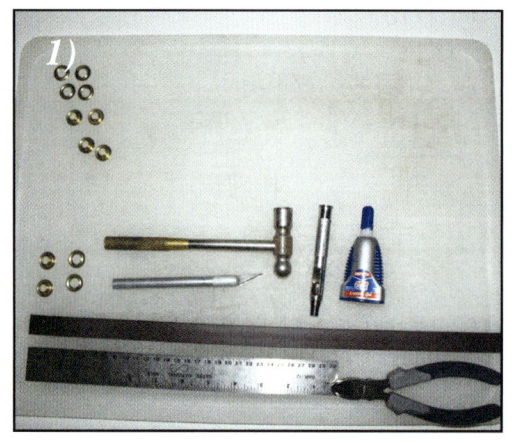

Equipment needed for making and fitting anklets.

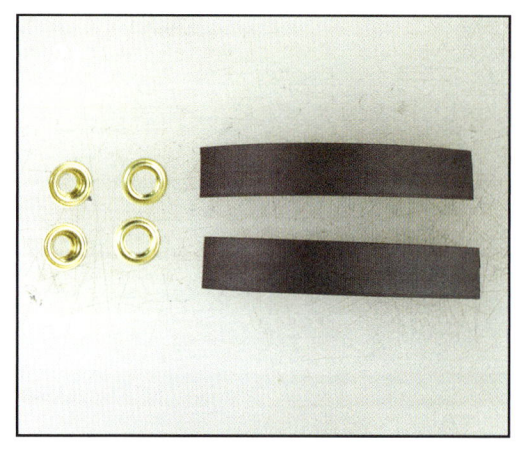

BioThane® or leather blanks and grommets.

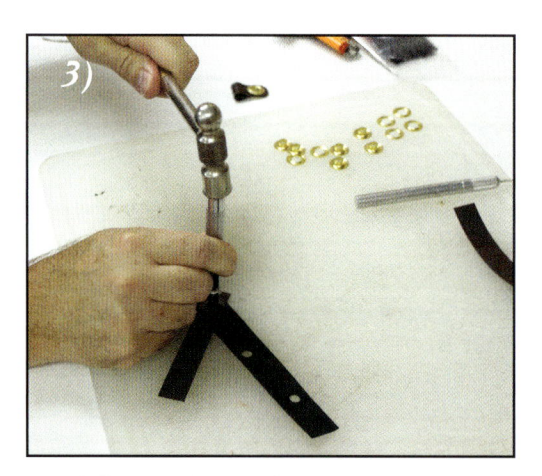

A hole is punched ¾ of an inch from one end.

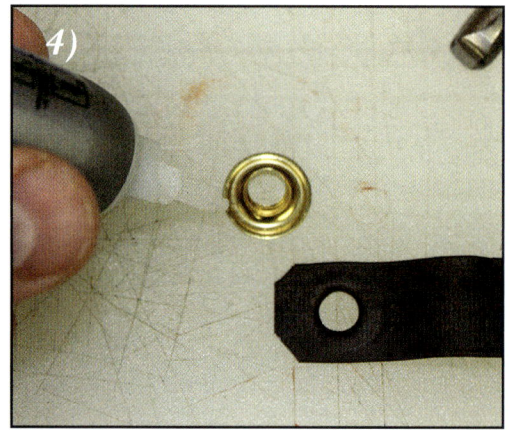

One half of the grommet is superglued in place.

Equipment and Housing for the Hawk

The anklet is placed around the hawk's leg and a mark made where the second half of the grommet needs to go.

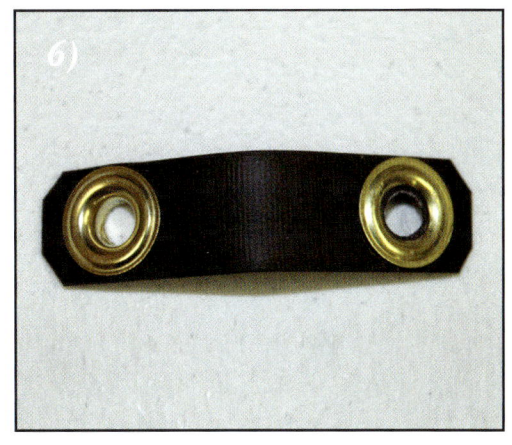

The second half of the grommet is glued in place. If desired, nicks are cut along the upper and lower edges of the anklet.

The anklet is placed around the hawk's leg to ensure a good fit.

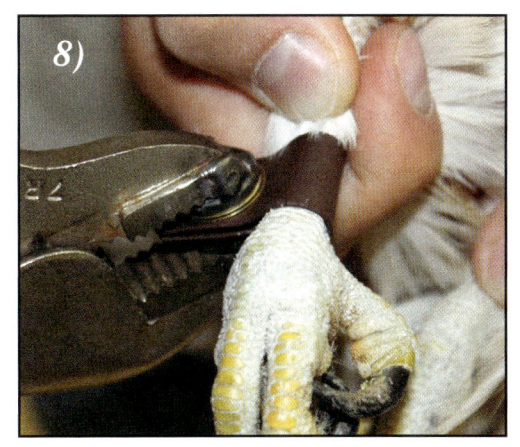

The grommet is closed with a grommet closing tool.

[77]

Falconry: A Guide for Beginners

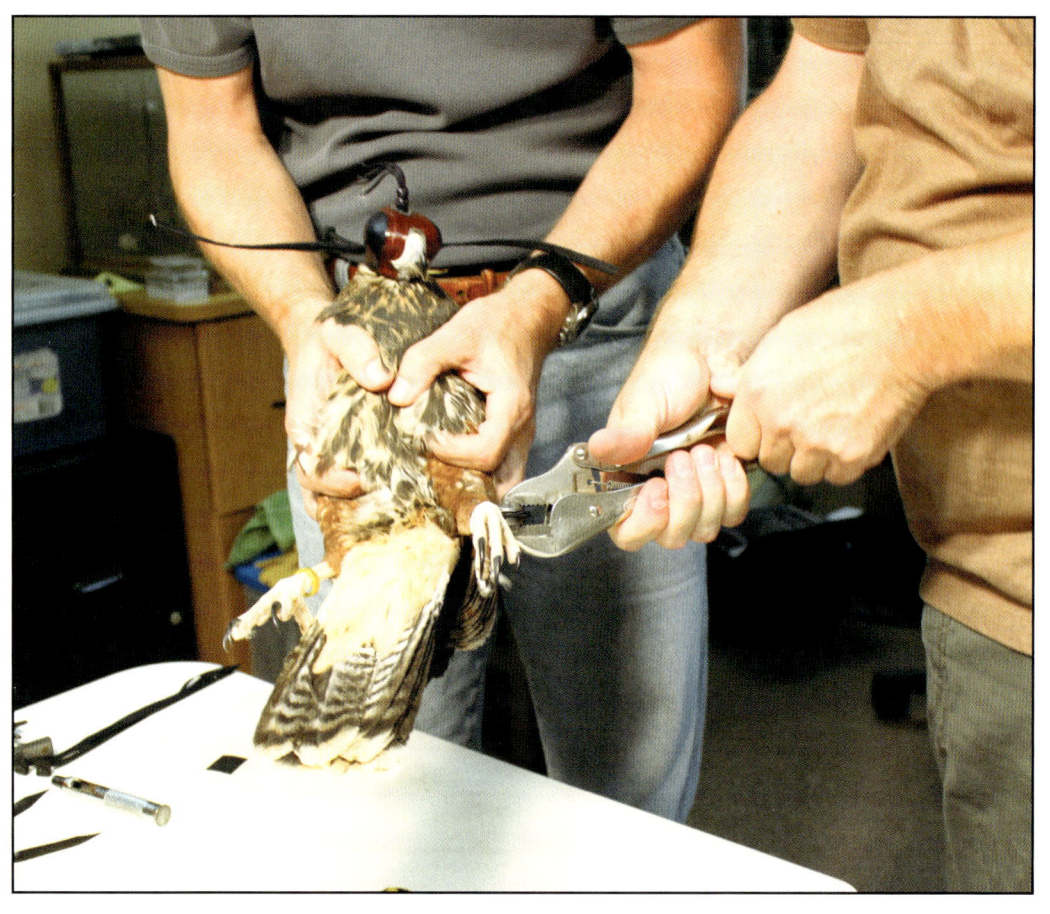

Casting a hawk so anklets, bells and reward tags may be fitted. This method is easier and safer than placing a hawk chest down on a cushion as it gives everyone much more room to work. Each leg is secured between the index and middle finger so that the person fitting the equipment will not be footed by the hawk.

While anklets and jesses were traditionally made of leather, new and experimental materials have recently shown great promise. Although anklets are still mostly made of leather, I have recently started using BioThane® with good results. The disadvantages of leather are that the breaking strain can never be known and that it weakens over time. Leather can also stretch. Anklets that once fit well can soon resemble loose fitting pants worn by a person on a crash diet. BioThane® does not stretch and does not weaken over time. BioThane® also offers the advantage of giving a certain amount of protection against squirrel bites. Care should be taken with both leather and BioThane® anklets to check for any wear on the legs of the hawk. I have known one goshawk and one gyr-saker hybrid that

[78]

Equipment and Housing for the Hawk

developed signs of wear on their legs when wearing BioThane® anklets but not when replaced with leather ones and Bingo, my black musket, developed signs of bruising when wearing leather anklets. In the latter case, fabric band aids placed under the anklets solved the problem.

The mews and field jesses themselves, while traditionally made of leather, can also be made from nylon and possibly other materials. Early attempts at making such jesses were often cumbersome, stiff and unsightly but there are now some decent braided jesses available. I fully expect over the next decade or so that leather will be phased out for jesses and possibly anklets as well.

Until that time, there is still need for a falconer to know how to make the Aylmeri jess system out of leather. The first consideration is the leather itself. Kangaroo is the best and is the only type of leather I recommend. Jesses and anklets should be made prior to trapping the hawk, and it is wise to make several sets of each to have spares on hand. Jesses should be inspected every time the hawk is handled, and if there is any sign of wear, both should be replaced. Many falconers have looked back regretting that they didn't take the few minutes needed to replace a pair of worn jesses and have come home to find an empty perch. Jesses should be greased weekly with lanolin or one of the jess greases available from equipment suppliers.

The making and fitting of anklets and jesses is shown in the accompanying DVD using templates available from Western Sporting.

Swivels

To keep the jesses from twisting together, they are both attached to a single swivel. There are a surprisingly large number of swivel designs on the market. The requirements of a swivel are that it be strong, as light as possible, that all the working parts can be visually inspected, and the shape or design keeps the jesses up and away from the joint where the swivel rotates. If the jesses can migrate down the swivel to the joint, they will interfere with its proper performance. Only one design meets all of these criteria, and that is the one pioneered by Martin Jones in England and now available in the U.S. from Western Sporting. I do not use or recommend any other design where the jesses are attached directly to a swivel though Sampo® swivels are acceptable for use in tethering systems. To attach the jesses to the swivel, one jess is first threaded through the other at the swivel slit located at the end of the mews jess. The two jesses are then threaded through the top of the swivel, and the bottom of the swivel is then itself threaded back through both jess slits. The jesses are then manually worked so that they end up on the top ring away from the joint. The diagram shows clear instruction of this process (see page 81).

Falconry: A Guide for Beginners

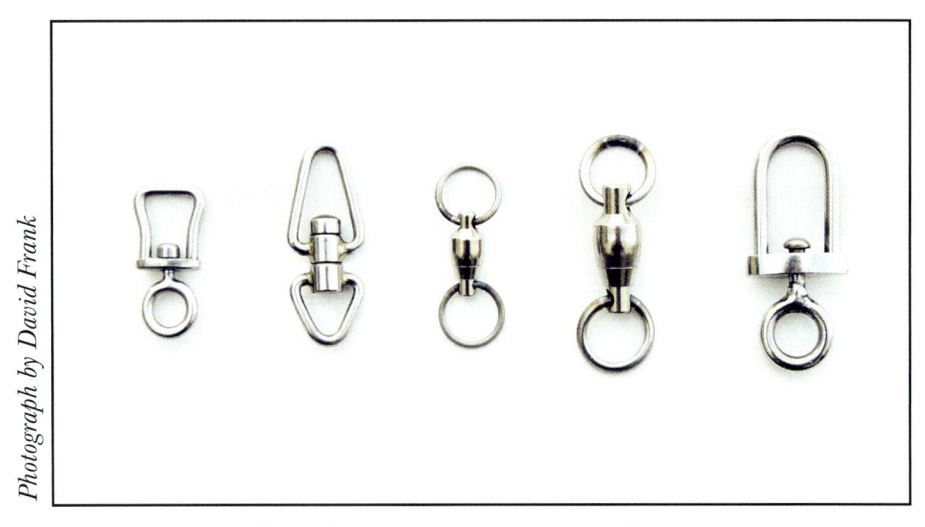

Photograph by David Frank

From left to right, Martin Jones D-type swivel, European type swivel, medium-modified Sampo® swivel, large Sampo® swivel and regular English D-type swivel. I only recommend the type on the left for use with leather jesses. Sampo® swivels are acceptable when used in tethering systems.

Under no circumstances should a spring clip of any kind be used for tethering a hawk to a perch. If spring clips do have a place, it is fastened to a small leash attached to the glove so a hawk's swivel can be quickly secured to the glove. Even then, I use the loop jess already described and secure it with a falconer's knot so I don't get smacked in the head by a spring clip swinging around attached to my glove while I'm running after the hawk. I've seen this happen to a number of falconers. Spring clips have a fascination for many, but they have also been the cause of many a lost hawk.

Leashes

Through the other end of the swivel to which the jesses are attached is placed a leash. Like jesses, leashes were traditionally made of leather but are now generally made with more modern materials. The number of hawks lost over the years by leather leashes breaking is surprisingly large. The wonder is that some falconers still use them, given the weight of evidence through history of their shortcomings and the current availability of better options. For leashes, I prefer square braided nylon leashes. I have used, with a lot of success, simple parachute cord leashes but the advantage of the square braid is that, having tied a falconer's knot, it will not tighten

Equipment and Housing for the Hawk

Attaching jesses to an English D-type swivel.

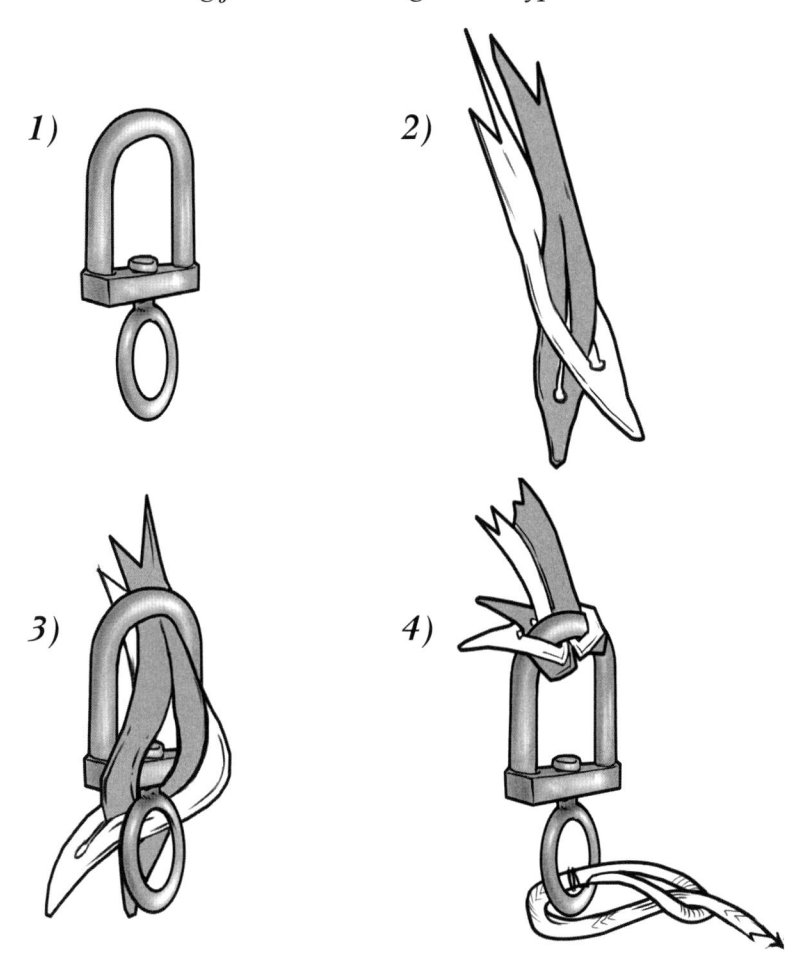

1)

2)

3)

4)

up like almost any other nylon leash will. One can come back later and even if the hawk has done a lot of bating, the knot will still be as it was when originally tied. With other types of braid and even with parachute cord leashes, they will, after a varying amount of time, begin to cinch up so tightly that untying them becomes difficult. Not so with the square braid. This leash is expensive when compared to the other types, but the investment is well worthwhile, especially for a falconer flying only one hawk. A leash with a button or knot at the end to prevent it from pulling through the swivel should not be used. Sooner, rather than later, this knot will end up between the jesses, causing the hawk to get twisted up because the swivel is then unable to operate. A loop at the end of the leash through which the rest of the leash passes back after being put through the swivel is a far better and safer method.

[81]

Falconry: A Guide for Beginners

The falconer's knot is used to tether the hawk to a perch. The advantage of this knot is that it can be tied and untied with one hand. The hawk should never be placed on the perch until the two knots are secured. A hawk is placed on the perch by bringing it close and holding it directly above the perch so there's no fretting in trying to get there before the knots are tied. The leash is released from the fingers of the gloved hand, but at all times the jesses are secured by holding them down through the middle of the hand, behind the thumb but in front of the fingers, then passing them out between the ring and middle fingers so that the swivel is on the outside of the gloved fist. This position, called the lock, should always be used for the jesses whenever the hawk is on the fist. The free end of the leash

Tying the falconer's knot.

Equipment and Housing for the Hawk

[83]

Falconry: A Guide for Beginners

is passed through the tethering ring on the perch, and about ²/₃ of the leash is drawn through. After the first knot is tied, the leash is then slid up tight to the ring and the second knot tied.

Tethering Systems

A disadvantage of the traditional leather jesses, swivel and leash arrangement was that the jesses would migrate down the swivel and interfere with its action, even with a good swivel. When this happened, the falconer, after having left a hawk alone to weather for a while, would find it all tangled up by the perch because the swivel could not operate and the jesses had twisted themselves into such a mess that the hawk's feet were effectively tied together. Alternatively, the swivel might flip through the jesses when the hawk flew back to the perch, or the leash button might get caught between the jesses, again causing the jesses to become twisted together. Some falconers used a leather extender between the jesses and the swivel to avoid twisting of the jesses, but a better system is now available.

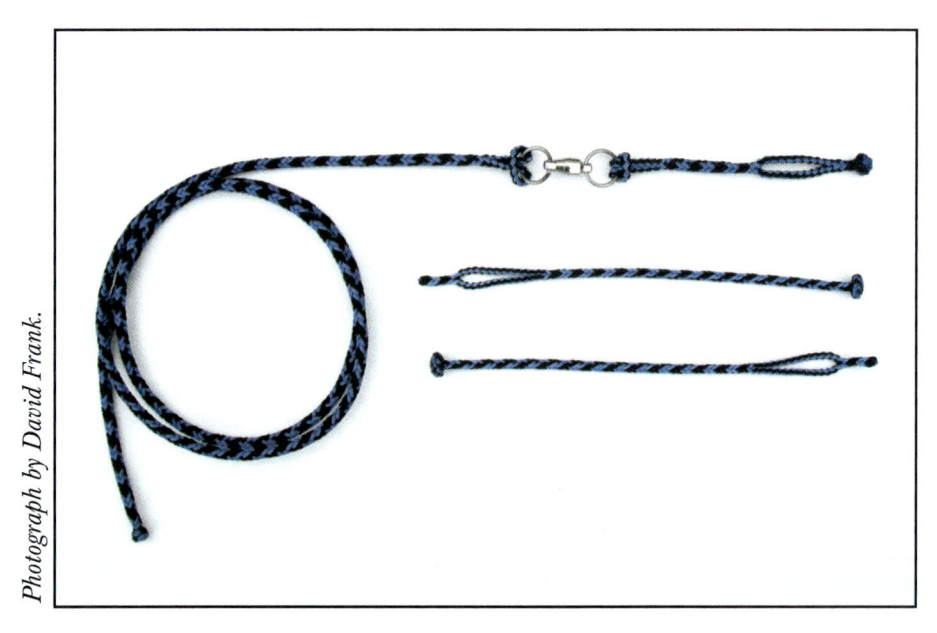

Photograph by David Frank.

The braided tethering system from Western Sporting.

Equipment and Housing for the Hawk

David Frank at Western Sporting provides what he calls the "tethering system," which consists of jesses, extender, swivel and leash all in one braided from nylon blind cord. After using this system for my own hawks, I now use nothing else. Gone is the fear of a hawk getting free because something has broken. Getting tangled up because the swivel cannot operate, either because the jesses have migrated down to the pivot so it cannot turn or because it has flipped back through the jesses, is another fear that has been removed entirely. Further, the material is much stronger than leather, and the breaking strain is constant and known, thus threat of a jess breaking is now completely absent from my mind. The system comes in two styles, the first with the leash permanently attached to the swivel and the second utilizing the Fox loop leash. My own preference is for the first type because I find it easier to get a bating hawk untied and up and away from its perch, but others prefer to use the Fox loop leash style.

Bells

Small bells specially made for falconry are used to help the falconer locate the hawk while it is flying or has become lost. They also make it possible to listen to the hawk on the weathering ground, and the falconer quickly learns from the bell sounds if the hawk is scratching its head or is bating madly because of a danger near the weathering area.

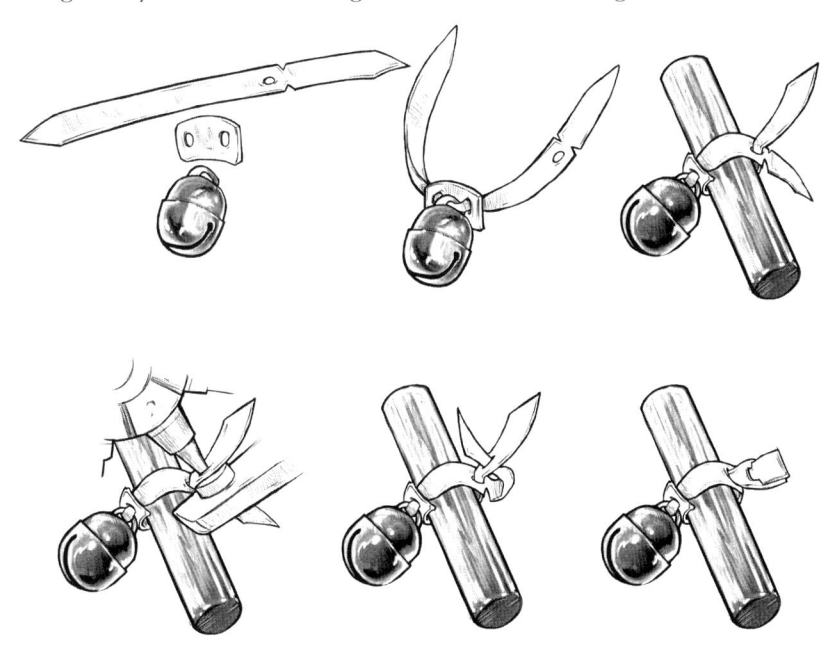

Attaching a bell to the hawk's leg with a bewit. This method is less likely to loosen than the traditional method and is therefore preferred.

[85]

Falconry: A Guide for Beginners

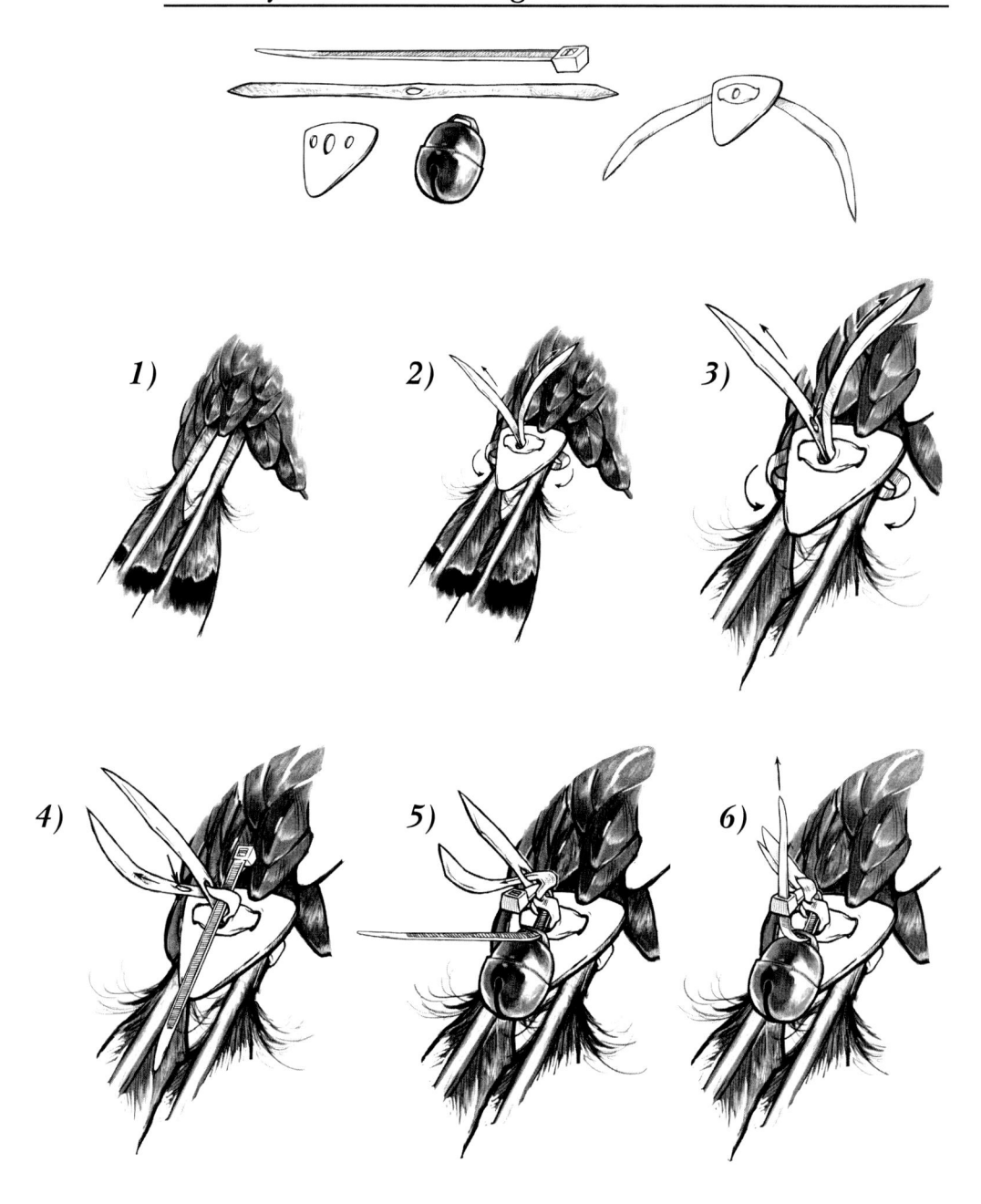

Attaching a tail bell. The materials needed are a guitar plectrum (pick), cable tie and a strip of leather 8 inches in length by ¼ inch wide. This method secures the bell using both deck feathers. If a transmitter is used, the transmitter tail mount is fitted just below the tail bell mount on the top deck feather or can be fitted directly to the plectrum.

[86]

Equipment and Housing for the Hawk

A trained Red-tailed Hawk or Harris' Hawk should carry at least two bells, one fixed to the leg by a bewit and the other to the tail or train as it is correctly called. Both methods are shown in the accompanying figures. An advantage of a tail bell is that even when resting, a hawk moves its tail, consequently ringing the bell and notifying the falconer of the hawk's location. Furthermore, when a hawk is on the ground, vegetation or snow may interfere with the sound of the leg bell, but the tail bell will still be up out of the way and ringing loudly. There are several types of bells on the market; my preference is for acorn type bells. They are slightly more expensive than others, but they last longer and ring better.

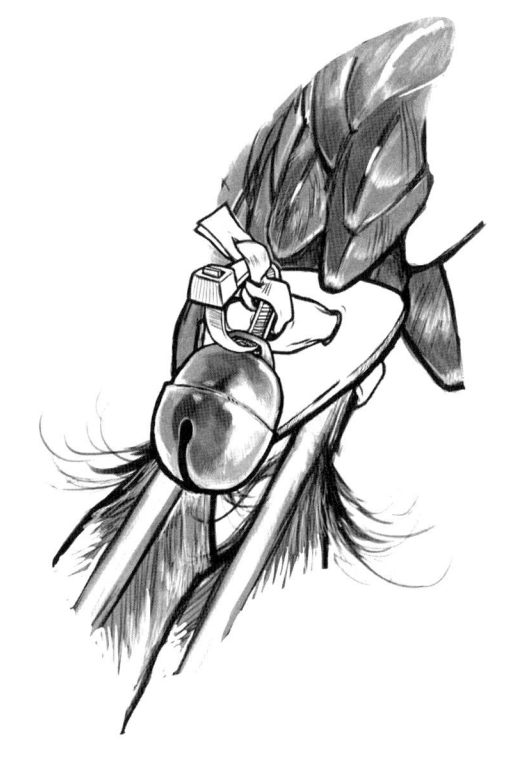

Completed guitar-plectrum tail bell fitted to the tail of a hawk.

Like many falconers, I use a reward tag on each of my hawks with my phone number on one side of the tag and the word "Reward" on the other. I secure the tag using a bewit on the leg without the bell. While a tag doesn't guarantee that someone who finds a lost hawk will pick up the phone and call the number, in most instances it definitely helps. One pigeon fancier on finding a lost gyr-saker hybrid of mine ignored the tag and tried to sell the hawk to a friend of a friend! But on another occasion, one of my employees lost a lanneret and tracked it using the transmitter to a palm tree where the hawk spent the night. The following day, an inspection at the base of the tree confirmed the fear that the tree was home to a Great Horned Owl because surrounding the base of the tree were castings from the owl's previous meals. Feeling dejected, my employee went home only to get a phone call three hours later, reporting that the hawk had flown down to someone who had called the number on the tag. The moral of the story is to never assume a lost hawk is dead!

Falconry: A Guide for Beginners

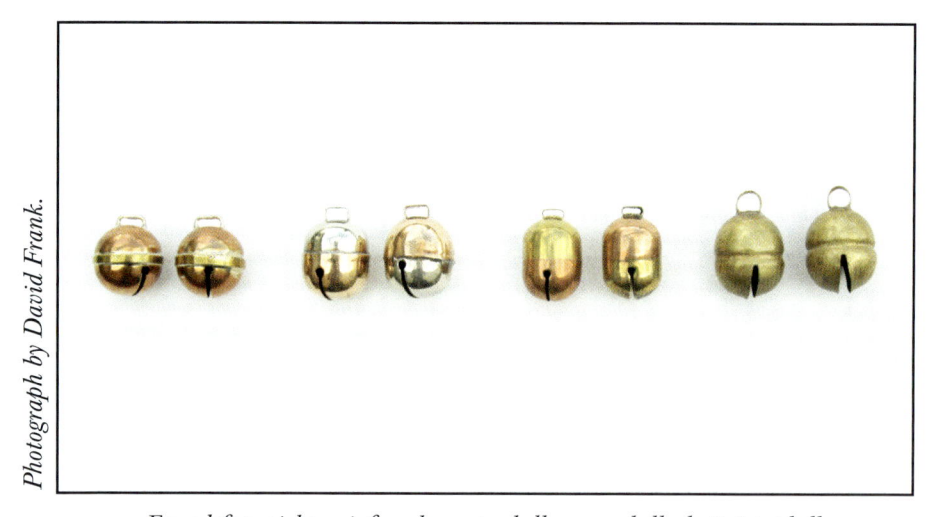

Photograph by David Frank.

From left to right: reinforced equator bells, acorn bells, butt-joint bells and Lahore bells. My preference is for the acorn style, though any bell, which is loud and lasts works fine. The rough opening of the slot on Lahore bells has been known to cause abrasions on the tops of hawks' toes if the bewits stretch at all, which they invariably do at some point.

Telemetry

Radio telemetry is a system used for tracking and hopefully locating a lost hawk. It consists of three main parts: a transmitter fitted to the hawk, a receiver that picks up the transmitter's signal, and a directional finding antenna connected to the receiver that tells the operator which direction the signal is coming from. The transmitter can be fitted to the hawk's leg or tail or placed on a rubber band around its neck or fitted to a backpack that is worn permanently. For a broadwing, my preference is one transmitter placed on the tail. For other hawks, I use one on the tail or back and another on the leg. The broadwings rarely need tracking, and it is generally safe to fly one with just a single transmitter. A transmitter carried on the tail, because it is higher up, gives out a better signal and is less likely to be damaged if the hawk hits quarry hard, as can happen with a leg mounted transmitter. However there is a risk with tail mounted transmitters of their hitting a fence or other obstacle while the hawk is chasing quarry and either falling off or worse still pulling out the feather to which they are attached. If this happens and the feather can be found, make every effort to gently reinsert it into the follicle from which it came. If nothing is done (even another feather or a grain of rice can be used) the follicle will close and the hawk will likely never regrow that feather. No method of transmitter attachment is completely foolproof. Substituting a transmitter for a bell should not be done; a hawk should carry both when free flown.

Equipment and Housing for the Hawk

A tail mount for bell and transmitter.

The receiver should be light enough to be carried by the falconer at all times. It often happens that a hawk is seen to go down after a rabbit or some such within a few hundred yards, but it can be hard to pinpoint the actual spot. If the receiver is carried with the falconer, a signal can quickly be found, but if there is a half mile walk to the vehicle to collect the receiver and bring it back to where the hawk was last seen, a lot of valuable time is wasted. During this time, the hawk may well take its fill from a kill. On many modern telemetry systems, the directional antenna, sometimes referred to as a "yagi," is fixed permanently to the receiver and is collapsible to make transporting it easier. This added feature is important for the falconer who carries a receiver.

While I have used several different systems, my preference now is the transmitters and receivers made by Marshall Radio Telemetry. For longwings I use their RT Turbo transmitter on the hawk's tail or mounted on a backpack as well as their RT+ or on a leg if using a backup. For broadwings and shortwings the RT+ on the tail or backpack is generally sufficient.

[89]

Falconry: A Guide for Beginners

The keys to successful use of telemetry are to get the best equipment available, learn to use it and keep it in good working shape, and make sure everyone who helps also knows how to use it. My job in bird abatement means that I have overall responsibility for a large number of trained hawks, most of them longwings, which are being flown on several different contracts by different employees. We have learned over the years to work out what does and does not work, not only with telemetry, but with many other issues. Some of these lessons, often learned the hard way, have been incorporated into our procedures. Transmitter batteries are changed regularly, so that if a hawk does fly off, the batteries are not going to run out before a good couple of days of tracking can occur. We change our batteries every Monday without fail on all contracts. Therefore, if a hawk goes off on the following Sunday, we know the battery will have had less than about 12 hours of use and we will have at least four remaining days to track it. If I am using a transmitter on only one hawk, I change the transmitter batteries on the first of each month. Every hawk is flown with two transmitters so that if one fails, we can switch to the second.

Each site has spare transmitters so that if one is lost or damaged or must be returned for repair, we still have enough to have two per hawk. All employees know the locations of the local

A Marshall Radio telemetry receiver in use.

Equipment and Housing for the Hawk

high spots so that if a signal is lost while tracking a hawk, they can go straight to the highest elevation in the landscape to search for the signal before resorting to the hiring of an aircraft. At each site, the location of the nearest airport that rents private planes by the hour is known so that if necessary, the hawk can be tracked via aircraft. Receivers and spare batteries for them are carried in the vehicles. Most important of all however, employees are taught how to track signals by sending them off to search for hidden transmitters. They learn how different factors affect the signal, particularly if the hawk lands on the ground or goes down into a ditch or behind a hill or over a mountain or into a building or follows any one of numerous other scenarios we have experienced when tracking lost hawks. They know they should never give up trying to find a signal if there is hope the batteries are still active. A lost transmitter is like a shining light bulb; if a person travels around enough to catch a glimpse, it can be homed in on. Because receivers come with instructions, more details here are not necessary, but the need to practice cannot be overemphasized, so that when a real situation arises, learning does not take place on the job.

A recent giant leap forward in telemetry took place with the introduction of GPS transmitters. While GPS transmitters have been available to wildlife researchers for some time, they were either too expensive, too big or did not send updates in a way that could reliably be used by falconers. These new systems, built specially for falconers, use transmitters to send the GPS coordinates via radio to the falconer, which is then converted using software to show the location of the hawk. One system also incorporates a SIM™ card of the type used in cellphones, which will send a text message with its location when contacted via a text message. While there are various systems available and each has its strengths and weaknesses suffice to say this new step is already revolutionizing the way falconers not only recover lost hawks, but also in how they fly them. By receiving real time data as to the location of the hawk, including height, speed, and direction of travel, etc. decisions can be made on whether to initiate a search or to wait and see what develops. High flying longwings can now be tracked as to their whereabouts in the sky and what was once a panicking falconer on the ground, scanning the sky for his hawk, has now been replaced by a calm falconer monitoring what his hawk is doing via a smart phone or other device, making decisions in real time as to what to do next in the best interest of his hawk. In the last year or so I have come to rely on GPS telemetry completely and will no longer fly a hawk without it.

Falconry: A Guide for Beginners

Hoods

A hood is a leather cap that goes over the hawk's head and eyes, thereby keeping it from seeing anything. Rather like people who put their hands in front of their eyes while watching a scary movie, this will generally calm down a hawk. In the early stages of training when the hawk is very fearful of the falconer, the hood is worn for most of the day. As the hawk becomes accustomed to the falconer through the processes of manning and training, time in the hood decreases until eventually it is only used to prevent bating at times such as when confined in the car while travelling to and from the hawking fields. There are several styles of hoods, and unfortunately, not many falconers or even some suppliers who sell hoods know the difference. In modern books on falconry, especially those written and published in the U.S., hoods have been misidentified, thereby adding to the confusion. To clarify this, three main hood types in common use are identified in the accompanying photographs.

> Braces. Straps traditionally made of leather, but nowadays mostly of the nylon-type waterproof fabrics, which are used to open and close a hood.

Dutch Hood

The body of the Dutch hood consists of three separate pieces sewn or glued together. The back of the hood can open or close by means of braces threaded through the hood. Dutch hoods are shaped on a block resembling the hawk's head but are larger on the sides to prevent the hood rubbing against the eyes. To open a hood is to strike it; to close it is to draw it. When a hood is in the open position it is referred to as struck, when closed, as drawn.

Photographs by David Frank.

The front of a typical Dutch-style hood.

The back of a typical Dutch-style hood showing the braces.

Equipment and Housing for the Hawk

Indian Hood

Developed in India hundreds of years ago, the body of this hood consists of one piece of leather. Because it is sewn all the way up the back of the hood, it does not open or close. It has no real place in modern falconry.

Anglo-Indian Hood

It is not known who actually thought of the idea to put Dutch braces on an Indian hood, thereby creating the Anglo-Indian hood, but we have a lot to thank them for. The Anglo-Indian hood consists of a one-piece Indian hood with the back open and Dutch braces inserted to allow it to be opened and closed.

A cast of lanners wearing Anglo-Indian hoods. Comfort is the most important aspect to consider when choosing a hood for a particular hawk.

Falconry: A Guide for Beginners

Arabian-style hood: This type of traditional hood has been made into many variations, especially with regard to modificatons at the closure in the back.

Photographs by David Frank.

The front of a modified Arabian-style hood.

The back of a modified Arabian-style hood.

Arabian Hood

The body of the traditional Arabian hood is also made from one piece of leather, but has a different shape entirely than the Indian hood. It has braces in the back that thread through the hood several times causing it to draw shut like a concertina. Arabian hoods are also lightweight compared to the original Dutch hoods, though recent improvements in hoodmaking have made Dutch hoods as light as the other types. Thus, any advantage the Arabian or Anglo-Indian hoods once had in this department no longer exists.

Equipment and Housing for the Hawk

Palmyra Hood.

A new type of hood was recently designed which tries to incorporate the best features of the three other types: the firmness of the Dutch hood, the wide opening at the back of the Anglo-Indian hood, and the soft beak opening of the Arabian hood. Called the Palmyra hood, the body is made of two pieces of leather. The front, which houses the opening for the beak, is made from soft, slightly thinner leather than the main body of the hood, which is made from thicker, firmer leather that helps the hood keep its shape. The opening at the back is cut high like the Anglo-Indian style allowing it to go on easily.

A passage Red-tailed Hawk wearing the newly designed Palmyra hood.

Choice of Hood

The most important thing about any hood is not style or price or attractiveness—it is fit. I have had good success with Anglo-Indian, Arabian, and Dutch hoods as long as the fit is correct. If it isn't, the style doesn't really matter, nor does who made it or how much it cost. Formerly, I made my own Anglo-Indian hoods, but there are now so many good hoods available from talented hoodmakers that to make one's own hoods is as practical as making one's own shoes, even though many falconers still enjoy the challenge. For those who do wish to try their hand at hoodmaking, I recommend they study *Hoods, Hooding and Hoodmaking* by Jim Nelson.

I do not generally use traditional Arabian-style hoods except on some Saker Falcons and on shortwings. For the other species, there is a tendency of having to push the Arabian hood onto the head with a little too much pressure for my liking; I prefer a hood that goes on smoothly and easily. The shape of a shortwing's head, and perhaps not surprisingly, of the Saker Falcon's, blend well with the Arabian hood. The window-backed Arabian hoods do go on nicely though, and being soft, they are very comfortable for hawks to wear. For other species, I use either Dutch or Anglo-Indian hoods, the latter preferably blocked in the same style as the Dutch. Martin Jones in England pioneered the idea of blocking Anglo-Indian hoods. To tell them apart from the traditional Anglo-Indian hoods, which were not blocked and were generally a lot softer than the blocked type, he referred to them simply as blocked Anglo-Indian hoods. Unfortunately, this term has not migrated across the Atlantic, so many equipment suppliers in the U.S. mistakenly refer to their blocked Anglo-Indian hoods by other names. Regardless, they make for a very useful type of hood that tends to cost less than the blocked Dutch style hoods.

The braces that open and close the hood were traditionally made of leather, which would stretch very quickly, especially if it got wet. Within a short space of time, the braces became loose with the result that the hawk could get the hood off. Some hawks become very adept at removing a hood if they are once able to succeed at it. In the last few years nylon braces or other outdoor breathable fabric has come into fashion. They are such an improvement that I no longer even bother with leather braces.

When buying hoods, it is best to order several in the size for the hawk being acquired. All hoods tend to vary slightly, and it is not unusual for them to need the slight modification of opening up the gape with a scalpel. It pays to have spares. A falconer can never have too many hoods. When a new hawk is acquired, the first thing needed is a hood that fits well. If only one hood is purchased and it doesn't fit, it is sufficient to say that the hawk is going to go through a lot more stress than necessary. Hooding will be covered in more detail in the section on training. Here, it is enough to know that for a passage redtail, any of the different types of hoods will work as long as it fits.

Equipment and Housing for the Hawk

To keep hoods in good shape and help them last a long time, I grease them at least twice a year and whenever they are put into storage. To keep them in shape while out hawking, I attach them to a clip on the outside of my hawking jacket. A useful alternative is to use a hood protector available from falconry equipment suppliers. This will protect the hood at all times and can be attached to the falconer's belt or jacket or bag. Hoods should be taken care of and cleaned when necessary. The hawk spends time wearing a hood each day there is an excursion to the field, and nothing is more annoying to me, and probably to the hawk, than a falconer cramming an ill-fitting, dirty hood onto the hawk, who must then put up with it. Any food that gets inside the hood should be scraped out as soon as it appears. It is useful to make a habit of blowing into the hood to remove any dust before placing the hood on the hawk's head. When not in use, the hood should be hung up somewhere dry and out of reach of inquisitive children and dogs. A damp hood should not be put on a hawk unless it is unavoidable, if, for instance, it rains while out hawking.

Perches
Outside Perches
The final requirement for the hawk is a perch. For outside there are three main perch styles—the block perch, bow perch, and ring perch.

Block Perches
Traditionally, block perches are reserved for longwings, it being noted that they normally sit with their feet in the flat, open position. Shortwings and broadwings, which normally perch in trees, tend to be more comfortable on a bow or ring perch that more resembles a tree branch. Different materials including wood, metal and plastic have been used for the actual block part. Metal should be avoided where cold temperatures are experienced as they can lead to frostbite on the hawk's toes. My preference is for a fairly simple design with a relatively shallow, disc-like top and a long stem. I developed this reasoning over decades spent training longwings and based it on what happens when a hawk bates as I am picking it up. In that instance, I like to quickly get the hawk up away from the ground as far as possible to prevent any feather damage.

A block with a low, fixed anchor point keeps both hawk and falconer near the ground where a lot of damage can be done before the hawk is up on the fist and calmed down. Some books state that a low fixed tie point puts less stress on the hawk's legs when bating, but I have seen no evidence of this, rather the opposite in fact. It is an advantage to have the ring travel up during a bate to give the hawk more room to get away from the block

Falconry: A Guide for Beginners

before being stopped at the end of the leash. With a fixed low point, the hawk may well bounce back into the block or ground with its tail, but with the block I prefer, no matter what direction the hawk bates, the act of the ring travelling up the stem will, even slightly, act as a brake slowing down the stress at the end of the bate on both the legs and equipment. If bating upward, as many hawks do, the ring will travel up the stem so that when brought to a stop at the end of the leash, the hawk will be further away from the block than if there is a fixed, low tie point.

While block perches are normally used for longwings, many other hawks also like them. Tradition should not dictate where a hawk sits. Redtails, for example, often sit on the tops of telephone poles with their feet spread wide. To give the hawk a choice, it can be tied to a block perch one day and the next to another type of perch to see if a preference can be detected. Merlins, in my experience, are much more comfortable on bow perches than the traditional block perches they have historically been forced to sit on. I assume this is because merlins often sit on branches of trees as shortwings do, so my merlins sit on bow perches, and we both remain deaf to the comments of other falconers stating that longwings should sit only on block perches!

A gyr-saker hybrid on a block perch of the style preferred by the author. The top is lathe turned Ultra High Molecular Weight Polyethylene or UHMW. This is the same material cutting boards are made from and it does not need varnishing as wood does, will not crack, is easy to clean, and is virtually indestructible.

Equipment and Housing for the Hawk

Bow and Ring Perches

Bow perches were traditionally made of wood, sometimes with dire consequences as the wood partially weathered and eventually broke, releasing the hawk with not only its jesses, swivel and leash attached, but the ring as well. Metal has now replaced wood, and where the hawk sits, the perch is padded with a varying array of materials including rubber, nylon rope, cotton rope, leather and Astroturf. It is important to remember that a hawk spends a lot of time on its perch, so the padding has to be comfortable. I prefer to give my hawk a choice, so I have perches with different types of padding that I use on alternate days. This helps prevent sore points from becoming established on the bottoms of the feet. If not detected, they can quickly lead to bumblefoot.

The bow perch is so named because it resembles an archer's bow stuck into the ground. It is the best and safest design for broadwings and shortwings. The top of the bow should be no more than 11 inches above the ground for a hawk the size of a redtail. If any higher, there is an increased risk of the leash getting hooked up in some way during a bate, causing the hawk to damage its tail feathers. The spikes should be at least 9 inches in length to eliminate any possibility of the hawk pulling the perch out of soft ground and then dragging it around. If there are other hawks nearby, one of them will likely end up dead. Another important feature is the angle at which the bow leaves the ground. There is a tendency, especially if the bow is made up by a welder with little or no knowledge of falconry, to put the cross bar that rests on the ground right where the angle changes from the vertical. If this is done, the angle will be too great to allow the ring to slide freely over the perch when the hawk bates. If the hawk has been tied with too long a leash, there is a chance it will walk around and back through the bow and become trapped. A friend had this misfortune happen to his Tawny Eagle who was thus trapped and unable to get up. As bad luck would have it, his ferret also escaped at the same time, attacked the eagle and killed her. In falconry, if it can go wrong, it will. When tethering a hawk to a bow perch, a leash need not be longer than 18 inches when tied. This is more than sufficient for the hawk to get clear of the bow when bating, yet not too long to allow the buildup of enough speed to put undue stress on the legs. Neither does it allow the hawk to double back under the bow and become entangled in the leash.

Falconry: A Guide for Beginners

Over the last four years or so I have begun to use high block perches with the top of the perch some 30 inches above ground level. The hawks seem calmer on these higher perches, are less likely to bate and are easier to approach and pick up during the early stages of manning. The perch is introduced as soon as the hawk has shown a willingness to jump back onto a regular height block perch. The leash should be tied so that the ring lies about 9–12 inches above the ground while the hawk is sitting on the perch. When the hawk bates, if the leash gets caught over the top of the perch she will flap to one side or another and free the leash and any hang up is generally momentary. It is a mistake to use a leash so long that the ring lies on the ground as there is then a danger that if the hawk bates in such a way as to end up with the leash hooked over the top of the perch, she is likely to continue to try to reach the ground, it being so close by, rather than flap to one side and free the leash. The actual block top used on these perches should be chosen carefully. Plastic tops with smooth sides and with a depression in which the Astroturf sits are preferred so that the leash can easily slide to one side. Avoid any type of block top on which the Astroturf sits directly on top, or with rough edges as both these will snag the leash.

Equipment and Housing for the Hawk

Intermewed captive-bred Harris' Hawk on a bow perch. Note that the angle of the perch sides as they leave the ground is less than 90 degrees thereby ensuring the ring moves smoothly and freely when the hawk bates.

While a ring perch is the same shape in cross section as a bow perch, the design is sufficiently different to warrant some caveats. It is crucial that when any hawk has finished bating from any kind of perch, the leash must be lying flat along the ground. If the leash is raised off the ground in any way, it will interfere with and eventually fray and break the tail feathers. The problem with the standard ring perch is that if a hawk bates toward the opposite side from that where the leash is hanging, the leash may well get trapped in the padding and not end up flat on the ground as it should. Some ring perch designs try to overcome this with a ring that is fixed to the side of the perch, which rotates as the hawk bates, thereby theoretically preventing a situation of the leash ending up over the top of the perch. The problem however, is that there is a higher tie point than necessary, so the leash will still end up splitting the tail feathers, resulting in frayed and broken feathers, and that is not

Falconry: A Guide for Beginners

acceptable. Furthermore, many hawks do not like a perch rotating beneath them. Despite improvements in ring perches, I see no advantage over a bow perch, and I do not use them.

Another perch is the so-called tail saver perch. This modification of a standard bow perch design ostensibly sets out to prevent damage to the tail by using the leash to lift the tail clear of the ground when the hawk bates. This will very quickly result in broken tail feathers, and it should not be used.

The problem of perches with high tie points, as shown here, is that the leash is lifted up through the tail feathers when the hawk bates from the perch and the leash at this angle will very quickly wreck them.

Equipment and Housing for the Hawk

For outside purposes therefore, my preference for a Red-tailed Hawk or Harris' Hawk is a bow perch. I use one padded with cotton line, and on alternate days, one with Astroturf or rubber. I am not against seeing a redtail on a block perch, but I prefer a bow perch.

A haggard African Hawk-Eagle. Every precaution has been taken to make sure she is safe and secure. The bow perch is pushed firmly into the ground so she cannot get the leash caught under or around any part of it. Where the bow goes into the ground, the angle has been lessened to ensure that if she does bate one way or another, the leash and ring will follow her so the leash is left lying flat along the ground where it cannot interfere with her feathers. The padding is not so long that it will affect the leash moving freely over the bow. The edges of the padding are finished with electrical tape so the ring may move freely, and the ring is plenty large enough to move freely over the padding. Finally, she is fitted with the Western Sporting tethering system so there are no leather jesses nor leather leash to break, and she wears anklets made of Biothane®, which will not break or stretch.

[103]

Falconry: A Guide for Beginners

For several years I have been using high rotating ring perches for broadwings and shortwings. A hawk on this type of perch is almost six feet off the ground and as such they feel much more secure and are less likely to spend their time idly bating as some hawks, particularly the accipiters, often do. The actual ring perch on which the hawk sits rotates so that if the hawk bates towards the opposite side to which the leash is tied, the ring quickly rotates freeing it to slide down to the ground. Hawks on this type of perch are not, as is often thought, tied with a six-foot-long leash, such a leash would cause problems when the hawk bated as it would allow it to build up too much speed before the end of the leash is reached. The usual leash is used and tied so that the ring hangs just below the rotating ring part of the perch. As such, when the hawk bates, the ring slides down the pole of the perch and rests flat on the ground. Hawks also get some exercise flying back up to these high perches.

Equipment and Housing for the Hawk

Inside perches

Inside the mews, I prefer the hawk to be perched up off the ground so that it can see through the window and so when I approach to pick it up, I am on its level rather than towering above, which might cause a bate, especially in the early stages of training. Traditionally, screen perches were used in the mews, but I now use table-mounted perches, either a block, bow, or loop perch depending on the species of hawk being flown. Along one wall of the mews, a shelf is built some 4 feet in width and 3 feet from the ground. For a block perch, a square section measuring 2 feet by 2 feet is cut out of the table top, and a corresponding piece is placed underneath the table. The perch is fitted into this depression and sand or corn cob litter catches the mutes. A 12–14 inch length of ½ or ¾-inch electrical pipe with fittings on each end is attached to the underside of the block and the top of the table. A 2-inch ring is fitted over the pipe before the block top is put in place. The bottom fitting is screwed or bolted to the tabletop. I use a 3-inch piece of 4 by 4 so that the bottom fitting, and more importantly the ring, sit above the sand or corn cob litter.

Table mounted block perches are very useful for keeping longwings inside a mews. They are far superior to screen perches, and in my opinion, are better than shelf perches.

Falconry: A Guide for Beginners

For a table-mounted bow perch, the shelf is built 4 feet in width, 3 feet from the ground, and the same length as the wall along which it is fixed. This shelf is surrounded on all sides with 2 by 4 lumber so that a depression is created which is 4 inches (actually 3 ½ inches) deep. This is filled with corn cob litter or sand. A bow perch is fixed to the base of the shelf. It is easiest to use a portable or indoor bow perch with a base that can be bolted to the shelf so it cannot move in any way. As an alternative to mounting the shelf directly to the wall of the mews, a table can be built along similar lines.

Male Harris' Hawk on a table-mounted bow perch.

Equipment and Housing for the Hawk

Loop perch

Another useful type of perch for the mews is the loop perch. The chief advantage of this perch is that it is almost impossible for the hawk to get caught up in any way. Also, because the hawk is able to move about the perch a bit, it can burn off excess energy by jumping or hopping from side to side. The loop perch can either be placed on the floor or on a shelf as described for the shelf-block perch. It is suitable for all species of hawks. It is fairly easy to make one from a length of 12-inch by 1-inch lumber that runs the width of the mews or between the partitions as appropriate. The metal loop part will need to be made by a welder, but it is fairly simple to construct. It is secured to the base of the shelf or to a heavy plate underneath a perch that will be placed on the floor. When the hawk bates forward, the leash lies flat on the ground as it should. If the hawk bates backwards, which few hawks do because of the limited space, the ring will flip over to the side of the perch the hawk is now on, again leaving it lying flat on the floor out of harm's way. I anticipate that this perch will come into more general use over the next few years.

A newly taken up, captive-bred male Harris' Hawk on a table mounted loop perch. The table itself is set at waist height so that when the hawk is approached, the falconer is not towering over it, which can cause alarm. It is imperative that the leash is tied so the hawk can only just reach the carpeted section at the front of the perch and cannot hang over the edge. On a 4-foot wide table, the perch is placed 18 inches from the back, giving it 30 inches at the front.

Falconry: A Guide for Beginners

Bath Pan

Once the hawk has settled into the routine of being handled and trained she should be offered a bath pan regularly. It may take her a while to become relaxed enough to use it but it should be offered to her as soon as she is weathering unhooded on the weathering lawn. The bath needs to be large enough for her to get thoroughly wet and deep enough so that she can dip her shoulders underneath the water. For a red-tail, a diameter of 24-30 inches and depth of 4-5 inches is sufficient. For hawks which are free lofted a bath pan can be left permanently in the mews. While the advice in many falconry books is to offer the hawk a bath before it is flown, many hawks like a drink after flying and so I generally, even if it is at the end of the day, perch a hawk next to a bath for a few minutes after returning from flying. It is surprising how often they will jump down and take a drink, then return to their perch without taking a bath. If not given this opportunity, they may become dehydrated. Many hawks will take a sip of water if offered to them regularly from a cup or small bowl after flying. Alternatively, some falconers dip some of the hawk's daily rations into water prior to feeding up the hawk after flying. I even had a Eurasian Sparrowhawk many years ago that would leave the fist and wade into the nearest puddle to take a drink while out hawking. Below is a group of longwings enjoying the morning sun and a chance to bath in clean clear water in a secure weathering area.

Equipment and Housing for the Hawk

Transport Box or Giant/Modified Hoods and Cadges

For transporting a hawk to and from the field, many falconers use a giant or modified hood, really a rather fancy name for a large box! Transport box is perhaps a better term. Transport boxes are useful for several reasons. For hawks which do not take, or have not been properly trained to the hood, the transport box is a far better option than leaving the hawk unhooded in the back of the vehicle where it is likely to bate and possibly damage feathers, not to mention draw attention to itself from anyone who happens to see it. If away from home, the transport box is a suitable place to let the hawk sleep. If left hooded she may have trouble casting through the hood whereas in a transport box this will not be an

Immature goshawk in the type of transport box made by Western Sporting. Note how the leash is tied to the outside of the box to prevent the hawk inadvertently escaping when the door is opened. Hawks should not be left unsecured in such boxes unless they will be opened in a closed room or mews.

Falconry: A Guide for Beginners

issue. It is crucial however, that adequate ventilation be provided and that the hood be cleaned thoroughly each time it is used. The transport box pictured and sold by Western Sporting has a fan incorporated to allow adequate ventilation and many falconers, especially in the UK, place a small container of freshly picked pine needles inside which act as a natural disinfectant.

My own choice for day to day hawking, is to transport the hawk hooded on a cadge of some kind and to reserve the transport box hood for periods when I am hawking away from home. Transport boxes, if not constructed properly or used too frequently can cause feather wear because more often than not, the feathers are apt to come into contact with the sides of the box. A hawk on a cadge can spread its wings to balance itself if the vehicle suddenly lurches, whereas the same hawk in a transport box hood would smack its wings into the side of the box. Therefore, a cadge on a bed of kitty litter that is cleaned out as often as necessary is my preference for transporting hawks when I will be returning the same day. Whether a cadge or a transport box is used, the

Passage Red-tailed Hawk on a cadge. The cadge is placed on a bed of kitty litter which is contained within a homemade coroplast container to keep everything neat and tidy. The advantage of this system over a modified hood is that the hawk gets much better ventilation and cannot damage its wings and tail feathers.

Equipment and Housing for the Hawk

hawk should ride to and from its destination at right angles to the direction of travel, in other words, facing either forward or backward, not sideways. In this way, it can maintain better balance against the turns of the vehicle.

The cadge pictured can easily be made from a length of 12 inch by 2 inch board some 14 inches in length. Two supporting feet, made from 2 by 4 lumber 12 inches in length are screwed securely to the bottom of the cadge to give it stability. I attach rubber matting to the bottom of the feet to give extra grip. Astroturf is fastened to the top of the cadge with glue and staples to provide a good surface to hold on to. A screw eye is fastened into the top of the cadge or on the front for tying the leash to.

Scales

Scales are used for weighing a hawk, which is an aid in determining its condition. There are two main types of scales, the counter balance or mechanical type and the electronic type. Electronic scales have improved greatly in the last decade. Provided that a check weight, which is an item of known weight, is used to verify accuracy at least once a week, an electronic scale is more than adequate. I do not use the triple beam balance used by many falconers; I think that electronic scales are easier to move around and are more rugged. Scales should be accurate to within ¼ of an ounce or 8 grams for a redtail. A perch for the hawk should be affixed to the scale, providing an adequate surface to hold onto.

Glove

A glove for a Red-tailed Hawk needs to be strong enough to prevent the talons penetrating through it into the falconer's hand, yet supple enough to feel the jesses and the grip of the hawk and to maintain a hold on the food. The glove should extend at least halfway to the elbow. While some falconers use a welder's glove, I find they look ridiculous. A falconer ought to at least try to look the part, not as if he has just finished his workday, left the proper equipment at home, and rushed out into the field to fly a hawk. Traditionally, hawks are held on the left hand, allowing the right hand to remain free for hooding and tying the falconer's knot, but if it is easier to hold the hawk on the right hand and do these other activities with the left hand, there is nothing wrong with that. When buying a glove, the falconer should make sure it is made with the rough side of the leather to the outside. If the smooth side is on

Falconry: A Guide for Beginners

the outside, it will quickly become too slippery for the hawk. It is worthwhile getting a new glove each year for reasons of hygiene, though if taken care of, gloves will last a lot longer.

Lures and Lure Lines

A lure has two purposes. One use is as an object that the trained hawk associates with food and that can be used to recall the hawk to the falconer. The second use is to teach the hawk that objects similar in appearance to the lure are food and should be chased. The first type of lure is known as a recall lure, and the second type, a dummy lure. It is not necessary to use only a single lure for both purposes, and where broadwings such as redtails are concerned, a different lure for each purpose is recommended. While redtails are trained to return to the fist just like other broadwings and shortwings, there may be occasions

Red-tailed Hawk on an electronic scale.

Equipment and Housing for the Hawk

when the redtail is reluctant to do so. Having made the hawk to the lure in addition to the fist may well prevent its loss. Furthermore, if the hawk is lost, it is much easier to walk around swinging a lure that can be seen from a long way off than to walk around holding up a fist. I therefore train all my broadwings and shortwings to the same type of recall lure that I use for all my longwings. Longwings, especially the larger ones, are normally trained exclusively to return to the recall lure for the simple reason that in the wild they tend to strike their prey at very high speed. Having to brake and land on the fist, is thus an unnatural act for them, although I have had a few that would do it. Also, because longwings are typically recalled from much greater distances than the broadwings or shortwings, a recall lure is more visible to them.

    I use a recall lure that is made from a rubber doormat available at large home improvement stores or from a black rubber inner tube. A length of rubber is cut that is approximately 12 inches long by 8 inches wide. Two inches in from the longest side, strips are cut every half inch, resulting in what looks like the makings of a grass skirt, albeit a rather small one! The whole thing is then rolled up, and parachute cord keeps it from unraveling. A separate piece of parachute cord is threaded through the center of the lure. It is used for tying food to the lure and for securing the lure to a swivel attached to the lure line. One side is

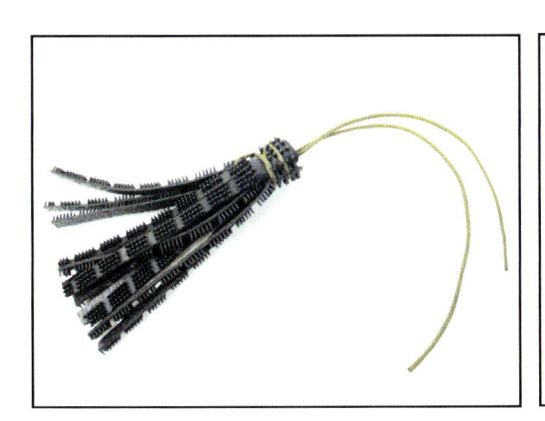

Photographs by David Frank.

On the left is a rubber recall lure made from a doormat. On the right is a lure stick and line. The weight and size of the lure can be modified by using less rubber, shortening the length of the strands or even by removing some of them. Such a lure cannot hurt a hawk, can be easily made up and cleaned, and will last a long time without losing its appearance. The strands on the one pictured, which I use for all my medium to large hawks, are about 6 inches long, while the lure itself measures about 8 inches long. One falconer found it also works well for swatting cows when they invade the flying ground!

Falconry: A Guide for Beginners

longer than the other, and this is the part threaded through the swivel. A square knot is then tied. By having one side longer than the other, the knot cannot interfere in any way with the free operation of the swivel.

The advantages of this type of lure over other types, such as leather birds or wings from quarry, is that they are cheaply made, easy to clean and disinfect (being made of rubber), and that they last a long time. Not only that, but after 6 to 12 months of use, they still resemble their original appearance. A pair of mallard wings used as a lure for 6 months, (or perhaps a lot less) will look nothing like it did at first. The deterioration is gradual, and the hawk slowly becomes conditioned to responding to something that ends up looking like two broken feathers and a piece of string. When the falconer finally decides to get a new pair of duck wings, the hawk may not recognize it as a lure at all. Not to mention there are many bacteria inhabiting such a filthy mess. Rubber lures can be easily cleaned, easily replaced, are virtually indestructible and therefore last a long time, do not change in appearance, and cannot hurt the hawk (or the falconer). It's easy to make up several at once, and if a hawk is lost, anyone available can rush out to swing a lure around. For all those reasons, I recommend a rubber lure as a recall lure.

A recall lure is attached to a lure line that is wound up on a stick when not in use. The line should be at least 4 yards in length. Many falconers use too short a lure line, and I have seen longwings lost because the falconer could not get far enough away from the lure to call a nervous hawk down. What happens is that the hawk is a bit spooked and doesn't want to come close to the falconer to land on the lure that is lying about 3 feet away as he or she holds onto the stick. The falconer kneels down to give the hawk more room, but still cannot get more than a few feet from the lure. Eventually the hawk stops making passes and goes off on its own, in one instance I witnessed, never to be seen again, all for the sake of a few extra yards of line. With a 4-yard lure line, a falconer can put out a lure a good distance away, thus giving a nervous hawk plenty of room to come in and land on the lure without feeling crowded or intimidated. I use a line of braided cotton, as it is a bit softer on the fingers than nylon when swinging it around, although parachute cord also works well. The stick is 8 inches long, and the line goes through a hole drilled in its center and is tied so it cannot fall off. In addition to holding the line when the lure is not in use, the stick adds weight, so that if the falconer does let go, it will bring the hawk down within about 50 yards. At the far end of the line is a swivel, generally a freely spinning one like a Sampo® swivel. Through the other end of the swivel, the lure is attached.

Equipment and Housing for the Hawk

A rabbit lure made from a canvas dog-retrieving dummy covered with fake fur from a craft store.

    The dummy lure is used to teach a hawk that "this is what prey looks like, and you should chase it." For the redtail, the most common dummy lure is a fake rabbit made from a rabbit skin, fake fur, or suitably colored leather. Soft dog retrieving dummies (not the hard plastic ones) can be used as a base for the lure with either a rabbit skin or fake fur glued or sewn around the dummy. Strings should be tied to the front end for attaching food, and the throwing handle can be used to secure the lure line or creance for dragging it. It is also useful to attach some leather ears at the appropriate end. This will help the hawk to orient to the end where the head is, which is where it should learn to secure its quarry. Most importantly, a rabbit lure must look like a rabbit. That may sound obvious, but I've seen some amazing lures including one about the size of a pillow that wouldn't fit inside the falconer's bag. Squirrel lures can also be useful to introduce a redtail to squirrels if the hawk is slow to recognize them as prey. I do not use bird lures for redtails. Once they are entered to other prey, most redtails will chase a pheasant or duck if it gets close enough, and bird slips with redtails tend to be infrequent compared to rabbit and squirrel flights.

Falconry: A Guide for Beginners

Creance

A creance is a long line used during the period of training before the hawk can be trusted to fly free. The simplest form of creance, and the one I use, is 50 yards of braided Dacron with a breaking strain between 120lbs and 150lbs. It is wound up on a stick when not being used and is always carried in the field whenever I am flying a hawk. Creances have other uses besides just being an insurance policy before the hawk is flying free. They can be used as a very long lure line to coax back a nervous hawk, or a dummy lure can be attached so the falconer can break the association of the lure following him or her. For instance, I frequently attach a dummy lure to the end of a creance, run the creance around a tree or through some bushes

Photograph by David Frank.

Fifty yards of braided Dacron wound on a stick makes a perfectly good creance and is easy to carry in the hawking bag or vest. A falconer leaving home with his or her hawk should never be without a creance.

and then out the other side to be pulled by someone else as I approach with the hawk. Creances can also be used to trap a very nervous hawk that will not allow itself to be picked up from the lure. This is done by unwinding the creance and putting the stick firmly into the ground. The falconer walks away from the hawk until the creance is at full length, then walks around the hawk, wrapping up its legs on the way. Circling one and a half times is generally enough as long as the falconer ends up on the side opposite to the stick so the slip knot just created can be pulled tight. The chapter on training includes more information on proper use of a creance.

Equipment and Housing for the Hawk

Lure Machine

I began using the lure machine some 20 years ago, and it revolutionized the way I trained my hawks, got them entered, and kept them fit. The design was pioneered by the late Tom Bianchi for use in training and exercising dogs, primarily sight hounds used for coursing rabbits. The heart of the machine is a starter motor, which is powered by a 12-volt car battery, or even better, a deep cycle marine battery. Many zoos now use them for exercising cheetahs, but falconers, at least in the U.S., have been slow to recognize their potential. The lure machine can be set up two different ways. The first is with a take-up wheel that holds from 800 to 1200 yards of line, and the second is with a continuous loop wheel. With a take-up wheel, the line is pulled out, around some pulleys if desired, and when the trigger is pressed, whatever is on the end of the line, be it a recall lure or dummy rabbit, is pulled back toward the machine at speeds of up to 40 miles per hour. With a continuous loop wheel, a course can be set up to run around a number of pulleys, continuing around the loop wheel

A lure machine with the take-up wheel fitted. The battery is disconnected here so the machine can more clearly be seen. To the front lies the trigger. My latest version is remote-controlled and can be operated from up to 100 yards away. This means I can set up flights for my hawk, and she will have no idea where the lure is coming from.

Falconry: A Guide for Beginners

in a never ending loop. While the initial cost may be a turn-off, (about $500 at the time of this writing), it is an item that can easily be shared by a number of falconers. A lure machine makes entering a hawk much easier, and it makes exercising a lot more fun and interesting for both the falconer and the hawk.

Hawking Bags and Vests

The final item needed is for carrying all the equipment the falconer takes to the field plus the hawk's quarry. This item can be either a bag or a vest. I used bags for the first 10 years of my career as a falconer, but once I switched to vests, I never changed back. A vest has many more pockets for holding the items a falconer uses in the field, and the weight is distributed on both shoulders, making it more comfortable to wear, especially while running. There are vests custom-made for falconry, or one can use a fly fishing vest with a few modifications, mainly something waterproof for carrying quarry that might be bloody. The items on the following list are always stored and carried in my hawking vest.

A hawking bag on the left and a hawking vest on the right. The choice is up to each individual falconer, but I prefer a vest.

Equipment and Housing for the Hawk

My list includes:
- Spare jesses, both mews and field. Swivel and leash.
- Creance.
- Rubber recall lure, lure stick and line.
- Tube of antiseptic cream in case the hawk is injured, perhaps by a squirrel bite. It is important to put antibiotic ointment on a wound within minutes to prevent infection from setting in.
- Knife that can be opened and closed with one hand.
- Sharpened screwdriver and pair of electrical wire strippers for dispatching quarry.
- A clip on the outside of the vest for the hood when it is not on the hawk.
- Food for the hawk. Before being put in a vest pocket, this goes inside a plastic sandwich bag that is used only once, then thrown away.
- Copies of permits. They are kept inside a waterproof bag in a zipped inner pocket.
- Hawking whistle. My first action after putting on the vest is to remove the whistle and place it around my neck. I use a referee's whistle because the sound tends to carry farther than that of other whistles.
- A larger plastic bag for any quarry that is caught. Quarry is placed inside the bag, then carried in the vest's big back pocket.

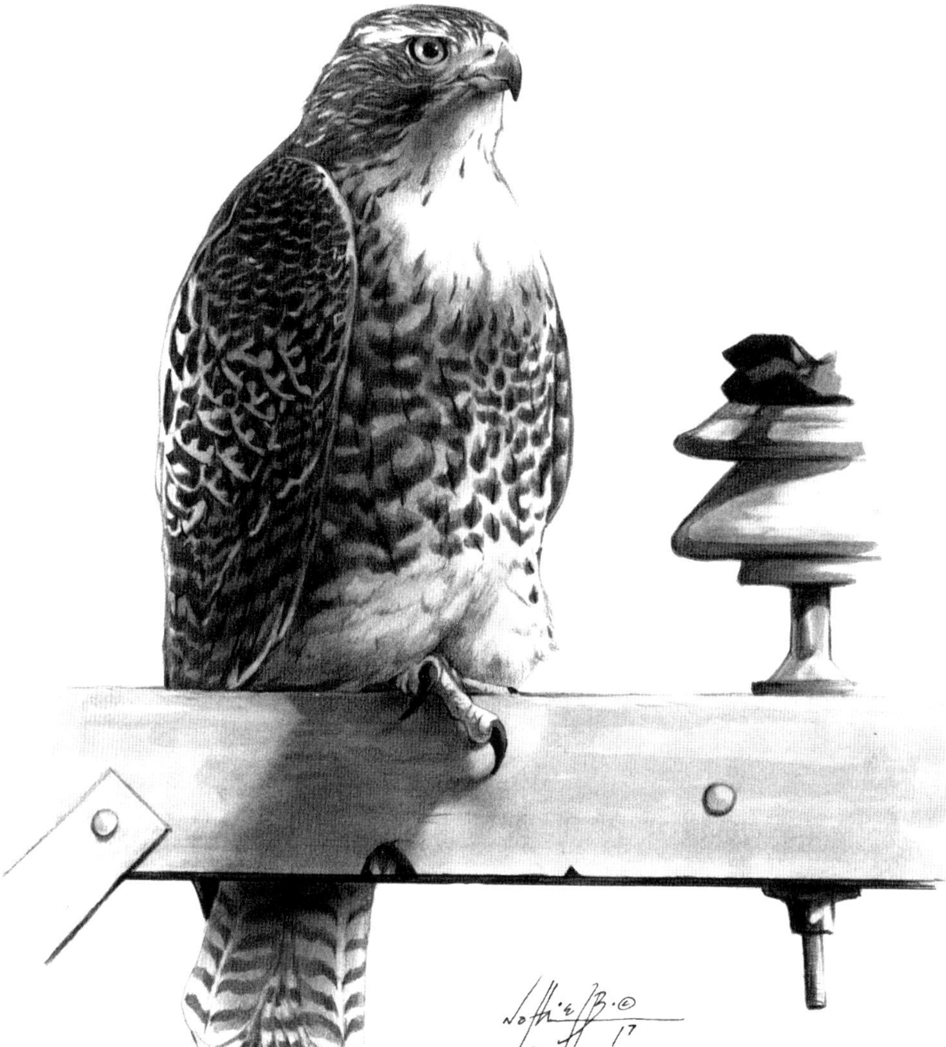

Chapter Four

Trapping

For a newcomer to the sport, it is helpful to know some of the interesting details of trapping history. Until very recently, federal regulations stipulated that an apprentice could possess only a wild taken passage Red-tailed Hawk, an American Kestrel or, only if in Alaska, a Northern Goshawk. Today, depending on the state in which the apprentice lives, he or she may legally be able to possess almost any species of hawk commonly used for falconry whether taken from the wild or captive bred.

But, legal implications aside, in my opinion, there are only two hawks that are suitable for someone coming into the sport of falconry, and those are the passage Red-tailed Hawk and the Harris' Hawk taken as a passager or captive bred. Because the passage redtail is a very good first hawk for the beginner, this book has been written with the redtail in mind. There are extremely few captive-bred redtails available in the U.S. simply because they are so common in the wild that no one bothers to breed them, but for those in other countries, it is important to know that a captive-bred redtail is not a good first hawk for an apprentice. I flew a number of captive-bred redtails while living in England (where they do not occur in the wild) and have seen many more flown by colleagues. Captive-bred redtails, and also eyasses, have a habit of being aggressive to the falconer, and many of them are confirmed screamers. With passage redtails so easily available in the U.S., there is no need to try a captive-bred hawk of the same species; the passage hawks are superior in every aspect. The Harris' Hawk is also a good choice for a beginner, but it does not have the range in the wild that the redtail does. It is thus not so easy for many falconers to take a

> Passager, Passage Hawk. A raptor trapped from the wild after it has left the nest and become independent of its parents, but has not yet molted.

> Captive bred. A hawk that came from an egg laid by a female held in captivity.

Falconry: A Guide for Beginners

passage Harris' Hawk, and most of those used in falconry are captive bred. A chapter on training the Harris' is included in this book, but it is still my recommendation that a beginner start with a passage redtail.

I do not recommend American Kestrels for beginners in the U.S. nor any other species of kestrel anywhere else. The smaller the hawk the smaller the margin of error when it comes to regulating weight and food intake. While a beginner may have many good qualities and intentions, such as enthusiasm and a desire to do the right thing, a hawk as small as a kestrel can be put at risk with even a small mistake. The American Kestrel, like the Merlin and the Sharp-shinned Hawk, is better left to falconers who have some experience. I would qualify my position in the instance where the apprentice has a sponsor living very close by who has experience with kestrels or other small hawks and is able to monitor both the apprentice and his hawk on a daily basis. In such a situation a kestrel might be adequately taken care of but the combination of a small hawk with a new falconer who is unsupervised does not often work out well for the either party.

Types of Traps

The main traps used for catching hawks, in no particular order, are the bow net, the bal-chatri (or BC as most falconers call it), the pigeon harness, the noose carpet, and the cage-type traps. In addition, though of limited use for redtails, but useful for other species, there are the dho-ghazza and the phai trap. The type of trap to use depends in part on how one plans to trap a hawk, in part on the species being trapped, and finally, on personal preference. There are three basic ways to locate a hawk to trap, and these methods affect the decision about which trap to use. The first method is to look for the hawk by driving, preferably on quiet, relatively untraveled back roads. The second is to try intercepting the hawk as it passes, probably on migration, and the third is to set up a stationary trap in an area frequented by hawks in the hope that a hawk will find the trap and end up in it.

For road trapping, which is how most hawks obtained for falconry are trapped, speed of the trap's deployment is an important consideration in the type of trap to use. The bal-chatri and the pigeon harness can both be deployed very quickly. With practice, the dho-ghazza and the phai trap can be rapidly set up, but they are more suitable for catching longwings such as the Merlin and Prairie Falcon, which tend to attack their prey at high speed. That's not to say redtails can't be caught in such traps but the bal-chatri and pigeon harness are simpler to use. The bow net, while it will catch any hawk that comes to it, takes time to set up and is therefore more useful if the hawk comes to the trapper rather than being actively sought,

Trapping

for instance while passing by on migration where the falconer is hiding in a blind. Cage traps, like the Palmyra trap featured in this chapter, can be set up quickly, but are not convenient to carry around in a car and toss out the window like a bal-chatri or pigeon harness. They are most suited for placing in an area where a hawk's presence is suspected, in the hope that a suitable hawk will find the trap and get caught. Cage traps are very efficient at catching hawks that come to them, though it generally takes a while for a hawk to figure out how to get in. These traps are also the only type that can be left unattended, though obviously they should still be checked periodically.

Bow Net

The bow net has been used for centuries and made famous by Dutch hawk trappers. The bow net is, as its name implies, a bow that has a net attached to it. When laid flat on the ground, the net is curled under the bow. Therefore, all that is visible is a thin semi-circle that

A bow net fitted with an automatic release trigger. Bait such as starlings, sparrows or gerbils is placed in the cage, and the whole set-up is camouflaged. When the hawk tries to get at the bait, it trips one of the lines, which triggers the release of the bow net. Hawks that come down to the cage get caught by this set-up very quickly.

[123]

Falconry: A Guide for Beginners

is easily camouflaged with some grass or other vegetation. The bow is attached to the ground at either end by hinges, and when the hawk attacks the bait in the center of the bow, the falconer pulls the bow up and over by using a long line that stretches to his or her hiding place. As the bow moves in an arc, it carries the net with it. Alternatively, the hinges can have springs attached to them, and the bow is held open by a trigger. When the hawk is in position, the falconer releases the trigger, and the springs carry the net over the unsuspecting hawk in an instant. The back of the net is tethered, often by securing it to a second, non-moving bow, and thus when sprung, a circle is formed by the two halves lying flat on the ground. Anything within the circle will be trapped by the net when the bow is triggered.

There are three basic ways to trigger a spring-powered bow net. In the first method, the trigger that holds the bow open is released when the falconer uses a pull cord. In the second method, the falconer releases the trigger by remote control, and the third method utilizes an automatic trigger that the hawk itself trips.

Attracting the hawk to the center of the bow net can be done in one of three ways. The simplest method is to place a bait-containing cage in the middle of the net. We'll discuss suitable bait later. The

The trip lines that spring the trap run across the top of the cage. They are shown here in white for clarity, but black Dacron is a better choice as it is almost invisible.

Trapping

hawk must be relatively near the net to see the bait, so this method is, in practice, most useful if there are a number of hawks already in the area or expected to be passing through on migration. I often use this trap and trigger combination on airports where birds of prey need to be relocated away from runways so they don't collide with planes. Such accidents are nearly always fatal to them and can be catastrophic for the aircraft involved. During migration, I keep several bow nets set up. I drive from one to the next, checking them every 20 minutes or so, or I set them where all can be seen from a central location. At some airports, it is not unheard of to trap 100 or so raptors during a two-month period. By observing the perches that raptors use (such as airport antennas, particular trees that are favored, or poles in open areas) and then setting bow nets close to such places, success can be greatly increased. As the hawks are drawn to the perches as part of their routines, it is easy for them to spot the bait in the cages placed close by, and down they come to trap themselves the instant they touch a bait cage.

A bow net set with an automatic trigger. Two starlings are in the bait cage.

Falconry: A Guide for Beginners

The second way to attract the hawk to a bow net is to use a live pigeon on a long line that can be made to flutter and even fly if the line is also run through a pole with a pulley at the top. Once the hawk takes the pigeon, the pigeon is dragged, hawk and all, into the center of the net and then the bow is triggered by the falconer. Such a set-up requires a blind for the falconer who has to remain in constant vigilance for a passing hawk. This method is most useful where hawks can be intercepted as they pass by on migration. Hawks, including redtails, tend to follow fairly well determined migration routes, particularly along ridge lines and the edges of large areas of water. Falconers who set up blinds in such locations can be rewarded with the sight of a redtail passing by at several hundred feet folding its wings and coming down in response to showing of the pigeon. The downside is the falconer might potentially spend many days in the blind waiting for a suitable day when hawks are passing through.

The third method of enticing a hawk to a bow net is to allow the hawk to kill a pigeon or other bait, then bump the hawk gently off it, set the bow net over the bait, and trap the hawk when it returns. In such a scenario however, a noose carpet is just as effective, yet quicker and easier to set up.

Bal-chatri

This trap was developed in India and is one of my favorites. If I were only allowed one trap with which to catch a passage redtail, this would be my choice. The bal-chatri, or BC as it is commonly known to falconers, is a wire cage covered in nooses. Hawks are attracted to the cage by the bait inside, and in trying to get at the easy meal, they usually run all over the trap, thus getting at least one toe caught in one or more of the many nooses. The bal-chatri is easy to use, easy to deploy, and can be kept in a car so that the moment a hawk is seen, the trap can be tossed out the window or placed out an open door in a suitable location very quickly. Hawks rapidly recognize when prey is easy to catch, and the actions of the bait animal, or better still animals, running around inside the cage, apparently trapped with nowhere to go, make a very tempting, easy meal for them. Two disadvantages of this type of trap are 1) a wary hawk may not be prepared to come down and 2) the trap is generally not suitable for species such as Merlins that try to grab their prey as they go past in high speed flight. However, we have trapped Prairie Falcons and even Gyrfalcons on bal-chatris when nothing else was available. The dome in the photograph is the best shape, but I have used all different shapes including very small, rectangular shaped bal-chatris for trapping large numbers of kestrels passing through on migration.

Trapping

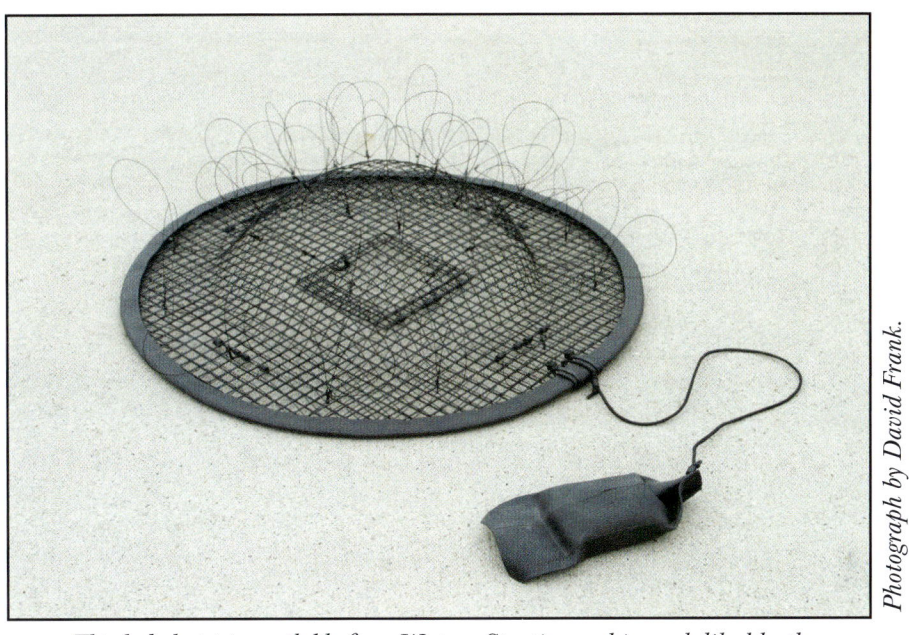

Photograph by David Frank.

This bal-chatri is available from Western Sporting and is much liked by the author because of the domed shape, making it easy for hawks to run over the trap, thus exposing themselves to the nooses that are made of nylon covered wire. These are an improvement over monofilament nooses because they hold their shape better, are easier to fit, the tension can be adjusted, and they will not break or decay as nylon does. Bait animals also cannot gnaw through them, an annoying habit of mice with nylon nooses.

American Kestrel trapped on a bal-chatri with a mouse as bait. The length of chain, used as a weight, is to prevent a larger hawk from flying away with the trap.

Falconry: A Guide for Beginners

Pigeon Harness

Pigeon Harness

Various pigeon harness designs have been used for centuries in the Middle East. While American falconers sometimes claim to have invented the leather jacket harness type, in *A Falcon in the Field* (1966), Mavrogordato claims it is an Arab invention. In Roger Upton's book, *Hood, Leash and Lure* (2004), mention is made of such a device to trap a wild Hobby. This was in 1934, over a decade before any known mention of American falconers utilizing the idea. Certainly the Arabs had made harnesses of materials other than leather for many centuries before the leather jacket harness was first used in the U.S., so the concept of nooses on a flying bait bird is a very old one.

Regardless of origin, the various types of harness are one of the most preferred methods for catching large longwings such as the Prairie Falcon and Peregrine Falcon. Nowadays, a typical harness is generally a soft leather vest made to fit on a pigeon, though a smaller version can be made for starlings. Nooses in the past were generally nylon or horse hair, but now are also made from the plastic coated wire mentioned in the bal-chatri description. Other designs utilize small wire frames to hold the nooses, and I even saw one that was made entirely out of nylon monofilament. It was so unobtrusive that when the pigeon wore it, nothing showed except a couple nylon nooses sticking up on the pigeon's back.

Trapping

To be successful, the harness must allow the pigeon to move about and preferably fly a bit. The harness is fitted to a bait bird and is itself attached to a line, the length of which can vary depending on the circumstances. At the other end of the line is a weight to prevent the hawk from flying away with the whole thing. For the redtail, it is necessary only that the pigeon be able to fly for a couple of yards. I use a 4-yard line attached to a 1lb weight. If I want the pigeon to stay exactly where I put it, I use a shorter line of about 1 foot attached to a 4lb or 5lb weight. Such a set-up is most useful when trapping near roads where the hawk might be able to drag the pigeon and the weight onto the road. If this happens, it may well be run over by a passing car, which no matter how remote the location, always seem to appear on such occasions.

While most of the nooses are placed on top of the harness jacket, it sometimes happens that the hawk, on catching the pigeon or other bait bird, will turn it over to eat it. If there are no nooses on the bottom, the hawk will not get caught. A problem however, is that if nooses are put on the bottom, the pigeon may well get its own feet or toes caught in them, trip itself up, and lie there motionless. My preference therefore is to place the nooses only on the top. If the hawk appears to have turned the pigeon over without getting caught, I approach to make it leave the pigeon, but only to the extent of flying to a nearby location. I then place a noose carpet over the dead pigeon, and the hawk will return once I leave. One drawback of the pigeon harness is that it is not good news for the continued health of the pigeon!

Mention must be made here of a method that uses a pigeon harness with either no drag line attached or a short line with no weight on the end of it. The Arabs have used this method for centuries, and it is mentioned in at least one falconry book published in the U.S. The advantage is that, to the hawk, the pigeon appears completely free flying, and thereby wary hawks are not put off by the unusual antics of a pigeon that can't fly very far because it is on the end of a short line. Arabs were often dealing with the Saker Falcon, which are notoriously hard to trap, but it must be noted that they were trapping in wide open spaces. Even if the pigeon flew for several hundred yards and was carried for several hundred more yards by the hawk, both could be followed and eventually chased down; it is difficult for a hawk attached to a pigeon to take off from level ground repeatedly to take flight. There are, however, very few places in America where such favorable conditions exist, and there are also a lot more flying predators that will take advantage of a hawk attached to a pigeon, coming in to kill it. For these reasons, the reader is advised not to use this method.

Falconry: A Guide for Beginners

Noose Carpet

The noose carpet is a simple circle, square or rectangle of wire mesh fitted with the same types of nooses used on a bal-chatri. It comes in useful when a hawk has taken a pigeon wearing a harness and has killed it and turned it over without getting caught in a noose. It is also useful for trapping a hawk that has been seen making a kill or has killed something such as a pigeon not wearing a harness, or a pheasant or other bait bird released by the falconer for just such a purpose. A hawk that has killed something will, if made to leave the kill in a gentle manner, generally return to the site to finish its interrupted meal. In the meantime, the carcass is covered by the noose carpet, and the hawk is forced to walk over it to get to its meal, all but ensuring it will get a toe or two caught in one of the many nooses. A noose carpet should be heavy enough so it will not move as the hawk walks over it, or better yet, surrounded by a frame that also helps keep its shape. If the hawk does return, it is apt to be caught fairly quickly if landing nearby and approaching the kill on foot. However, if the hawk lands directly on top of the kill and doesn't move its feet, getting caught can take some time.

A modification of the noose carpet is as follows. At an airport where I was responsible for relocating raptors, there was a problem with Ospreys. Because they generally only eat fish (although we had seen them at another airport where they hunted and caught mice in open fields) it is almost impossible as well as impractical to use bait to trap them. It was noticed however that the Ospreys had certain perches, in this case radar antennas that they favored and regularly used. We modified one of these antennas by placing a circular, 12-inch diameter wooden disc on a pole high above the nearby surrounding perches so that it would be the most obvious perch available. On top of this was another circular wooden disc covered with wire that in turn was covered with nooses—in essence a small, circular, noose carpet. Just underneath the circular piece of wood used as a perch, a nylon line was secured and ran at a 45-degree angle down to the ground where it was secured again. From the wire noose carpet, there was a short line that was fixed to a ring around the down line. The theory was that when the Ospreys landed on the perch, their feet would get caught in the noose carpet and as they tried to fly off, they would take the carpet with them, and both they and the carpet would slide down to the ground. My colleagues were rather skeptical of this whole design, but in less than two hours of the noose carpet being placed on the perch, we had our first Osprey. The method can easily be modified for use with other species of hawks. When hawks are attracted to a bait bird, be it a tethered bird or bait in a cage, they will often veer off at the last second if they suspect something is amiss. If

Trapping

A noose carpet on top of a pole. The carpet can be made to any shape. I used one that was 4 feet long by 2 inches wide and was placed on top of a radar tower for trapping and relocating Ospreys that were causing a problem at an airport. The nooses can either be attached directly to stadium Astroturf as in the photograph or to ½-inch hardware cloth that is secured to a wooden base. Of paramount importance is that the carpet itself is free to leave the perch on which it is placed so the hawk cannot be left hanging by one or two toes. The type used here is secured to a short line. When the hawk tries to fly off, the carpet comes with it, secured to one or more of its toes by the nooses. It goes only a foot or so and then slides down the pole to the ground.

[131]

Falconry: A Guide for Beginners

there is a perch nearby, they will generally make straight for it so they can sit and contemplate what to do next. If an upright post or pole is placed close to the bait and a noose carpet affixed on top and attached to a down line, a hawk that lands on it will probably get caught very quickly without ever getting close to the bait. While this method cannot be set up quickly, it is useful for those who trap hawks on migration or are able to put out stationary traps and check them periodically.

Winding Up

The section on equipment briefly mentions a method of using a creance to trap a nervous trained hawk on a kill. This is known as "winding up." Though opportunities to use this practice do not come along very often, hawks on kills, even wild ones, can often be approached fairly closely. In such a situation, especially if no other equipment is available, "winding up" is a good option. Instructions for this method are as follows:

1) Secure one end of the creance to the ground as close to the hawk as it will allow. For a creance 50 yards in length, try to get within about 25 yards. If the tie point can be raised off the ground by an inch or two, perhaps by putting the creance stick into the ground or by securing the line to a hawking knife and sticking that in the ground, so much the better.
2) Unwind the line to the full extent while walking away from the hawk.
3) Now walk in a circle around the hawk, taking care not to spook it. (Avoiding eye contact definitely helps.) Keep the line tight so that it begins to wrap up the hawk when it comes into contact with its legs. Surprisingly, to those who have not tried or seen this, a hawk will not normally lift its legs up to allow the line to pass harmlessly beneath it, so fixated will it be on keeping hold of its prize. Walk so that the first contact with the legs comes from the front. If it comes from the back, the tail will interfere with the creance getting wrapped around the legs.
4) Continue walking around until completing 1½ circles and ending at the side of the hawk that is opposite to where the creance is secured to the ground.
5) The creance will have formed a loop around the hawk, and by gently pulling it tight, the hawk's legs can be snared with the noose thus formed.

I have trapped several wild redtails this way, all of them immature, and have had many opportunities to do the same to a variety of hawks including peregrines and a Prairie Falcon.

Trapping

Winding up a hawk using a creance.

Cage Traps

Cage traps, and I include the well-known Swedish goshawk trap in this category have been around for centuries. They are not just used for trapping hawks but for catching all manner of birds from small songbirds on upwards. Cage traps generally have two compartments; on the bottom is a smaller compartment used for holding the bait bird or birds, and on top is the catching compartment. The perennial problem with all the cage traps I've used or seen is the triggering mechanism. On the Swedish goshawk trap in the photograph on the following page, the top two doors are held open under some considerable pressure by a piece of wood hinged in the center. When the hawk enters the trap, the wood collapses, thereby releasing the two doors and trapping the hawk. Getting the tension just right on such traps is very difficult. If set too light, the wind or the hawk landing on the doors can set them off and if set too heavy, a lightweight hawk or one that lands lightly on the trigger will not release it. The other issue with the Swedish goshawk trap is having very little room left to hold the trapped hawk after the doors close. If left too long, the hawk can and will damage itself by attempting to escape. Furthermore, if made too small, as has happened, the doors close with such force that they can cause serious injury to the hawk, in one case breaking both its wings, not an auspicious start to the career of a trained hawk!

[133]

Falconry: A Guide for Beginners

Swedish goshawk trap. The trap is triggered by the hawk landing on the hinged board which is holding open the two doors. This trap is not as safe or as effective as the Palmyra cage trap.

  To overcome the weaknesses of other cage traps, I developed the Palmyra cage trap, and it has proven to be remarkably successful. The release mechanism is a mousetrap that is set at the side of the cage and is triggered by two or more thin lines running across the cage bottom. The hawk, on entering the top compartment, has to be completely inside to trip the lines, and they can be set with such sensitivity that I have even caught sparrows in this trap. My first design had four trapping compartments on top and caught, in the first year of use, sparrows, starlings, doves, kestrels, a Marsh Hawk, redtails, Barn Owls, Sharp-shinned Hawks by the dozen, and Cooper's Hawks—all that from one trap. The four-compartment trap is shown in the photographs. It is really only useful for trapping large numbers of hawks either for banding or relocating them from airports or other sites where they are causing problems. The single compartment trap is of more use for falconers. The netting on top should be soft, yet strong. This is the only trap in which it is safe to leave a hawk unattended for any length of time. A hawk doesn't tend to panic until approached closely, and it is safe inside the compartment, which should be at least 2 feet square to give the hawk room to sit and perhaps move about a bit. Even a hawk the size of a female redtail is safe in this type of trap.

Trapping

Two American Kestrels trapped in separate compartments of the four-compartment Palmyra cage trap. Note how the other two compartments are still set. The cage is 4 feet square and 3 feet high. The bait cage is 1 foot high with trapping compartments that are 2-foot cubes. The mouse trap triggers can be seen on the sides of the trapping compartments. The bait birds, in this case starlings, are visible in the bottom bait compartment.

The triggering mechanism. The lines, finely braided Dacron that trigger the mousetrap thereby releasing the door, can be seen extending from the mouse trap into the trapping compartment. They are secured on the opposite side of the trap. As soon as they are touched by the hawk, they trip the mouse trap, releasing the door and thereby trapping the hawk.

Falconry: A Guide for Beginners

A passage Red-tailed Hawk caught in a single compartment Palmyra cage trap. Made of aluminum square tube for ease of construction and light weight, the cage should be spray painted black or green to make it less conspicuous. The hinges are spring loaded door hinges available from any hardware store. The door closes gently yet quickly and will not harm the hawk in any way as the more heavily sprung Swedish goshawk traps have been known to do. In this particular design, the trapping compartment and bait cage are two separate pieces held together by tie wraps. As such, they can be transported to the field separately. Also, if the weather is going to be inclement, the bait cage can be brought inside and the trapping compartment left where it is. In this version, the door to the trapping compartment opens through 180 degrees. This makes it easier for the hawks to find their way in than with a door that only opens through 90 degrees as in those pictured previously. The bait compartment is 1 foot by 2 feet by 3 feet and the trapping compartment, 2 feet by 2 feet by 3 feet.

Trapping

The release mechanism is a mouse trap.

Dho-Ghazza

Another trap that has been around for centuries is the dho-ghazza. In its simplest form, it is a net hung between two poles. Bait birds are placed on the side opposite the one from which the hawk is expected. As the hawk attacks the bait, it becomes caught in the net. Throughout the years, there has been much debate on the size of net, the types of poles, and especially the release mechanism for the net. This trap is most useful for Merlins and the large longwings that tend to attack their prey at high speed. For redtails, which generally come in at a slower rate, a bal-chatri works just as well. Removing a hawk and re-using the trap are more easily done with a bal-chatri than a dho-ghazza. Falconers often make nets for Merlins smaller than for the large longwings on the principle that a smaller net is harder for the hawk to see and thus to avoid. I thought the same until I started trapping hawks with large mist nets of 30 by 9 feet, which were not very difficult to see. Nevertheless the hawks, especially Merlins, came in and got caught anyway. The last-minute sudden change in direction that often takes a Merlin around a small net is not necessarily made in response to seeing the net, but in an effort to make the bait birds flush—since a bird just getting off the ground is at its most vulnerable. I now use dho-ghazza nets 3 feet wide and 2 feet high or even larger, even for Merlins, and they work well enough. More important are the thickness and visibility of the poles. Hawks will treat thin poles

[137]

Falconry: A Guide for Beginners

like stems of vegetation and will attempt to fly right through them. Thick poles, especially if placed close together, may cause a hawk to fly around them. The thicker the poles, the wider the net should be. This allows the hawk plenty of room to fly between the poles and to make a sudden move right at the end if it so desires.

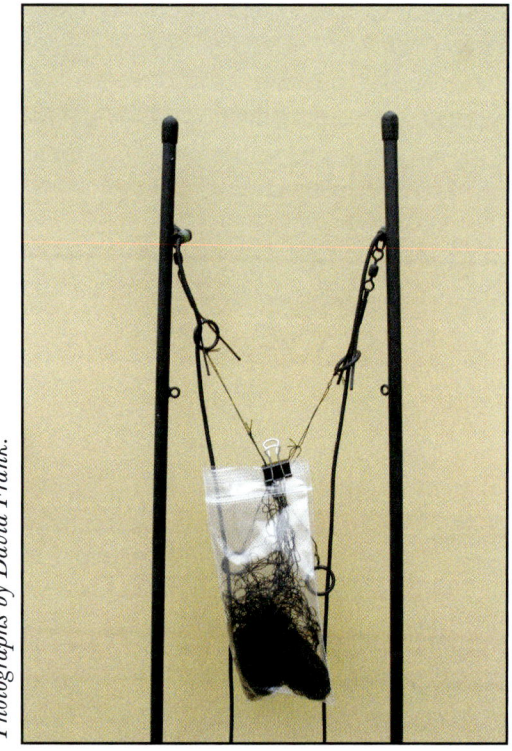

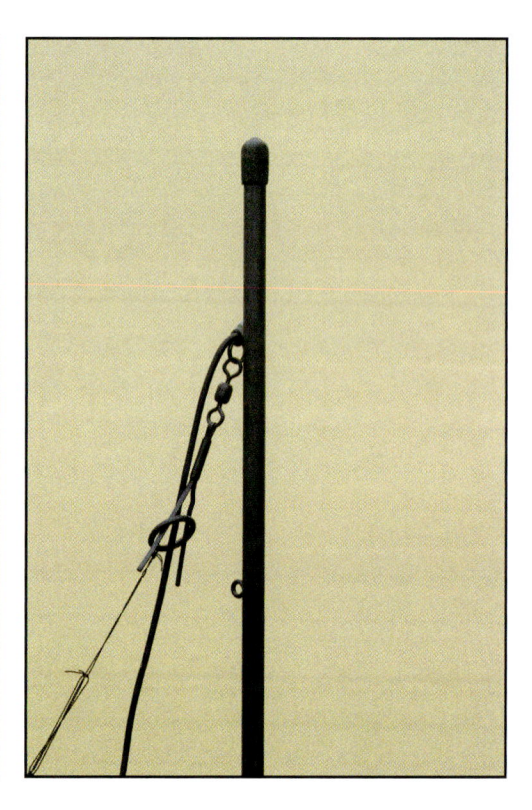

Photographs by David Frank.

The photograph on the left shows the storage method for a dho-ghazza with the net semi-permanently attached to the poles. This method allows for very quick deployment of the net. The photograph on the right shows a method of releasing the net. Each corner of the net is secured to a small ring as shown. The rings are held gently in place by a hair clip that will release the net when the hawk hits it. The rings are secured onto a bungee cord that runs from the top to the bottom of the poles.

The release mechanism for the net is of paramount importance. Some falconers have the net held at all four corners by paper clips or hair clips that hold it taut, yet allow for instant release when struck by a moving hawk. In such a case, the net must either have a drag line attached to it or be attached to a separate line such as a bungee cord secured to the poles (as pictured). Another method is for the tops of

Trapping

the net to be securely attached to the poles while the bottoms are fixed to rings that slide easily up the poles when the hawk hits. The pole bases are fixed to lead weights that hold them upright, yet easily topple with a small amount of pressure anywhere on the poles. As the hawk hits the net, the poles topple over, the rings slide up, and the hawk is encompassed by the net. This method allows for a much quicker deployment of the trap than one that involves setting up the poles and securing the net. In the quick method, the poles are brought together and the net bunched up and pushed into a stocking or empty snack canister. Merely opening up the poles will cause the net to pull out of its container and slide down the poles and into place, ready for placing on the ground in only a matter of seconds. The size of the net mesh is yet another consideration. In theory, the bigger the mesh, the less noticeable it is. However, my mist nets have mesh ranging from 1 to 2 ¼ inches. All of them trap hawks, and so I use the mist net that happens to be lying around. They all seem to work well regardless of size. What definitely helps is to set the net with a background behind it. Even the best sighted hawk will have trouble spotting a net with bushes in the background.

Phai Trap

While not one of my favorite designs, the phai trap does have utility, particularly for trapping Gyrfalcons and Merlins. Experienced Gyrfalcon trappers say that a sparrow placed in the middle of a phai trap will bring in even a Gyrfalcon with a full crop. The phai trap is another design originating in India. It consists of large nooses, typically four inches in diameter, which stand upright in a ring around the bait. The one pictured here is a modification based on a design by Hubert Quade in which the plastic coated wire nooses are permanently attached to a base and is called the phai hoop trap. The bait bird, usually a sparrow or starling, is attached to a weight and placed in the center of the trap.

Bait

In the 1960s, Jack Mavrogordato wrote that if he could have only one type of bait, it would be the English or House Sparrow. Nothing has changed since then. Whether in a bal-chatri, behind a dho-ghazza, in a Palmyra cage trap, in a cage around which a bow net is set, or in the center of a phai trap, active sparrows will pull in more hawks than any other type of bait bird or mammal. Next in order of preference comes the European Starling, which is almost as good as a sparrow. Both these species are active, legally and usually readily available to

Falconry: A Guide for Beginners

anyone with even the most basic knowledge of bird trapping, and can be kept in large numbers in darkened cages with a minimum of effort. They will attract almost any kind of hawk from the smallest sharp-shin to the largest redtail.

Obviously, the bait for a pigeon harness is a pigeon. Freshly trapped barn pigeons work well, as do free flying homing pigeons. Pigeons from a pet store will likely sit still and not make much effort to fly, thereby resulting in their being ignored by many hawks. For bal-chatris, mice also work well, but I don't consider them any better than sparrows and starlings. Mice bought at a pet store are likely to be rendered immobile if the weather is at all cold as is often the case when trapping. I do not use hamsters though they are used with success by other falconers. Gerbils work very well for redtails. The chosen bait should be taken care of, not just for humane reasons, but because if properly looked after, bait will be more active when in full view of a hungry hawk. Bait that remains immobile because it is cold and hungry will not attract that hawk. Bait that is well fed, lively and accustomed to being in the open is much more enticing to a hawk. Except where pigeon harnesses are concerned, I do not use only a single bait bird if it's possible to use more. Two or three sparrows or starlings in a bait cage are almost certain to guarantee that at least one is active enough to attract the hawk that is so desired.

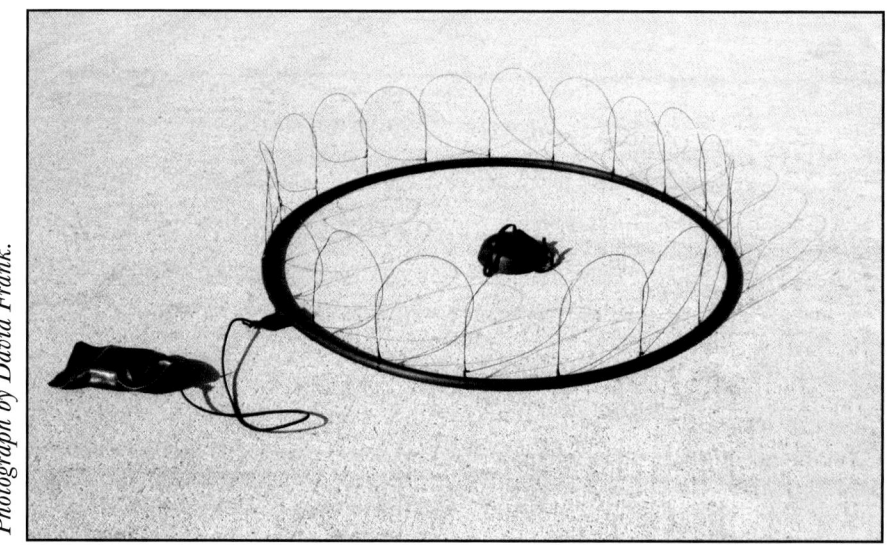

Photograph by David Frank.

The phai hoop trap as sold by Western Sporting. Though not especially useful for redtails, it will catch them. It is normally reserved for the longwings which attack their prey at high speed. It is said to be particularly effective for trapping Gyrfalcons, and some falconers use a variation of it for catching Golden Eagles by using a rabbit as bait.

Trapping

Trapping Tactics

It is possible to set up stationary traps along a migration route but road trapping is easier when only one hawk is wanted for training. Though it may not be quite as exciting to some, it takes a lot fewer man hours. As mentioned, stationary traps such as the Palmyra cage trap and the automatic bow net can be semi-permanently set up near a place where they are readily observed. If one's job is in a location surrounded by some open ground, it is possible, with the necessary permission, to set up such a trap and keep an eye on it while working. Hawks are sure to pass by from time to time even in locations in town where they are normally not seen. To someone who hasn't tried them, it is surprising just how successful such traps are. A couple of sparrows or starlings in the bait cage will live quite happily if they have food and water and a small box to hide in when the weather turns inclement. The trap should be brought in at night so it doesn't attract cats or owls and for other occasions when it isn't possible to observe it often enough. If trapping in a setting where there are lots of people, any hawks caught will already be partially manned and virtually immune to seeing people nearby. Such hawks, even the passage shortwings, can be remarkably tame right from the first day.

Photograph by David Frank.

The photograph above shows the transport box the author uses to keep the trap stored safely, yet still available for quick deployment. The box in the center contains the weight to which the bait bird, usually a sparrow or starling, is attached. When the box lid is closed, the bait container remains dark, thus keeping the bait bird quiet. In the left hand corner is a compartment that holds the trap weight and line. The trap itself is held in place by two Velcro straps so it doesn't move about, causing disruption of the sensitive nooses.

[141]

Falconry: A Guide for Beginners

Road Trapping

    Let's assume that most beginners will catch their first redtails by road trapping. The traps most suitable for this are the bal-chatri and the pigeon harness. The dho-ghazza and phai trap also work, but not as well for redtails as for other species. The bow net and cage trap take more time to set up, and the cage trap may require the hawk's studying the trap a long while before coming into it. If using a pigeon harness, it is also wise to have a noose carpet in case the hawk kills the pigeon but does not get caught. The hawk can then be bumped off and the carpet placed over the dead pigeon. Most hawks will return to a kill in a short space of time as long as they are not initially terrified into flying away.

    The most difficult part of road trapping tends to be finding a hawk to trap. It pays to become familiar with the trapping area beforehand so that time is not wasted driving unsuitable roads, plus it will be easy to recognize places where hawks have previously been spotted. I have a slight preference for early morning and late afternoon, but have trapped hawks at all times of the day. Most hawks however, take the middle part of the day off, so a hawk that ignores an offering at 1:00 p.m. may well come down immediately if offered the same bait an hour before sunset. Though I have trapped hawks within 10 minutes of leaving home, it pays to be prepared to make a long day of it. Friends often want to come along, but unless they are falconers, it is often best to ignore such requests. It's very frustrating to listen to someone whining about boredom after covering 100 miles of back roads without seeing a hawk. Looking for a hawk to trap might require a concentrated effort, and distractions are not wanted.

    Redtails are often found on high perches such as telephone or power poles or in the trees of wooded areas. In early autumn before the leaves fall, they can be difficult to see even when close by. In more open areas, they are readily visible on exposed power poles, so those are good places to start. Once a hawk is found, an effort should be made to identify it as male or female, immature or adult. If a red tail makes it obvious that the hawk is an adult, it is best to leave it alone and move on, but if there is any doubt about the age, it is better not to risk bumping the hawk trying to get a closer look.

    If facing a suspect redtail so that the color of the tail is difficult to see, another indicator of immaturity is a light-colored diamond on the chest. It is normally absent in the adults, but Red-tailed Hawks do vary enormously in color. I tend to make a cursory look and then deploy the trap. Trapping an adult redtail is not an offense, but possessing one is, so if one is inadvertently trapped, it should be released immediately. While it may seem preferable to place the trap the way the hawk is facing, this is not always necessary because

Trapping

A passage male redtail trapped on a Western Sporting bal-chatri. Two gerbils are used as bait.

with time, a hawk is likely to look over its shoulder. If placing the trap in view of the hawk, it helps to position the vehicle so that the trap can be deployed out the opposite side from the one in the hawk's view. It is best if the hawk doesn't see what is taking place, and above all, it is important not to stare at the hawk. It is amazing how hawks will ignore vehicle after vehicle until the occupants stop and stare at it. That sets a hawk on edge and may well cause it to leave. A trapper should be nonchalant in all actions taken which is easier said than done!

Falconry: A Guide for Beginners

How close to place the trap is another matter of judgment. I've placed traps directly under hawks that have ignored them, and then a different hawk appears from the other side of a wide field and takes the bait right beneath the hawk that showed no interest. The fact is that if a hawk is interested and can see the bait, it will come in from a great distance, certainly in excess of 100 yards and often half a mile or more. The temptation of course is always to place the trap within 10 or 20 yards of the hawk so it merely has to drop off its perch and get the bait, but a lot of hawks are unintentionally bumped that way. One consideration is how far from the trap the falconer is waiting. It must be possible to observe and get to the hawk quickly once caught. A hawk on a trap is vulnerable to attack from other predators including larger hawks, dogs, and coyotes. A trap must therefore not be left where it cannot be observed unless it is a cage trap, the inside of which is relatively safe.

Enough time must be given for it to catch at least one toe in a noose once the hawk is down on a bal-chatri or pigeon harness. A good pair of binoculars will help to watch for difficulty in lifting a toe or for an attempt to move on the trap without being able to. If using a dho-ghazza or phai trap, there will be no doubt as to whether or not the hawk is caught. As soon as it's determined the hawk is snared, no time can be wasted in getting to it. It is easier to take a hawk out of a noose than a dho-ghazza. If using a dho-ghazza, the hawk is taken up off the ground by grabbing its feet in a gloved hand and trying to figure out which way it went into the net. Once that is known, the opening can be found so the net can be gently worked back over the hawk. It is easier to cut the net with a pair of scissors to remove the hawk, but this ruins the net, so the price paid for it is a consideration. If trapped on a bal-chatri or pigeon harness, the hawk will likely flip over on its back or side as soon as the falconer gets really close and will stay in this position for a few seconds if the falconer moves slowly and deliberately. This is one time when it pays to look a hawk directly in the eyes to meet its gaze, thus keeping it focused away from what the gloved hand is doing. After determining which foot is caught, the other foot is slowly approached with the gloved hand held down close to the ground, and the leg is grabbed above the foot. The leg that is noosed is also secured with the gloved hand so both legs are held firmly in the one hand. It is normally simple to loosen the noose, but a pair of wire cutters should be handy just in case. When caught on a phai trap, a hawk is usually snared by just one noose that will have pulled tight and become extended away from the rest of the trap. The free leg should be gathered up as with a bal-chatri, and then the other leg is grabbed so the noose can be worked free.

Trapping

In the photograph on the left we are disentangling a freshly trapped redtail from a pigeon harness. Note how she is already hooded and how each leg is secured by one hand while her wings are held in by the forearms. On the right, we are examining her feet for any signs of bumblefoot, bites, etc. She could easily be jessed while in this position.

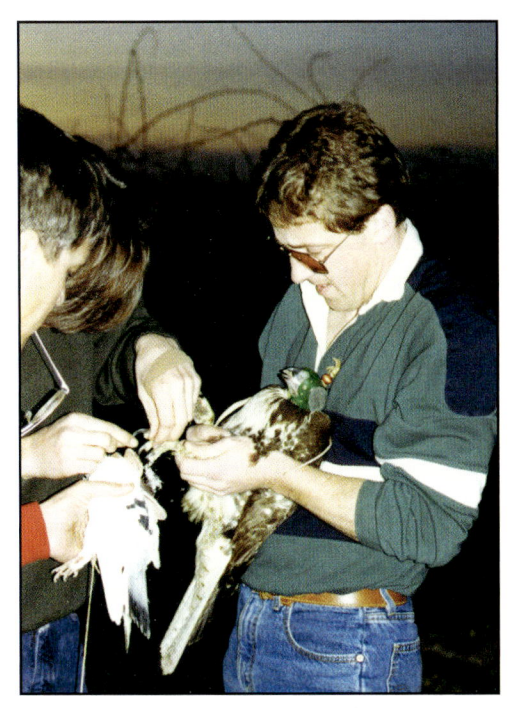

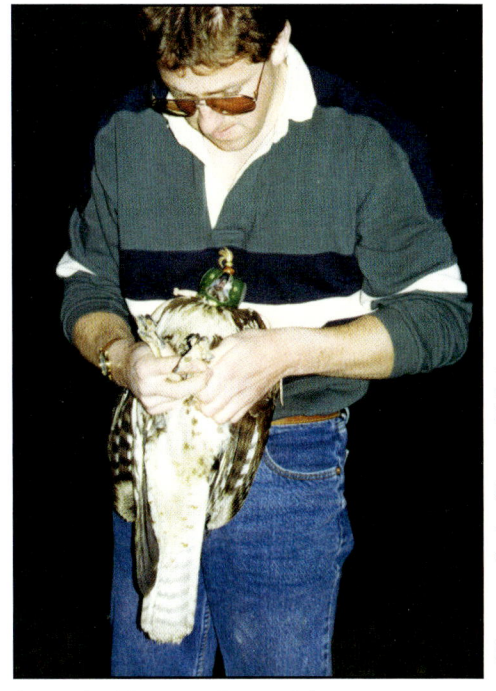

Photographs by Sharon Zobrist.

As soon as practical, the hawk is picked up off the ground and a hood put on. Once free of the trap and hooded, the anklets and other equipment can be fitted right there in the field or vehicle, or the hawk can be socked for the journey home. If putting the equipment on right away, the hawk should be up on the fist in order to settle down before being transferred to a perch for the journey. It will also help to spray the hawk with mist from a water bottle to help calm it. Some hawks will travel well when hooded and on a perch immediately after capture, but this is not always the case, so preparations to sock the hawk are needed. An abba is a piece of cloth into which two pockets are sewn. The hawk's wings are put into the pockets, and the rest of the abba is wrapped around the hawk's body. Some falconers put the hawk into a pantyhose stocking after having cut a small hole for its head to emerge from. Once the hawk is equipped, the pantyhose can easily be cut off. Another option is wrapping the hawk in a towel and holding it on one's lap as long as someone else is driving. No matter how the hawk is secured, it is necessary to be wary of its feet, for if possible to get hold of something, the hawk is not likely to let

[145]

go. At all times, it must be handled with care so the feathers are not damaged in any way. Many trapped hawks have lice or mites or both, so it is a good practice to spray any newly trapped hawk with a mite spray available from pet stores.

The decision on whether to keep a hawk or try to trap another is a personal one. I like a hawk to be feather perfect because it cannot be made that way if there is damage to the feathers; frayed or broken feathers will not really improve even if well imped. Some redtails have bites to the toes if they have been catching squirrels, and this can be a mixed sign. It may be that they have learned to catch squirrels, and the bites are old, learning wounds, or it may be that after getting bitten by squirrels, the hawk won't chase them anymore. There is simply no way of knowing. Another questionable sign is a hawk that is very thin. I don't like to train them, but I am often reluctant to let them go because they may not be doing well in the wild and may be having trouble fending for themselves. If released, it may well die. If I do release such a hawk, I leave a pigeon or other food so it can get a good meal. Ideally, the hawk I am looking for will be well muscled, in good feather condition and with clean feet. With regard to sex of a redtail, if the hawk will be flown at jackrabbits, it will be preferable to trap and keep a female. I would recommend the same for squirrels although there have been a number of good males flown at squirrels. If cottontails will be the main quarry, either sex will be fine, but my choice would be a male because it will usually give a more stylish flight.

Road trapping can really only be learned by experience, but it is no more difficult than fishing once a hawk to be trapped has been found. The details are endless and the variables limitless, so giving too much guidance is to risk making the whole process sound like a science when it isn't. With good bait, good traps, and enough time to find a number of hawks, one will be caught sooner rather than later. With each one caught, something new will be learned. With experience, what once was thought to be set in stone may even be unlearned!

For more information on trapping, I refer readers to the excellent book, *Trapping Essentials* by Ben Woodruff, published in 2008 by Western Sporting.

Trapping

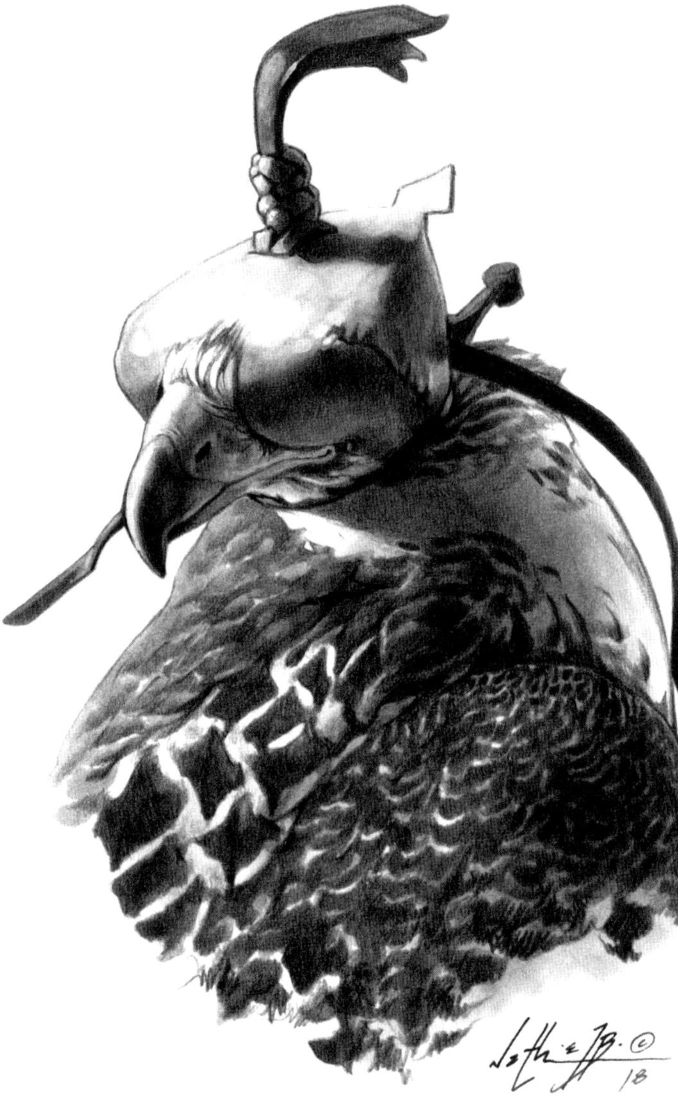

Chapter Five
The Basics of Training a Hawk

    A hawk is trained to come to the falconer for a reward of food. It therefore follows that the hawk must be hungry enough to want the food before flying to the falconer for it. A desire to eat is not the only principle used in training a hawk however, for if not properly conditioned to accept the falconer, the hawk could be starving, yet still might not fly to the falconer for food. A hawk must be familiar enough with the falconer and calm enough in his or her presence to accept the food being offered and to do what is asked. The process of taming a hawk to first accept the falconer and then everything associated with life as a trained hawk is called manning. A well-manned hawk fears nothing associated with life as a trained hawk and is not fearful of the falconer or of the daily routine of being handled and flown.

> Manning. The act of taming a hawk as opposed to training it.

    It is not possible on a daily basis to deduce the mood and physical condition of a trained hawk by simply looking at it. Though a hawk may give outward clues, such as bating toward the falconer when he appears wearing a hawking jacket, such obvious signs can be misleading. The easiest way to judge the condition of the hawk and the method all falconers rely on, at least in Western countries, is to weigh the hawk every day. What is known of the hawk's previous performances at certain weights can determine whether it is likely to behave as expected. Simply put, if yesterday our trained redtail went out into the fields with us, followed from tree to tree as we tried to flush rabbits and other quarry, returned when offered a piece of food on the fist, and perhaps ended the day by catching a rabbit and being given a meal at the site of the kill, and then if today our hawk weighs the same, we can be reasonably certain it will perform the same.

Falconry: A Guide for Beginners

> Flying weight. The weight at which a hawk is in the correct condition to be flown at quarry. If flown overweight, it may refuse quarry or refuse to come back to the falconer. If flown underweight, it will be more susceptible to disease and may lack enthusiasm and energy for flying.

The weight at which the hawk performed this way is called the flying weight. Understanding it, how to determine it, and how to know when the hawk is or is not at flying weight are some of the most important lessons the falconer needs to learn. If the falconer makes a mistake and releases a hawk when not at flying weight, or to put it another way, in flying condition, it will only be luck if the hawk is brought home at all. Understanding flying weight is therefore a key to successful, consistent falconry. Lack of understanding this principle can result, at best, in inconsistent behavior or at worst, in the loss or even death of the hawk.

Flying Weight

A hawk in training should be weighed daily and its weight marked on a chart. Weighing should take place at the same time each day because we are trying to learn how much food is required to keep the weight the same over a 24-hour period. Once we know that, we can determine how much is needed to maintain, lower or raise the hawk's weight. The amount of food received from the falconer is the main factor that determines what a hawk weighs on a day to day basis. Other factors are 1) the weather, or more specifically, temperature, 2) the amount of flying the hawk has done or will do, 3) the type of food given, such as low quality rabbit or high quality quail, and 4) whether the hawk's weight is going up, coming down or staying level since the same time yesterday. Scales need to be consistent and accurate to ¼ ounce or 7 grams for a hawk the size of a redtail. Whether to use grams or ounces is a personal preference but having used ounces for the first few years of my hawking career, I now use grams.

Food intake is the most crucial part of overseeing weight control in a trained hawk, so the falconer must be aware of how much food is eaten by the hawk on a daily basis. There are three ways of doing this. One is to know in advance that the food given to the hawk always weighs the same. For instance, day-old cockerels, also known as day-old chicks and obtainable from hatcheries and from major food suppliers for raptors, weigh the same within a few grams. The second method is to weigh the hawk both before and after feeding it, and the third method is to weigh the food prior to giving it to the hawk. The second method of weight control is often used by falconers flying the smaller species such as Merlins

The Basics of Training a Hawk

and sharp-shins. It pre-supposes that the falconer will finish feeding the hawk where the scale is so the hawk can be topped up, as it were, until the desired weight is reached. That is not always practical. My own practice therefore is to use a combination of the first and third methods. When I know the food is of a standard size, such as day old chicks, then I use that method. If the food varies or if I am using portions of a large bird or mammal, I weigh the food prior to leaving for the flying ground. This is clarified in the following examples.

A trained hawk has to be correctly conditioned to fly at its best. Here Lee McGrorty's captive-bred goshawk closes with a brown hare showing she is fit, strong and in perfect flying condition to take on such formidable quarry.

[151]

Falconry: A Guide for Beginners

HAWK: Scruff	SPECIES: Harris' Hawk	SEX: M							
	September 1985 / December 1985								

WEIGHT	1lb 7oz		1lb 6oz		1lb 5oz	DATE:	FOOD: Heads	Bodies Legs	Quarry Taken
			X			31	3	3 6	Rabbit
			X			30	3	3 6	Chicken!
			X			29	3	3 6	Rat
			X			28	3	3 6	3 Doves in Barn
			X			27	3	3 6	3 Rabbits
			X			26	3	3 6	Cock Pheasant
			X			25	3	3 6	
			X			24	3	3 6	Cock Pheasant
		X				23	2	3 6	
		X				22	2	3 6	
			X			21	3	3 6	LBJ Oops!
			X			20	3	3 6	Partridge
			X			19	3	3 6	Mallard Duck
			X			18	3	3 6	Rabbit
			X			17	3	3 6	
			X			16	3	3 6	
			X			15	3	1 6	Rabbit
				X		14	3	2 6	Rabbit
			X			13	3	1 6	
			X			12	3	1 6	
			X			11	3	1 6	Mallard Drake
		X				10	2	1 6	
			X			9	3	1 6	Coot
			X			8	3	1 6	Moorhen
			X			7	3	1 6	Woodpigeon
				X		6	3	2 6	
			X			5	3	1 6	
			X			4	3	1 6	2 Moorhens
			X			3	3	1 6	Rabbit
			X			2	3	1 6	
			X			1	3	1 6	

The Basics of Training a Hawk

Example 1: Scruff

The first example is Scruff, a rather exceptional male Harris' Hawk that I flew in the early 1980's. He maintained his weight early in the season on one whole day-old chick plus the legs and heads from two others, or to put it another way, one body, three heads and six legs. As the weather got colder and the amount of flying increased, Scruff's food intake needed to be adjusted to keep his weight level until, in the depths of winter, he would need three whole chicks a day to keep him level. Scruff's flying weight, once trained and fit, was 1 pound 6½ ounces regardless of temperature or length of day or any of the other factors that sometimes affect an individual hawk's flying weight. If I made a mistake in feeding him and his weight crept up or down by ¼ ounce, his food intake would be adjusted accordingly by adding or subtracting one or two chick legs or heads.

This chart to the left is for Scruff, an intermewed captive-bred male Harris' Hawk. The first half of the chart covers September of 1985, and the second half covers December of the same year. There is a difference between flying during relatively warm September weather versus cold December weather on the food requirements of the hawk. The food fed was day-old chicks. For ease of use, I divide them into heads, bodies and legs. The food is easily adjusted by adding or subtracting a head, body or leg when necessary. A hawk will need more food to raise its weight than it will to lower it. On the days that Scruff dropped or gained in weight, the food he had been given the previous day was the normal amount generally required to keep him level. Weight control is not an exact science, and occasionally a hawk will drop or gain weight slightly even when not anticipated. It is for this reason that hawks should be weighed every day, even if they have a day off from being flown.

Falconry: A Guide for Beginners

HAWK: Scrumpy	SPECIES: Lanner Falcon	SEX: M	MONTH: August 1981

WEIGHT										DATE:	FOOD:
						X				31	1 ½
						X				30	1 ½
						X				29	1 ½
						X				28	1 ½
						X				27	1 ½
						X				26	1 ½
						X				25	1 ½
						X				24	1 ½
						X				23	1 ½
						X				22	1 ½
						X				21	1 ½
						X				20	1 ½
						X				19	1 ½
						X				18	1 ½
					X					17	1 ¼
						X				16	1 ½
						X				15	1 ½
						X				14	1 ½
						X				13	1 ½
						X				12	1 ½
							X			11	2
						X				10	1 ½
						X				9	1 ½
						X				8	1 ½
						X				7	1 ½
						X				6	1 ½
						X				5	1 ½
						X				4	1 ½
						X				3	1 ½
						X				2	1 ½
						X				1	1 ½
		16 oz		15 oz		14 oz					

[154]

The Basics of Training a Hawk

Example 2: Scrumpy

The second example is Scrumpy, a lanneret that I flew in 1981. In the month of August, his weight varied only twice from his flying weight of 15½ ounces. Once he went up ¼ of an ounce, and once down ¼ of an ounce. This accuracy was achieved by weighing Scrumpy's food beforehand. For almost the entire time, 1½ ounces, of food (quail) kept him level. And so I took one 1-ounce piece and four ¼-ounce pieces with me when I flew him. To keep him level, he got the 1-ounce piece and two ¼-ounce pieces. The other two ¼-ounce pieces were spare. The day he went up by ¼ ounce, he got 1¼ ounces. The day he dropped, he got the full 2 ounces, because it takes more food to put weight on a hawk when its weight has dropped than the amount of food it takes to lower the weight when the hawk has gained.

For flying small hawks, the danger of dropping too low in weight is very real. If a hawk the size of a redtail is found at flying time to be ¼ ounce underweight it might not make any real difference to how it flies but for a hawk the size of a kestrel, such a difference can be very serious and dangerous to its health. Years ago, when flying a Eurasian Sparrowhawk named Star, I developed the habit of weighing her twice each day at set times. In this way I was able to anticipate in advance what her condition would be at flying time some eight hours later. Her weight chart is on the following page to show how this method works in practice. This method should be used when flying small hawks.

The chart on the left is for Scrumpy, an immature lanneret. The food used was breast of quail with the occasional part of liver and heart of quail added. By weighing out the food before flying him, it was easy to maintain his weight almost exactly. Using this method, it is easy to maintain a hawk's weight using any type of meat cut into suitably sized portions. For a redtail, one could use several ¼oz pieces for recalling the hawk and keep a 1oz or 2oz piece as a trade-off for when the hawk makes a kill. It is a simple matter when weighing the hawk to work out how much food it needs during the following flying session, and is easy when out in the field to keep track of exactly how much food the hawk is eating.

Falconry: A Guide for Beginners

HAWK: Star	SPECIES: Eurasian Sparrowhawk	SEX: F	MONTH: September 1978								
WEIGHT		9 oz	8 ¾ oz	8 ½ oz	8 ¼ oz	8 oz			**DATE:**	**Food AM:**	**Food PM:**
					O		X			1		1 ¼
				O		X			2	⅛	1 ¼
				O		X			3	⅛	1 ¼
				O		X			4		1 ¼
				O		X			5		1 ¼
			O		X				6	⅛	1 ¼
			O		X				7	⅛	1 ¼
			O		X				8	⅛	1 ¼
				O		X			9		1 ¼
				O		X			10		1 ¼
				O		X			11		1 ¼
				O		X			12		1 ¼
				O		X			13		1 ¼
				O		X			14		1 ¼
				O		X			15		1 ¼
				O		X			16		1 ¼
			O		X				17	⅛	1 ¼
				O		X			18		1 ¼
				O		X			19		1 ¼
				O		X			20		1 ¼
				O		X			21		1 ¼
			O		X				22	⅛	1 ¼
			O		X				23	⅛	1 ¼
				O		X			24		1 ¼
		O		X					25		1 ⅛
				O		X			26		1 ¼
				O		X			27		1 ¼
				O		X			28		1 ¼
				O		X			29		1 ¼
				O		X			30		1 ¼

[156]

The Basics of Training a Hawk

Finding the flying weight can be a great mystery for beginners and even some experienced falconers but it is the key to successful, repeatable falconry and is crucial to the health of the hawk. To show how we arrive at the flying weight, let's use a freshly trapped Red-tailed Hawk as an example. When first removed from the trap and taken home, the redtail is fitted with jesses, hood, etc. If the hawk will stand properly, it is weighed. In any case, it should be weighed as soon as possible after trapping as long as there is no food in its crop. To check for food in the crop, which is situated just below the beak at the top of the chest, a falconer pushes a finger lightly into it through the feathers. If there is resistance, the hawk still has food in there. If there is a lot of food in the crop, it will be a visible bulge. In addition to food in the crop there may also be food in the stomach and waste material in the gut. Any food, whether in the crop, stomach or gut will pass within about 24 hours and the hawk should be weighed again at this point. The old falconers called this passing empty, in acknowledgement of the fact that what they were dealing with in the hawk, both physically and mentally, was not being masked by the presence of food. It is this passing empty weight that should be the starting point upon which further decisions are made.

Weighing a hawk is not simply a matter of putting it on a scale and reading a number. The scale must be placed on a level surface and be secure so that it will not topple over and frighten the hawk. The perch should allow the hawk, even a longwing, to grip onto it. For this purpose, I use an 8-inch length of 2 by 2 lumber that is covered with Astroturf. Although of no benefit to a wild caught hawk, a newly taken up captive-bred hawk recognizes the feel of Astroturf under its feet. It settles down more quickly, thus allowing a more accurate reading to be taken. Weighing the hawk should take place inside a closed room so that the hawk cannot escape if it takes fright and jumps off the scale. I

This chart is for Star, a Eurasian Sparrowhawk I flew in 1978/79. Her a.m. weight is marked by an O and her p.m. weight by an X. Her weight loss from 8:00 a.m. until 4:00 p.m. when she was flown was a regular 3/8 of an ounce. By weighing her every day at 8:00 a.m. I was able to anticipate if she would be at flying weight at 4:00 p.m. If her weight was predicted to be too low, she was given a small piece of food, generally 1/8 of an ounce, to give her a boost. If her weight was too high, there was nothing I could do except refrain from flying her that day or delay flying though I avoided that because it tends to have knock on effects for the following day. This method helps prevent a hawk, especially a small one, from falling below its flying weight and becoming more susceptible to disease.

Falconry: A Guide for Beginners

weigh my small hawks with the hood, jesses and swivel on, but without the leash. It is important that the leash is taken out of the swivel. If not, it either drags on the tabletop or needs to be held up away from the table and scale. This will make it impossible to get an accurate reading. If using a tethering system, then before weighing, the falconer should remove the leash, swivel and extender, leaving only the jesses in place. For larger hawks, including redtails, it is permissible to let the leash hang down and rest on the table as long as you do this each time. Sometimes a falconer is seen moving the leash up and down in an attempt to get the scale to give a desired reading. This is rather like a person weighing himself with one foot on the floor exerting various amounts of pressure to get the scale to say what he wants it to. The hawk should always be weighed while wearing the same equipment. There is no point weighing the hawk with the hood on one day and the next day without it, or one day without a transmitter and the next time with it. Some falconers subtract the weight of the equipment but this is not necessary as long as the same equipment is used each day, for what we are trying to ascertain is whether the hawk weighs the same or has gone up or down in weight.

At the same time the hawk is weighed, its physical condition needs to be ascertained. Is the hawk on the high or heavy side, or is it on the low or thin side? This is determined by feeling the breastbone and the muscles under the wings where they join the breast of the hawk. The easiest way of doing this is to lightly pinch the breastbone below the crop between the thumb and the index and middle fingers of the right hand while the hawk sits, hooded, on the gloved left fist. To feel the wing muscles simply open the fingers and thumb wider and move them to the muscle area at the base of the wing.

Manually feeling the condition of the hawk should be done whenever a new hawk is taken in hand. Many falconers, myself included, regularly feel the breastbone and wing muscles of a hawk in training at least once a week or whenever we suspect something is amiss. At this early stage however, with a freshly trapped passage hawk, this reveals only whether the hawk is on the heavy side or on the thin side. If the breastbone can barely be felt and the hawk feels rather like a Thanksgiving turkey, then this hawk is in fairly high condition and may not respond when offered food on the fist for some time. If the breastbone can be felt, but is not unduly sharp, training can proceed.

It is important to understand what these signs, the condition of the breast and wing muscles, are telling us as we learn to use them, in conjunction with other signals the hawk is giving to make the decision on whether to raise the hawk's condition, keep it the same or

The Basics of Training a Hawk

lower it. And this is something that may need to be constantly refined during the hawk's career. For instance, a young captive-bred hawk, freshly taken up from an aviary will have very little muscle tone but during training, as it does more and more work to increase its fitness these muscles will grow and its weight must be raised accordingly. It is possible, if the falconer does not increase the hawk's weight while trying to improve its fitness to actually lower the condition of the hawk. This will retard its training and a hawk that was progressing along nicely will begin to go backwards, may start to land, will appear weaker in flight and may even start to scream at the falconer for food. If the falconer doesn't pick up on this quickly he can ruin his hawk and, in this lowered condition, she will be more susceptible to disease. For a passage hawk which will already be fit when it is trapped, the longer it takes to train, the more muscle loss it will have. Then, once trained and flying free, the falconer must remember to increase its weight as it builds these muscles back up. It is through weighing the hawk daily and taking into account how it looks, reacts and feels that the falconer decides if it needs to go up in weight, stay the same or be lowered in weight. Some falconers, especially some beginners, seem to think that there is some magic weight and if only they can find it their hawk will perform to perfection all the time, rather like finding the combination to a safe they assume once they have it, the hard work is over. That is not the case.

Occasionally, a hawk is trapped in very low condition and the breastbone will feel very sharp and the hawk may appear weak or have difficulty standing. Such a hawk will need a minimum of two to three weeks of unrestricted rations to bring its condition up. During the same period, mutes should be checked by a vet, and if the hawk refuses to eat well, other tests should be carried out by a vet to ascertain if there is an underlying illness. The problem here is how to persuade a recently trapped, very scared hawk to eat as much as it can. The only real solution is to turn the hawk loose in the mews and leave it with food it will hopefully recognize, preferably something nutritious like pheasant or if previously frozen, pigeon. Quail generally also works, but rabbits are too low in nutritional value to raise a hawk's weight, even a redtail that regularly eats them in the wild.

> Mutes. This is a term used to describe the fecal droppings of a hawk.

To feed a hawk in this condition, the food is torn open so the meat is easily seen, and the mews window is covered with shade cloth so some of the light and most of the distractions are hidden. After leaving the hawk alone for an hour or two, the falconer will hopefully find on

[159]

returning that the hawk recognized the food and took a good feed from the carcass. The falconer then continues in this way, only going in the mews twice a day, once to give food and once to remove what has been left. Weighing the food beforehand and then weighing what remains will provide an idea of the amount the hawk is consuming with no need to catch and weigh the hawk itself. At this point, when a hawk has undergone no training, any handling will have negative associations and will hinder training that comes later. Handling such a hawk at this time only builds a very bad impression of the falconer in the hawk's mind. As long as the hawk is consuming over 4 ounces of nutritious food each day, its weight will probably be going up. If otherwise healthy, a hawk that has simply been having a hard time catching prey in the wild is likely to eat a lot more of this free food for the first week or so and then naturally reduce its own intake. Once that happens, the hawk can be left for a day without food, and training can then progress as laid out in the next chapter. If the hawk does not eat, even when left alone with food that is reasonably recognizable as such, the hawk should be immediately handed over to the care of a veterinarian. No wrong has been committed if this is a freshly trapped hawk; in fact, its life may have been saved. Some hawks are easy to catch because they come into a trap when they are starving, either because they just have not been able to kill enough food for themselves or because they have an underlying illness.

Ideally, a falconer starts with a hawk on the high side and lowers the weight to get some kind of response. This is because it is much easier to arrive at the flying weight by coming down to it than by coming up to it; reasons for this will soon become clear. Assuming the hawk is not overly thin as described above, training can proceed.

Here we return to our newly trapped redtail. Had the hawk simply been weighed without first feeling its breastbone, what would have been learned? Absolutely nothing except a weight, and this brings us to the key point about flying weight and weight management. The actual value revealed by the scale in terms of grams or ounces is irrelevant. It is whether the hawk's weight is going up or down or staying the same, how this applies to the hawk's bodily condition, and what the hawk does during the following training session that is important. The reading on the scale simply gives us a way of judging the condition of the hawk in a language we can understand. We can use it to determine how much to feed the hawk and to gauge on the following day whether we have fed too much, too little, or just the right amount. For readers who like analogies as I do, it compares to the gas gauge of a car that is driven for the first time. If the gauge's reading is half full that means

The Basics of Training a Hawk

nothing to us until driving the car reveals that the tank is empty after 100 miles. It is then known that when the gauge says half full, the car will go 100 miles before more gas is needed. In terms of trained hawks, in a simplified example, if the hawk flew three feet yesterday and weighs the same today, it will probably also fly three feet today, all other things being equal. But unless there is previous information to put the matter in context, then the reading on the scale, just like the gas gauge of the new car, doesn't tell us a thing.

It is the hawk's behavior that tells us the correct flying weight, not some figure we make up in advance. I sometimes hear falconers weigh a freshly trapped hawk or one taken up from an aviary and then announce the weight at which it will fly. Whenever I've tried that and then compared the true flying weight with my prediction, the two are often wildly different. There is no point in thinking a male Red-tailed Hawk for instance, is going to fly at 30 ounces because it was trapped at 36 ounces. It may, or it may not. The flying weight depends on the skill of the falconer, the hawk's natural tendency for tameness, its physical condition when it came into the trap, and many other factors.

The falconer uses the scales along with an honest assessment of the behavior of the hawk in relation to where it is in the training and manning process, and its physical condition (gauged by feeling the breastbone and wing muscles) to make decisions on whether to raise or lower the hawk's weight or keep it the same. Scales have a habit of having a rather perverse effect on falconers—especially more experienced ones. Simply put, sometimes I think we believe the scales more than we do the other signs the hawk is giving off. If for instance a hawk that last season flew at 930 grams and flew quarry well and was responsive is now, this season, refusing quarry at the same weight, we are often reluctant to admit that the hawk's weight needs to be lowered. And so we tend to soldier on day after day, coming up with various excuses as to why the hawk isn't performing up to the same standard it has in the past. It may of course be that the hawk isn't as muscled-up as it was when it was catching quarry at 930 grams and so the extra weight it is carrying is actually internal fat. We have the option of waiting the hawk out, hoping it will gain muscle (if that is indeed the problem) while it burns off the fat or we can hope that in some other miraculous fashion it will start to perform properly again. The problems with that approach are two fold; firstly, the hawk may learn some bad habits if consistently allowed to refuse quarry yet still get fed and secondly, we are missing out on some good hawking. If the falconer continues to ignore such signs he may even lose the hawk. On the other side of the equation some falconers will keep a hawk at a weight they think is the correct one when it is becoming increasingly

Falconry: A Guide for Beginners

obvious, or at least it should be, that the hawk needs to be raised in weight. So the falconer must take note of all the signs the hawk is giving him and use the weight he reads on the scales to determine whether he needs to keep it the same, or raise or lower the weight. And he uses the scales over the next few days to confirm he is doing just that.

It must also be noted that weight control is not an exact science. Even the best falconers will err more than occasionally and of course hawks are individual creatures with moods and feelings that we do not always understand. We may be able to feel if a hawk is on the heavy or thin side judging by the feel of the breastbone but our judgment in this area cannot be perfect. We can certainly not judge to the nearest quarter ounce just by feeling the breastbone. Neither can we see what is going on inside the hawk physically. Also, hawks, just like humans, change as they mature and I suspect there are other things going on that we, or at least I, will never fully understand. Of one thing I am sure, if the outward signs show that the hawk is either over or under weight, use that information to decide

> Made. A hawk is said to be "made" when there is no doubt that it will fly a particular quarry. For instance, a hawk is said to be "made" to rabbits when it will chase them without hesitation.

how much to feed the hawk and don't rely on what the hawk did at this weight last year, or even last month to cloud your decision making. In practice, at least with a made hawk, if it is not performing to the standard it has before, it often only needs an adjustment of a quarter or half an ounce one way of the other to get it back on form. To use our gas tank analogy, if the car starts to run out of gas after only 90 miles instead of 100 miles like it did in the past, we can either keep driving and getting stranded each time, or we can make an adjustment and accept that perhaps the engine is not the same as it used to be and that now, a half tank reading on the gas gauge means we have 90 miles before we run out.

Finding the Flying Weight

So let's look at how we arrive at the hawk's flying weight. During training, hawks are weighed once a day just before the training session begins. Hawks perform most consistently when fed and flown on a

> Cast. To eject the indigestible portions of a previous meal in the form of a pellet. Hawks normally cast about 18 hours after eating.

cycle of roughly 24 hours provided they have cast, so it follows that the training session and the daily weighing routine should be at the same time each day. From the hawk's point of view, this is best done either early in the morning or near the end of the day. If a falconer works a shift that ends at 2:00 p.m., then flying time will be in the afternoon. The time of day doesn't matter too much as long as the hawk is accustomed to it and

[162]

The Basics of Training a Hawk

as long as it is the same each day. A hawk, even at flying weight, will not necessarily perform up to its usual standard if it is flown earlier or later than the previous day. Following weighing, the training session proceeds with the falconer judging how much to feed the hawk.

Early training for most broadwings follows a pattern. Each day, we handle the hawk for an hour or so, doing some hooding practice and trying to persuade the hawk to take food on the fist. Some hawks feed the first time food is offered; others may wait for up to a week or more. As long as an attempt is made for at least one hour per day in a quiet place with no distractions when the hawk is hungry enough that hunger will overcome fear, it will eat. I once had a passage goshawk wait 14 days before taking food, and Scruff, mentioned earlier, took 9 days. I also had a passage Cooper's Hawk that fed on the fist, unhooded in broad daylight, with another person in the room, 10 minutes after having her jesses put on and only 30 minutes out of the trap. The first two hawks were fairly heavy when training began; the last was close to starvation when I trapped her. So let's assume the redtail in our example has just fed on the fist for the first time, three days after being trapped. We weighed it before, so now we know the weight at which it will, all things being equal, feed on the fist. If we want the hawk to do nothing more in its life as a trained hawk than feed on the fist, we have a basic, feeding-on-the-fist weight. Of course we'll require more, but even at this stage, the hawk is what determined the actual physical condition it is in to feed on the fist, and we have used the scales to convert that into a language, or number, that we understand. In all probability, as the hawk fears us less, the weight at which it will feed on the fist will increase, and this has similarities to flying weight. With simply feeding on the fist however, if we continually raise the hawk's weight, there will come a time when it will refuse to eat either because it is not hungry, or more likely, it lacks the incentive to overcome its natural fear and carry out even this simple task. That incentive is satisfying the hawk's hunger. This is not the hunger of "I'm starving to death and I must eat or I'm going to die," but rather the hunger of, "I want to eat, and the food is right here, so I will overcome my fear of the strange, somewhat frightening situation I find myself in and bend down to eat." More and slightly different incentive will be needed to get the hawk to fly into the wind and overcome a fast fleeing quarry that will be difficult to subdue. For this, the hawk needs to be sufficiently trained and conditioned to think along the lines of "there is a jackrabbit 200 yards away that I can catch, and I'm keen enough to fly into the wind and give my best effort because if I catch it, I'll get to satisfy my hunger."

Falconry: A Guide for Beginners

The first time the hawk feeds on the fist, it should be given as much food as it wants, since it is not yet known how much food will keep the hawk level. Most hawks at this stage will stop eating once fear returns and overcomes the desire to satisfy hunger. On the second day, once the hawk has been weighed, the same procedure is followed, but this time we will have an idea about how much food is needed to keep the hawk at a consistent weight. Here is where the technicalities start. The parameters of the previous day were different because the hawk had never fed on the fist before and may not have eaten for some days previously. Therefore, although it may weigh the same today as it did yesterday, the hawk may not appear quite as hungry, or, on the other side of the equation, it may appear keener because its fear has decreased after an increase in trust from yesterday's training session. When a hawk is keen for food being offered her, and later, keen to fly quarry, she is said to be sharp set. Not until the parameters from one day to the next are the same can we determine the flying weight. Up until that point, we always give the hawk the benefit of the doubt and do not feed rations that would reduce weight until we are absolutely sure we need to do so to make progress. At this point, experienced falconers with a memory bank of many hawks for comparison might take shortcuts. They may know from the attitude of the hawk that it needs to be keener, but beginners or those flying a species for the first time should always err on the side of feeding the hawk too much. While it may take slightly longer to get the hawk into the field, at least it will get there. Trying to regulate a hawk's weight without sufficient reason or experience may well put its life in danger.

> Sharp Set. A hawk is said to be sharp set when she is keen for the food being offered her but neither too low, nor too high in condition.

Once a hawk is trained it is normal for flying weight to vary if the parameters under which it is flown are changed. These parameters include new quarry, a new flying area, increasing or decreasing day length, a temperature change, the onset of breeding season, migration tendencies, the quality and type of food, and probably many others. My Saker Falcons, to give one example, are used for bird control during the heat of the summer, when they fly at lower weights than during the winter. This is because I need to sharpen their appetites to keep their incentive up, and to keep them sharp set, and this is why many hawks have different flying weights at different times of the year. These same Saker Falcons also do a complete molt while being flown, something they could not do if they were in too low a condition. My Lanner Falcons, on the other hand, generally do

The Basics of Training a Hawk

not need their weight reduced, at least not by as much, as the Saker Falcons. That's simply a difference in the two species. Dixie, a Falcon I flew in the relatively cold high desert around Reno, Nevada, at about 710 grams would behave abysmally if I tried her at the same weight in the warm, quarry rich areas of northern California less than 100 miles away. That's because the parameters changed, and she needed to be at a lower weight to bring the incentive back. It doesn't mean she is lower in condition, although she would be if I took her back to the high desert and flew her at that lower weight.

Even in the early stages, if the parameters are changed from one day to the next, the hawk may react differently. For instance, if for the first feed, the hawk was fed inside a room from which it could not see out, then moved to a room where it can see out or to a room where another person is present, it may not act as keen because there is now something else to focus on. In practice, the sensible thing to do with a new hawk is allow it for the first four or five feeds to eat as much as wanted in a quiet room with no distractions. If its weight is increasing, but the hawk is still completing the session well by eating quickly without too much persuasion, all is fine. If however, as its weight increases, the hawk needs increased persuasion or more time, or spends too much time bating, this is the point at which to reduce the amount of food so that the hawk's weight drops back slightly and the incentive returns. This procedure will be followed repeatedly during the next few months as we alter the parameters and determine the maximum flying weight of the hawk for the conditions in which we fly it. It must be noted however that simply lowering the hawk's weight will not train it. Manning the hawk begins at the outset, the training part, when it is taught to first fly to the falconer and then work in cooperation with him, comes a little later but you cannot simply replace manning with weight reduction.

Training thus continues in normal fashion with the hawk being taught to fly longer and longer distances to the falconer as we closely monitor the hawk's weight and her reactions. During the time that we are teaching the hawk to fly to the fist outside on a creance, we can even try increasing the weight slightly. Here again, the reaction of the hawk following a weight change, whether increase or decrease, must be heeded. If the parameters have changed, so it will take one or two more days to get an accurate assessment of the hawk's reaction at this new weight. For example, perhaps our redtail hesitates when the distance we want it to fly to the fist increases from 15 yards to 20 yards. We keep everything else the same—the flying field, time of day, diet, clothes we wear, etc. Then we drop the weight by ¼ ounce by giving

Falconry: A Guide for Beginners

it slightly less food, and the hawk again responds quickly. We need to determine if this happened because of the increased hunger caused by the drop in weight, by having less food the previous day or if this is the actual weight at which our hawk has enough incentive to fly 20 yards to the fist. So we keep it at the new weight for a few days while increasing the distance, and as long as it continues to perform well, we keep it at that weight. We may even, as a check to make sure we are not relying simply on hunger to train the hawk, raise the weight back up. If the hawk then performs okay over the next few days, it can stay at this new, slightly higher weight or even be given another increase. In training a hawk, a falconer strives to fly it at the heaviest weight at which it performs the task we require (taking wild quarry) within the parameters under which we both must operate.

At this point, I want to dismiss a common fallacy. Trained hawks, at least if they are trained correctly, are not in low condition. They are, in fact, in a condition similar to a wild hawk that feeds itself because it is hungry. There is a habit among some falconers to fly their hawks as heavy as possible believing that they are better falconers because of it or that their hawks are healthier, or that bigger hawks are better. This concept must surely arise from the misguided belief that bigger is always better. I would even suggest that this attitude has been responsible for the loss of many trained hawks over the years as falconers try to compete with themselves and with each other to have the largest hawk. Whether a hawk flies at 40 ounces or 50 ounces is completely irrelevant, it is how it behaves that is important. Hawks that are flown overweight in the mistaken belief that bigger is better often end up getting lost or killed while getting into mischief away from the falconer instead of concentrating on the job at hand.

It is important that the trained hawk meets certain standards otherwise it cannot be considered fully trained. I expect a hawk to take the quarry that is available in a style that I have set and know is achievable and I expect responsiveness to the lure (for longwings) or fist (for shortwings or broadwings). The scale's reading in ounces or grams is only one way of making it easier for me to understand that one of the parameters, the physical condition of the hawk is easily understood and remains within my control. There is absolutely no merit in flying a large hawk if it doesn't meet the standard in the field. If one falconer has a female redtail that flies at 48 ounces, and I have one that flies at 40 ounces, that doesn't mean the other hawk is better than mine or that the other falconer is better. If both hawks are doing what they should in the field,

The Basics of Training a Hawk

it's merely a difference in individual hawks that can occur even among sisters from the same nest. But, as more commonly happens, if the heavier hawk is not as responsive in the field, it may mean the falconer has focused on what the scale reads and on trying to fly a large hawk instead of on what is revealed by the hawk's body language and behavior. If one falconer's Merlin flies at 190 grams, and another flies at 175 grams, and they are both flying well and taking quarry, what does that tell us? One Merlin is larger than the other! It's as simple as that. Another example of the differences between individual hawks is provided by 22 young produced from a Saker Falcon and a male gyr-saker hybrid over a period of five years. The females flew anywhere from 930 grams to 1200 grams, and the males from 710 grams to 830 grams. Even among sisters and brothers, we can see that hawks vary naturally in the size and weight at which they fly best. To reiterate, scales are merely a way to know in advance, after learning from the hawk's previous reactions at that weight, what the hawk's condition is.

As training progresses, our goal is to keep the hawk's weight steady while we increase the distance from which the hawk is called. Training, manning, and weight control affect each other. There is a common misconception that if a hawk will fly five yards at 40 ounces, it will fly further if its weight is lowered. This is not always the case. Many captive-bred longwings are, in fact, the reverse. Once they have learned what to do, their weight can be increased. Broadwings will normally fly free at the same weight at which they came quickly to the fist over a distance of about ten yards while in training on a creance. However, it sometimes happens that with an increase in the distance it is called, the hawk's response slows down. A hawk may be slow at flying longer distances or may completely refuse to do so for one of three reasons, assuming other parameters remain the same.

1) The hawk is being called too many times in one training session.
2) The distance is being increased too quickly.
3) The hawk lacks incentive, and its weight needs to be dropped slightly.

A fourth reason is that the hawk is so low in weight, it lacks the energy to fly that far. If unsure whether the hawk is too low, feeling the breastbone can help. If the breastbone is very sharp, the hawk's weight has been dropped too much. It will need at least ten days off with as much food as can be eaten before starting training again.

Falconry: A Guide for Beginners

Having a more experienced falconer nearby may be of help because he or she should know by feeling the breastbone if the hawk is too low. I say should know, but it pays to take such advice with more than a pinch of salt. Even after years of training and flying hawks I am loathe to advise someone to lower a hawk's weight until I have seen it fly and felt its breastbone. Such advice should never be given without having seen the hawk and felt the breastbone and then confirming that training has been going smoothly up to that point. If there is any doubt as to whether the hawk needs to be raised or lowered, raise the hawk's weight for a few days. The worse that can happen is you will slow down training for a few days but rather that than get the hawk so low in condition that it starts to shut down and refuses to do anything at all. While it may seem that the solution when a hawk is too low is to simply raise the weight that will not necessarily make the hawk suddenly fly well. In practice, the hawk will need to be taken up quite a bit in weight, given a week or more off and then slowly brought back down to its flying weight. A hawk is a living creature; if taken too low in weight it will need time to rebuild its reserves and to feel well again just like a person does following an illness.

If a hawk's weight needs to be reduced, it is never wise to guess at an amount. It is not appropriate to say, "she's overweight, so I'll reduce her by an ounce." Once the hawk has reached the stage in training at which it comes more than 10 yards or so, it is close to its final flying weight and should not be reduced by more than ¼ ounce, per day. Furthermore, after having been dropped, the weight should then remain level for at least two days before considering dropping the weight any further. Merely reducing a hawk's weight will not get it trained any faster and may lead to the hawk's starting to mantle or scream as it gets too low in condition. This ensures that the hawk is flying at the heaviest weight possible within the set of parameters determined for it. Again, experienced falconers can and do take shortcuts because they have a memory store of other hawks with which to compare the behavior of their current hawk. An experienced falconer is one who has achieved success in the field and has trained at least a dozen hawks. There is a tendency, especially among falconers who have only trained a few hawks, to be a little too sure in their relatively small amount of knowledge gained in working with only a few hawks. I did it, and most other falconers do as well but it is not until the falconer has trained over a dozen or so hawks that he will really begin to see the vast difference that is found among individual hawks.

The Basics of Training a Hawk

In our example, let's next assume we're at the point when our redtail is flying 50 yards to the fist and lure quickly and in different flying fields. This, for the time being, is our hawk's flying weight. For a passage hawk that already has a certain amount of base muscle tone, this flying weight is likely to remain the same for the next few months. A captive-bred or eyass hawk does not have as much base muscle tone at the beginning of training as a passager does. With more flying, it is thus more likely there will be a need to increase its weight in small, incremental steps, taking into account response and other factors. Every other week or so in the first season, I may experiment with my newly trained hawks by raising their weights about ¼ ounce (or 7 grams). As long as their behavior remains the same given the parameters in which they are being flown and their incentive does not diminish, I keep them at this new weight. However, in my experience, broadwings and shortwings do not increase much in weight from the time when they are first flown free. Scruff, mentioned earlier and whose praises I never tire of singing first flew free at 1 pound 6 ounces. I experimented with his weight during the first season and flew him as high as 1 pound 7½ ounces, but at this weight he would mess around a bit in the field and although he still took quarry, he lacked the necessary incentive to fly at his best. His eventual flying weight, which really just accounted for increased muscle mass once he got fit, was 1 pound 6½ ounces, and that remained his flying weight for the next three seasons. Bingo, my black musket, first flew free at 1 pound 2 ounces, with an eventual flying weight of 1 pound, 2½ ounces. There are a few situations in which hawks will fly considerably heavier than when they were first flown free. One is with hawks trained during the summer and then flown in cold climates later in the season. Another is when a hawk is flown at quarry that is not particularly taxing, especially if flown over the same terrain each day.

Sometimes I hear a falconer say that his hawk flies at a certain weight range, for example between 30 ounces and 33 ounces. He is actually saying that his hawk responds to his satisfaction between these two weights. If that is truly the case, he should always be aiming to keep his hawk at 33 ounces, for 30 ounces is 3 ounces lower than the hawk needs to be, and that is not good for its health. However, it is possible that the hawk's best weight is 30 ounces, but this falconer is willing to settle for less than the best from his hawk when he inadvertently gives it too much food and lets its weight creep up. This falconer will be lucky indeed if he does not lose this hawk or repeatedly go looking for it because it is not paying attention to him in the field, going off on its own instead.

Falconry: A Guide for Beginners

Flying Weight Summarized

- The flying weight is determined during the process of training the hawk.
- Hawks have only one flying weight for a given set of parameters. These include the type of quarry, the flying area, the day length, temperature and other weather conditions, time of year, diet, and other factors.
- The flying weight will stay the same unless one of the parameters changes.
- Although there is only one true flying weight, a hawk may respond at a wider weight range by performing to an ever-decreasing standard that the individual falconer is either willing or unwilling to accept. We all draw our lines in different places; what is unacceptable to me in a trained hawk may be tolerated by other falconers, and vice versa.
- Hawks at flying weight are not, if they have been trained correctly, low in condition.
- An increase in flying weight will not result in better flights or a healthier hawk unless the falconer's original idea of the hawk's flying weight was incorrect or one or more of the parameters has changed.

A falconer's goal should be to have a hawk that flies well all the time. This requires being honest and critical about weight management and the true flying weight of the hawk. If the parameters are altered, a different response can be expected for a while. This period of time may pass quickly, or it might be necessary to alter the condition of the hawk as well. If this is not desirable, the parameters should not have been changed in the first place. If a Cooper's Hawk doesn't fly well in company because it doesn't very often do so, the falconer should either man the hawk more thoroughly or avoid flying it in company. Lowering the hawks weight, while it may make it respond in company, also lowers the hawk's condition and that should be avoided if at all possible. For myself, I want my hawks to perform with others in the field, so I man them sufficiently and keep them that way as one of the parameters I set for myself and my hawks is that they will fly in company. It must be remembered however, that we falconers draw our lines in different places and have varying expectations for our hawks. The expectations from a hawk should be established very early on and the hawk conditioned to accept the parameters defining those expectations. Once trained and made, the hawk's performance, health, and even its life can best be guaranteed by staying at the flying weight that brings out the best performance within the established parameters. Raising or lowering

The Basics of Training a Hawk

the weight should, for a conscientious falconer, cause a corresponding change in the hawk's performance. When even just a little bad luck is added (which in falconry is often preceded by bad planning), a lost or dead hawk may result.

Diet

What the hawk is given to eat is critical for maintaining good health. As a basic diet for all my trained hawks, I use a mixture of day old cockerels, quail, and mice. All are commercially produced either for human food consumption (in the case of quail and of chicks that grow into chickens) or specifically for those of us who keep birds of prey or reptiles (quail and mice). During the hawking season, as long as it's been frozen first, I might also feed portions of larger animals such as rabbits, squirrels, pigeons, pheasants, or ducks that my hawks have caught. Generally though, prey caught by the hawks is kept frozen and fed during the molt when weight control is not as critical. It is much easier to keep a hawk at a certain weight by adhering to one type of diet.

> Molt. The process whereby a hawk replaces its feathers. Generally the mold occurs once each year beginning in the spring and lasting on average of six months.

When the hawk is catching quarry, I do not make a habit of feeding what has been caught. One reason for this is that I don't want to feed anything I haven't examined and frozen lest my hawks pick up a disease from their prey. Secondly, it is extremely difficult to judge the hawk's condition and stay at flying weight if feeding a varied diet. Let's say the Red-tailed Hawk in our example is getting a regular diet of day old chicks or quail. Within this established parameter, we know how big the portion of quail or how many chicks to feed to keep the hawk's weight level. If our hawk now catches a jackrabbit and we follow the advice in many falconry books to give it a gorge, allowing it to eat as much as it wants, we've firstly changed the diet. This altering of the parameters will have an unknown effect on the hawk. Secondly, after a gorge, it will be necessary to reduce the amount of food eaten over the next few days to bring the hawk back down to flying weight. This will not only reduce condition, but fitness as well, because the hawk can't be flown while overweight. Plus we are missing out on hawking opportunities! Had we given the hawk the usual daily ration of day old chicks, its condition would remain the same and we could confidently expect to go out tomorrow and have the hawk repeat the performance. What was done yesterday at 44 ounces will, in all probability, be done today at this same weight, assuming the other parameters remain unchanged.

Falconry: A Guide for Beginners

Passage Red-tailed Hawk on a squirrel. She does not need to eat the squirrel in order to gain more incentive, she already had enough incentive to catch it. As long as she gets a reward at the site of the kill, she will continue to want to take squirrels the next time the opportunity occurs.

If a hawk is flown over weight, as is often the case when gorged on a kill and then flown before it has returned to its flying weight, bad habits such as refusing difficult slips, flying wide, taking its time to return, etc. can easily develop. Once these habits are learned, they are very difficult to unlearn. It is important to remember that a hawk has no comprehension of right and wrong. So if it flies wide of the falconer because it is a bit too high in weight, although the falconer will consider such behavior bad, the hawk doesn't understand this behavior as bad or unwanted. Hawks simply do not know good from bad or right from wrong. It is up to the falconer to only put his hawk in situations where it is likely to do things that he wants repeated so that when he rewards it, the likelihood of it repeating them is increased. If he flies the hawk overweight and it learns a bad behavior for which it ends up getting a reward, it is likely to repeat it but is not the hawk's fault. The blame lies with the

The Basics of Training a Hawk

falconer who took the hawk out overweight thereby encouraging the behavior he does not want. Furthermore, reducing the weight to where it was before it learned the unwanted behavior, will not necessarily correct the behavior, especially if, in the hawk's mind, such behavior paid off. Everything the falconer does with his hawk that ends in success for the hawk, the hawk will want to repeat, both the good and the bad. A good falconer only puts his hawk in situations where she is likely to do something he wants repeated and so when he rewards the hawk the likelihood of such behavior being repeated in the future is increased. It is for this reason that the best falconers, those whose hawks fly well season after season, are the ones with the most discipline.

Many falconers think that by allowing a hawk to gorge on its first few kills, the likelihood of a repeat performance is increased. That is not correct. A hawk chases a rabbit because it has incentive that comes from knowing, partly through training and partly through instinct, that there will be food when the rabbit is caught. Nothing we do can increase the incentive that went into catching it. In other words, a hawk doesn't receive more incentive because it ate more food; the incentive it already had before catching the rabbit was, and is, sufficient. Allowing a gorge, followed by the need to give the hawk several days off without flying, will only allow it to forget how clever it was while also reducing its level of fitness. Furthermore, the hawk does not need to eat the rabbit or whatever it is it caught, but will quite happily eat the quail or the day old chicks it has become accustomed to during the course of training. By all means, the hawk can be given a full day's ration for at least its first 10 kills or more if you prefer, but gorging will not make it into a better hawk or make it more determined. After having taken quarry with numerous hawks throughout the last 40 odd years and witnessing several thousand kills, I can testify that trained hawks do not need to eat what they have caught. Giving the hawk a gorge is not therefore part of my routine after a kill though I do, generally, feed a hawk more each Saturday and then feed either reduced rations or nothing at all the following day as I do not hawk on Sundays. So it should be clear that giving a gorge in itself is not a bad thing; only that it is not necessary as a way of increasing the incentive of the hawk in the field by giving it more to eat when it has killed.

There are also stories within the experience of any group of falconers about what has gone wrong after feeding a hawk from its kill. Obvious horror stories include the hawk dying from disease or poisoning. More common are subtle stories that require reading

Falconry: A Guide for Beginners

between the lines. Perhaps the performance of the hawk was lowered because the falconer altered its condition either up or down, generally up, thereby reducing incentive. If the hawk was then flown, even though not at flying weight, and was allowed to refuse quarry or sit on a pole and was rewarded for coming back, a foundation for future disaster was laid. The falconer has inadvertently taught the hawk it can pick and choose when it wants to chase quarry and it will still get fed. Maybe the hawk flew wide, killed something a long distance away and got pounced on by an eagle. The eagle alone didn't kill the hawk; the falconer set the stage by flying it above weight. My standard practice is to feed the hawk its regular food at the site of the kill for at least the first 10 kills. Once made, I may feed a smaller portion of food for the first kill and then fly the hawk again if I think there is a good chance for a second kill. If the hawk kills again, I will let it feed up on the remainder of its rations for the day at the second kill site. If not, I will end the day by presenting the lure and letting the hawk feed up after the lure is taken. The lesson being taught to the hawk is that while it gets a small reward each time it comes to the fist, there is a larger reward for actually catching quarry.

The Basics of Training a Hawk

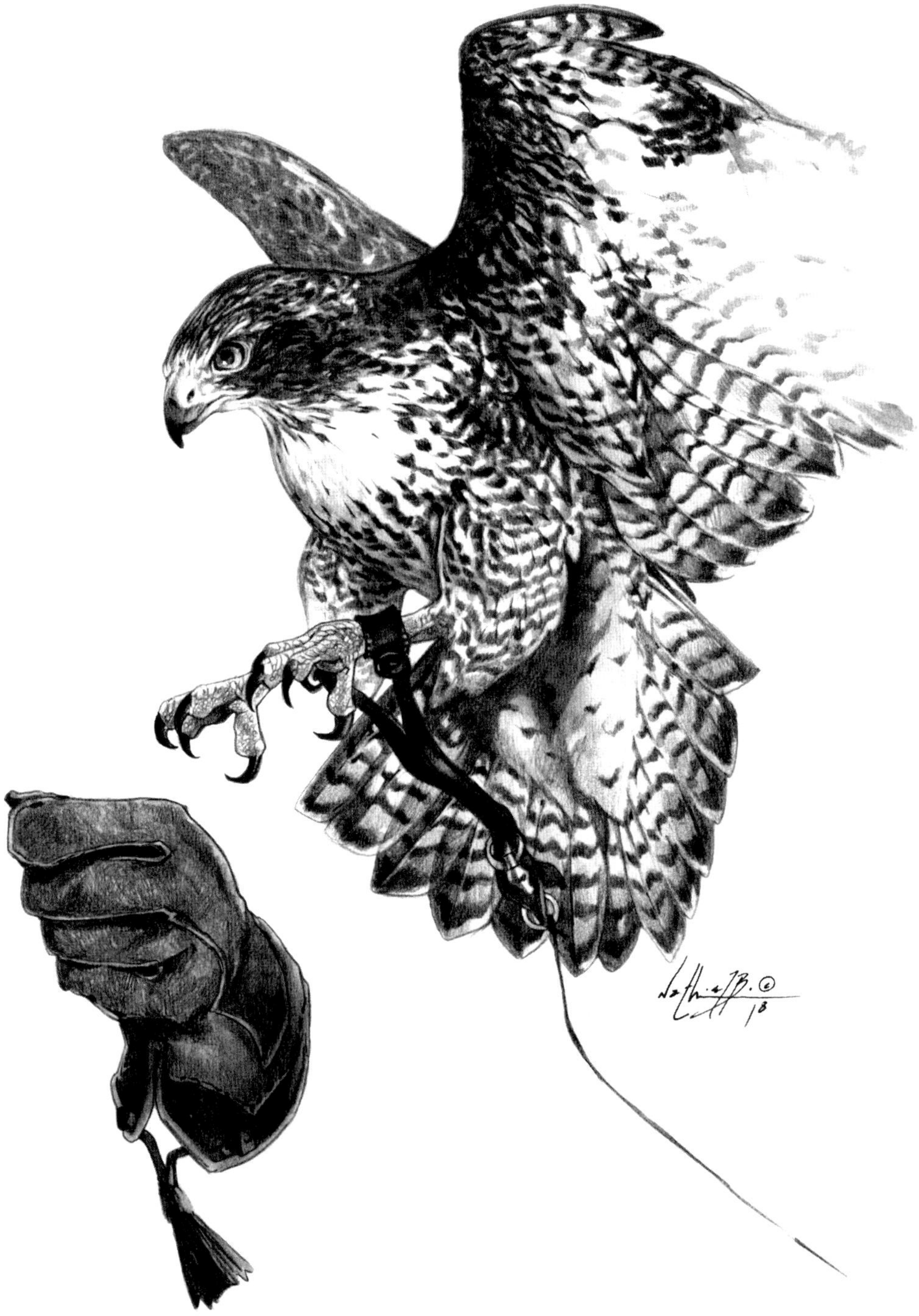

Chapter Six
Training the Red-tailed Hawk

Overall Goal

With a basic understanding of weight control, we can now move on to the subject of training our newly trapped redtail. Anyone embarking on the task of training a hawk or any other animal should have a thorough idea about the goal to be achieved. I try to meet these goals by the end of the first season. Before that time, the falconer should not judge the hawk negatively nor consider passing the hawk onto someone else without very good reason. I find it unfortunate and tiresome that some falconers fly a hawk for a few weeks and then either release it or pass it on because it isn't doing what they think it should be doing. Our society is filled with disposable items that are quickly discarded to acquire something else. That attitude should not apply to hawks. A falconer makes an investment in a living creature that should last for the life of that creature. While it is permissible to put a hawk into a breeding project after two or three seasons or to release a passage hawk at the end of the season, to give up flying an individual hawk before the end of its first season should happen only for a reason that is extremely compelling.

Falconry: A Guide for Beginners

Goals to be maintained or achieved by the end of the first season are the following:

1) The hawk should be alive and in good feather condition. If the hawk is lost or has died I will consider it my fault for only in that way can any lessons be learned to prevent the same thing from happening again.
2) The hawk should fly the type of quarry I have selected in as stylish a manner as the two of us can together achieve. While we may have our minds set on a certain quarry species, it must be remembered that some passage hawks have learned that certain species should be avoided and there is little the falconer can do to change their minds. While all hawks differ, I consider it my responsibility to bring out the best each individual hawk has to offer by flying her as often as possible thereby allowing her to develop and improve.
3) The hawk should be well trained, responsive to the fist and lure. I expect a certain standard of responsiveness from my hawks. I do not like to sit under trees or telephone poles waiting for a hawk to come down. I have no regard for falconers who repeatedly use live lures to recover their hawks. Such practices represent lazy, undisciplined falconry and are repugnant to others, falconers and non-falconers alike. A falconer relying on such techniques has not mastered the art.
4) The hawk should take the hood well at all times. How a falconer's hawk takes a hood is a direct reflection of the falconer's ability. I expect my hawks to take the hood at the first attempt unless there is an unusual reason.
5) The hawk should fly well in the presence of others. Occasionally a falconer will, because of circumstances, hawk alone. Some shortwings especially, when flown this way, can be difficult to persuade to fly in the company of others. Because I like to hawk with others, I expect my hawks to behave accordingly.

From the Beginning

After removing the hawk from the trap, it is given a quick check for broken feathers or injuries, then a decision to keep or release it is made. I like a hawk to be in good feather condition and to have a relatively round chest showing that it has been taking care of itself and regularly catching prey. I do not like to keep a hawk that has broken feathers, is covered in lice, or has a really sharp breastbone although I am often loath to return such a hawk to the wild because evidence

Training the Red-tailed Hawk

One of nature's wonders, a wild, passage Red-tailed Hawk. A falconer who traps this hawk or any other is responsible for how she turns out as a trained hawk. She's already survived long enough in the wild to prove she has what it takes. She must be treated with care and respect by a falconer putting forth only the best of efforts to make sure she reaches her full potential as a trained hawk.

shows it has not been doing too well. When I do release one, I try to leave a large item of food nearby, one that will be recognized so the hawk at least gets a good meal from the experience. I also spray the hawk with a lice spray to rid it of these pests, thus further giving a helping hand. If the hawk is of the species and sex I am looking for and is in good condition, I will generally keep it. The hawk is restrained in an abba; a square or rectangular piece of cloth with folds sewn into two corners and a tape attached for tying. The hawk's wing joints are inserted into the folds and the rest of the abba is wrapped around it and secured with the tape. Alternatively, it can be socked in pantyhose. It is worthwhile placing masking tape around the front three toes and around the back toe and talon to keep the hawk from damaging the

[179]

Falconry: A Guide for Beginners

Freshly trapped passage redtail secured for transportation in an abba.

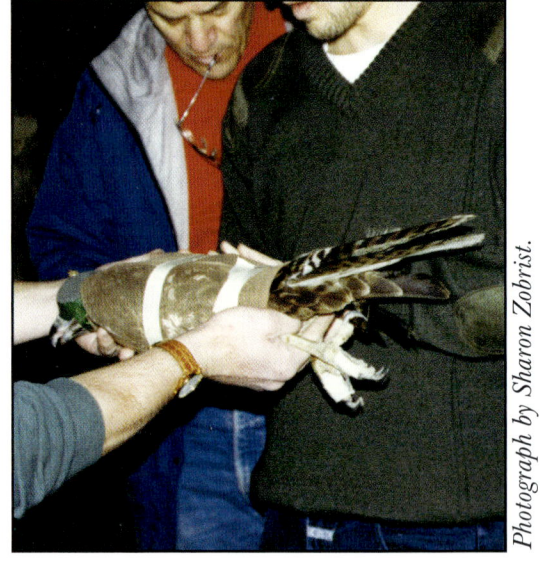

Photograph by Sharon Zobrist.

On the left, this freshly trapped redtail is securely held. In this position she can either have her equipment fitted or she can have her toes wrapped prior to inserting her into a nylon stocking as shown in the photograph on the right.

Training the Red-tailed Hawk

undersides of its feet if it is going to be a while before equipping the hawk. The hawk is hooded and placed chest down on a folded towel for the journey home. If the journey will be a long one, I usually fit anklets, jesses and a swivel and leash immediately after removing the hawk from the trap and hooding it, then I try to persuade it to sit on a cadge. If the hawk refuses to grip the perch, but sits relatively calmly on the carpet underneath the perch, I leave it there for the journey. Spraying water from a bottle is useful to calm a hawk, so I give it a thorough soaking after which the hawk generally sits quietly if handled gently.

Once home with the freshly trapped hawk, the first thing to do, if it was not done out in the field upon removal from the trap, is to attach anklets, bells, jesses, swivel and leash or the tethering system, whichever is chosen. The hawk was hooded as soon as it was removed from the trap, and it is important to remember that hood training begins with the hood on the hawk. Whether to begin working now or to let the hawk rest for a while depends partly on how tired the falconer is, but there is no rush, and it helps to let the hawk settle down for a period. It should be placed somewhere safe and tethered to a low, portable bow perch with two falconer's knots. I like to be able to keep an eye on a new hawk and do not, at this point, put it in the mews on the bow perch, but rather bring it inside my house where I place the perch on some paper spread out on the floor. This lets me keep an eye on the hawk to make sure, for instance, it is not constantly scratching at the hood, which might be a sign the hood is too small. Being in my presence, even though hooded, the hawk can hear activity that is happening around it, and this will start the manning process.

Hooded hawks are traditionally picked up by pressing the gloved hand against the backs of their legs about half way between the top of the foot and the knee joint. With a push forward, this will unbalance the hawk, and it will step backwards. There is however, another preferred way of getting a hooded hawk onto the fist or any other perch, and both the new falconer and new hawk should learn it. 1) Gently lift the middle toe of the hawk's right foot with the thumb and forefinger of the ungloved hand. 2) Place the glove under the toe so that it is resting on the glove. 3) Lift slowly, at the same time saying "step up". 4) Continue slowly upwards, and the hawk will lift up its other foot, and there it is, sitting on the gloved fist. The words "step up" mean nothing at this point, but if said every time, the hawk will come to know what they mean and will soon be stepping up smoothly often without the need to lift the middle toe.

Falconry: A Guide for Beginners

An advantage of getting a hooded hawk on the fist with this method is that the hawk is doing so of its own accord rather than because the falconer is unbalancing and thereby forcing it. Psychologically, it is always better if the hawk does something, however small, because it wants to rather than because it is forced. A second advantage has more practical purposes. Unbalancing the hawk with a push of the glove against the back of the legs will almost always cause it to quickly open its wings while trying to regain balance and avoid being tipped over. If this is done in a confined space, the hawk may well end up damaging its primary feathers, something the falconer must take every precaution to avoid. At this point, the hawk may be on the open floor on a bow perch with nothing to strike its wings against, but if the falconer always relies

This freshly trapped female redtail is ready to start training. Since being trapped, she's been hooded on a low bow perch with people and sounds to listen to. In essence, her training has already begun.

Training the Red-tailed Hawk

on unbalancing a hawk and if the time comes when the hawk must be picked up in a confined space, such as a transport box, damage to the feathers could result. Teaching the hawk how to step up on cue is fairly straightforward, and the benefits are well worthwhile. Incidentally, if it's decided to pick the hawk up from the back, and there are times when both methods may be necessary, saying "step back" before doing so will teach the hawk to do just that. Most of my trained hawks will either "step up" or "step back" on hearing the words even without feeling the touch of the glove under a middle toe or gently pressing against the back of their legs.

Watching how a falconer picks up a hawk can be revealing. I have little respect for falconers who are rough at handling their hawks. They grab the jesses unceremoniously and scoop the hawk up, knowing it has no choice but to follow the upward movement of the fist. When they feed their hawks, they sometimes stand with the wind blowing against the hawk's back. This makes it uncomfortable, and it wants to turn around. Or a falconer may fiddle with the jesses while the hawk is feeding, unmindful that this is causing the hawk to flap around to maintain balance. The falconer should care about the hawk, both its mental and physical well-being. A hawk should not be treated as a captive who has no choice about whether to sit on the glove, but rather as a treasure to be persuaded that the glove is a safe, comfortable place to be.

The falconer should keep his most useful hand free for hooding and unhooding, tying the falconers knot, etc. so most falconers hold their hawks on their left hand keeping their right hand free for these tasks. If you are left handed it is better to hold the hawk on the right hand in which case the following should be reversed. While the falconer is standing with a hawk on the fist, the hawk should be sitting comfortably with the toes of the left foot resting on the thumb and/or thumb joint, and with the right foot on the thumb joint or wrist. The wind, if there is any, should be blowing into the hawk's chest. The jesses come down between the thumb and forefinger and out between the ring and middle finger with the swivel resting on the back of the gloved hand. The leash, having been grasped in the middle, should have one firm loop wrapped tightly around the little finger, then the end of the leash is also brought up around the finger so that two smaller loops are all that show below the glove. Alternatively and wisely, especially for new falconers, the end of the leash can be tied to the ring on the glove. If the leash is merely left hanging down and if the hawk bates, it will probably get its wings caught up in the leash and a real fuss will ensue as the falconer untangles the hawk and gets it settled again. This damages not only the sensitive barbs on the feathers, but also and just as importantly, the hawk's frame of mind.

    While standing with a hawk, a falconer should take care that no one can pass behind it until the hawk is so well manned that doing so will not cause alarm. A conscientious falconer should be constantly thinking of the hawk, and if there are other hawks around, of them as well. It is easy to tell which falconers are in tune with hawks by watching how they walk through a gathering of falconers at a field meet, especially in the weathering area where several hawks may be present. A sensitive falconer will walk smoothly around other hawks, never passing behind the back of one. He or she will be constantly watching, not by staring directly at a hawk, but out of the corner of the eye, to see if any hawk gives a clue that it is nervous about being approached. He or she will then quickly veer off if necessary so as not to upset the hawk in question. Conversely, some falconers march straight through a weathering ground, heedless of the hawks they are disturbing, perhaps swinging a bath pan back and forth, remaining oblivious to the bating or unrest they might be causing. To master the art, as all falconers should at least be trying to do, it helps to put oneself in the hawk's position by pretending to be a captive of aliens who are now trying to make friends. If one imagines being held by an alien, being offered strange food and being carted around to see other aliens, one can imagine how to respond. Anything that can make the adjustment to a new life a smoother one will be met with less fear and quickly accepted. A hawk will likely respond to the same understanding, approach, and treatment that a human captured by aliens would like to receive.

    At this stage when the new falconer is handling a new hawk for the first time, there is a lesson to learn, one that will be used and refined every time the falconer is around a trained hawk. The falconer must learn to read a hawk's body language and the signals it gives in order to gain the hawk's trust and confidence and to learn how to act around hawks. A hawk gives off signals, some subtle and some not, when afraid or wary. Bating or trying to fly away from the perch or from the glove of the falconer is the most obvious sign, but there are often a number of precursors to this action that if noticed, could prevent the bate in the first place. Bating is ultimately a sign that the hawk is trying to distance itself from the falconer. A new hawk, assuming it has not been handled by anyone else, comes to the falconer with a clean slate. It is like an empty book waiting for the falconer to write in the story. How will that story read? Will the hawk live long enough and be in good enough condition to go hawking in cooperation with the falconer and perhaps a dog and other falconer friends year after year, or will the hawk be lost or end up with bad feathers or die from disease because it was not taken care of? The story is for the falconer to write, and reading the hawk's signals from the very beginning can make the story one to be proud of.

Whenever the falconer picks up a hooded hawk or even when passing close by, talking to the hawk will alert it to the falconer's presence so it is not startled. At this stage, having never been handled or asked to stand on the glove, the mere sound of the falconer's voice may be enough to make the hawk spread its wings slightly and puff out its feathers and open its beak slightly in an effort to make itself look bigger and more threatening. This is the hawk's first warning that it is afraid and is preparing for either fight or flight. Even though hooded, this first sign that the falconer sees should also be the first one to gradually diminish over the next couple days as falconer and hawk work together. It is encouraging to see the hawk beginning to accept the voice of the falconer as he passes close by and talks to the hawk while it is hooded on the perch. Most redtails quickly realize within a matter of hours that no harm is being done, and so they open their wings and beak less and less. The goal of the falconer when manning a hawk is to take it through the process with as few bates as possible. A bate should be considered a setback because it may mean the hawk has been tried beyond what it is ready for. A few bates are inevitable, but it is amazing how many can be avoided by just a little forethought on the part of the falconer who is watching the hawk's body language for signs of nervousness. It is during the manning process that the hood is most useful. Ronald Stevens, in his book, The *Taming of Genghis*, relates that he has trained hawks, in this case large longwings such as peregrines, to the point of flying free without a bate. My personal best was a total of less than 12 bates from the time I took the hawk out of the chamber, in this case a lanneret, to the time he flew free 14 days later. While some species tend to be more highly-strung than others, as do some individuals, the fact remains that many bates can and should be avoided. This is accomplished by moving training along at the pace that the hawk, not the falconer, sets.

Let's get back to our hooded redtail sitting on a bow perch in the house. It is getting used to noises in the background and will, after a couple of hours, or perhaps much less time, cease to show alarm when someone walks by while talking, perhaps calling it by name. The time for the first picking up of the hawk has arrived. A falconer who is right-handed wears a glove on the left hand, and a left-handed falconer

Falconry: A Guide for Beginners

wears a glove on the right. Traditionally and going back hundreds of years, hawks were carried on the left hand because this kept the right hand free for the sword, but practically the falconer should keep the most useful hand free for such things as hooding and tying the falconer's knot. To pick up the hooded hawk, let's use the method of lifting the middle toe of one foot. It doesn't really matter which foot, but I generally pick the one nearest me, which will be the right foot if I am approaching from the hawk's right side. If I am approaching from the front, it will be the left foot, place the glove and life under the toe. Even at this early stage, the hawk is less likely to bate if picked up from the front, so that is what I normally do. I untie the leash and wrap it firmly around my right hand once or twice before attempting to pick my hawk up, so that if it should bate, I can quickly lift it clear of the ground so it doesn't do damage to its feathers by striking them against the ground or the perch. Feathers can be repaired, but it's far preferable that they aren't damaged in the first place.

Let's assume that the hawk has stepped up nicely and is now sitting on the fist, still hooded, wondering what is happening. Before taking a step, the jesses are secured between the thumb and the fingers by passing them down into the palm of the hand. The jesses are now taken out the back of the hand between the ring and middle finger as close to the palm as possible before closing the hand. Placing the jesses in this position, which I call "the lock," allows one to grip them firmly and means the falconer is not relying on only the leash to hold the hawk. Whenever a hawk is on the fist, one's first reaction should be to put the jesses in that lock. After placing the jesses in the lock, the leash is taken at about the halfway point and looped around the gloved little finger, then wrapped around again so there is one tight loop around the little finger. Now the end of the leash is either tied to the ring on the glove, or it is brought up and grasped about two inches from the end around the little finger. Often, this can all be done even before the hawk is asked to step up.

If all was done smoothly and correctly, the hawk should now be sitting on the fist, having not bated. When a hawk bates, there are two ways to help it back up if it shows no sign of wanting or trying to do so on its own. At this early stage, if hooded, a hawk will probably not yet have mastered how to recover from a bate. After a couple of bates unhooded, it will probably learn how, but to leave a hawk hanging too long will wear it out and put a strain on its back. The first way to help the hawk recover is to cup the right hand, place it under the hawk's chest and lift it back above the fist,

Training the Red-tailed Hawk

The correct method of holding the jesses, swivel and leash.

at the same time maneuvering its feet into contact with the glove. Once the hawk feels the glove, it will likely grip it when the bare hand is removed from its chest. The second method, often used by those working with longwings, is to place the hand behind the hawk's back and lift it up, again maneuvering the feet into contact with the glove. However, it is difficult with a hand on the back, to position the feet into contacting the glove because the hawk must actually be tipped off the hand before contact with the glove is made. The result is often another bate. In addition, hawks are instinctively more afraid of a hand on the back than on the chest and will try to distance themselves by bating as soon as they can. The reason the latter method is preferred by some with longwings is that unlike most broadwings and shortwings, longwings will bite. A bite from even a small longwing can be painful. I find the chest method preferable, even for longwings, because of the added fear that placing the hand on the back causes.

A hawk will, if it moves its feet, always move them to a higher position if one is available. For this reason, when carrying a hawk, whether hooded or unhooded, the falconer's fist should be slightly higher than the elbow. If the hawk tries to move its feet, it will move away from the elbow, and finding no room beyond the end of the fist, will stop there. If the fist is held lower than the elbow or if, as is the case with many non-falconers holding a hawk for the first time and finding the hawk moving about, the hand is pointed downward in an effort to make the hawk move further away, it will begin to move up the arm, moving naturally to the higher location. The gloved hand should be angled slightly inwards at the bottom, in other words the little finger should be closer to the falconer's body than the index finger. This prevents the tail from coming into contact with the back of the glove, which may cause wear if it happens a lot. In practice, with a hawk the size of a female redtail, this means that the ball of the left foot is placed almost directly over the gap between the thumb and index finger.

Once our hawk is comfortable, we can take it for a walk around the house, talking all the while so the hawk becomes accustomed not only to sitting and being carried on the fist, but to our voice. The hawk should not be unhooded yet, that will come a bit later. At this point, we are simply teaching our hawk to ride on the fist and letting it know that we mean no harm. If desired at this point, the hawk can also be weighed as long as no food can be felt in the crop, situated just below the beak. As explained, the weight doesn't reveal anything unless we also feel the breastbone. If the sponsor or another experienced falconer is nearby, asking him or her to also feel the breastbone will provide another opinion. If the hawk is really thin, most falconers with true experience will be able to point that out if there is any doubt. Assuming the hawk is not thin, the next step, which should take place no later than the evening of the second day, is to start hood training and offering food on the fist. If I have trapped a hawk in the morning, I begin hood training the evening of the same day.

If trapped late in the day, I wait until the next evening, though earlier because I also want to offer food on the second day regardless of the trapping time on the previous day. Hood training begins by getting the hawk used to having the hood struck (opened) and drawn (closed). This is done with the right hand and the teeth. Denture wearers must be careful! The hood is gently struck and drawn several times; it simply cannot be done too many times. At first, the hawk may show signs of alarm by raising its wings, puffing out its feathers and opening its beak, the same signs it showed when first trapped, but these will diminish over time. We practice leaving the hood struck for a while, then drawing it. We leave it drawn for a while, then strike and draw it many times within 10 minutes. We practice walking with the hood struck. The more practice we both get, the better.

We now find a quiet place in a dimly lit room. Evening, after the sun has gone down, is a good time because our hawk cannot see daylight through a window. We can either sit down or stand. Sitting on a high stool can be useful because there are no chair arms in the way, and the rungs can serve as a foot rest. My favorite chairs for working with hawks resemble an office or computer chair with a comfortable arm rest, an upright sitting position, and easy in-and-out access. We now strike the hood and pull it ever so slightly forward until the hawk's right eye can just barely be seen, then the hood is popped straight back on again. We go back to striking and drawing the hood for a few minutes. Our hawk will, in all likelihood, show the same alarm signs that we are now used to seeing, but if we pop the hood back on quickly, our hawk will just as quickly calm down. Now we try again, bringing the hood off just enough to catch a quick glimpse of the hawk's eye then pop it back on again. We keep repeating the process, taking the hood off ever so slightly, then putting it back on, moving the hood a little further off the hawk's head and leaving it just a little longer before we put it back on each time. If the hawk looks like it is going to bate, slow down, go back to drawing and striking the hood for a few minutes then try again. Do everything you can to avoid a bate. It is here that the suitability of the freshly trapped passage redtail for a beginner becomes appreciated. Redtails tend to be calm by nature compared to other species, and as long as they are not pushed too far, it is fairly easy to avoid a bate. A redtail also has a fairly large head that gives a big target for a beginner with the hood.

A hawk should be trained at the speed at which it is ready to progress. There is no point in trying to rush it and cause a bate that will make the process go back a few steps. Many times, I have seen falconers take up a new hawk from a breeding chamber, put its equipment on, get it up on the fist, and promptly unhood it. The result has almost always been a bating, hanging, hissing, mad, and terrified hawk with an anxious falconer trying to get the hood back on to restore calm. Absolutely nothing is gained by such an experience, most certainly not the trust of the hawk, so the only answer is to take one's time. The first session should last a half hour to an hour. By the end of that

Falconry: A Guide for Beginners

Hooding a gyr-saker hybrid.

time, all being well, we will have progressed to taking the hood off the head entirely for a second or two, maybe more, and popping it back on. It is important not to overdo it by removing the hood so far that the hawk is frightened enough to bate. It should only be removed as far as the body language of the hawk indicates. If the session ends with being able to take the hood off for a few seconds, then gently put back on, our goal has been achieved, and we are well on the way to hood training the hawk. If there have been one or two bates along the way, it may mean we are pushing the hawk too much and moving it along too quickly, although some hawks will bate the instant the hood is even slightly off, no matter how careful a falconer is. This attitude of moving slightly slower than the pace at which the hawk is thought to progress,

Training the Red-tailed Hawk

Drawing the braces using the teeth and right hand.

trying to prevent mishaps on the way, will pay dividends later when out in the field. It may seem that I have been overly cautious in this section, especially to experienced falconers, but this is the time when the new falconer should be learning the most. The wrong lesson for future hawks is learned if nothing happens other than helping a hawk back on the fist after countless bates. At this point, the new falconer needs to learn how to avoid causing a bate in the first place. More experienced falconers, those who have trained a dozen or so hawks successfully, are quicker to recognize signs that the hawk is ready to progress, but for a first hawk, taking one's time will not be regretted.

We have not, as yet, offered the hawk any food. If it was trapped in the morning, and the first hood training session took place in the evening, the hawk does not need to be offered food that day. If convinced that the hawk is low in condition, my approach would be turning the hawk loose in the mews as explained earlier. If trapped late in the day, the first hooding session can take place at any time during the next day, but I find hawks to be calmer in the evening, so I generally wait until then. Regardless, on the evening of the second day, the hawk should be offered food for the first time. We will need a quiet room where there will be no

Falconry: A Guide for Beginners

disturbance. The room doesn't need to be too bright, but the hawk must be able to see the food in its feet. I suggest placing a table lamp, one with a three-way bulb on the lowest setting, in a far corner of the room.

Finding a comfortable chair is a good idea because the process may last an hour or so. The best type of food to offer the hawk is something easily torn up, but still recognizable as food. A mouse will suffice, but failing that, if quail or chicks will be the staple diet, a quail will probably also work even though the hawk may never have seen one, let alone have caught one in the wild. If the breast meat is exposed, our hawk will recognize it as food. The food is placed between the front side of the thumb and fingers of the gloved hand. We hold onto the legs of the quail by taking them out through the ring and middle fingers, then close the fist back up so that our hawk stands with a foot on the food yet without being able to wrap a foot around it. The alternative method used by some falconers is to hold the food behind the thumb, but this way is more uncomfortable for the hawk because it almost has to put its head between its legs to take a bite. If feeding on its own, a hawk would not hold food in such a position,

This male Harris' Hawk has just been unhooded for the first time. The hawk is staring at the falconer (who should not look directly at him) and opening his wings to make himself look bigger and more threatening. These signs of his nervousness will soon pass, but while a hawk is exhibiting them, one must move very slowly so as not to provoke a bate.

Training the Red-tailed Hawk

but would hold it under the front of its foot, taking bites from in front of its toes, as is possible if the food is held in front of the thumb. There are other problems with holding the food behind the thumb. First, the jesses and the food cannot both be held securely at the same time. Secondly, one's hand will nearly always end up in the vertical position, meaning that the hawk's tail is in almost constant contact with the back of the glove as the hawk feeds because the position is uncomfortable and the tail must be used for balance. This interferes with the fragile webbing of the tail feathers and causes them to wear unnecessarily. Later, after gaining experience, the beginner can try both methods as I have done, to see which is preferable. For now, food held in front of the thumb creates a more natural feeding position. Held thus, if the hawk looks down, it will see exposed meat under, or very close to, its front toes.

After doing 30 minutes of hooding practice we now remove the hood and put it to one side, moving slowly so as not to frighten the hawk as we sit back and try to relax. We do not stare at the hawk, but periodically move thumb or fingers inside the glove to see if the hawk will look down at the food. Sometimes a hawk will look down, see the meat, then quickly look away. The hawk knows it's food and knows it's there, but is just not ready to let hunger overcome fear of strange circumstances to bend down and eat. No matter, it will eventually do so, even if it takes an hour a day over five or more days; eventually the hawk will eat. It can be helpful to tear a small piece of food off the meat or to have some food previously prepared that is raised up to the beak. As the food gets close, the hawk may well bring its head back and raise it up slightly while opening the beak. With enough dexterity, it is often possible to put the food just inside the beak and leave it there. The hawk will likely just sit with the food in its mouth looking rather foolish, but eventually it will either fall out, or the hawk will deliberately drop it (not a good sign) or will swallow it. In my experience, most hawks will take pieces of food in this way for two or even three days before plucking up the courage to bend down and tear at the food for themselves. It can be helpful in keeping digestion going to give a couple of pieces this way, and it shows a hawk that I am trying to give it food. If the hawk flicks the food morsels away time after time, and especially if it also begins to bate repeatedly, it is not hungry enough, and we might as well put the hood back on and wait 24 hours until the next day when hopefully our hawk will be more inclined to accept the offering.

Falconry: A Guide for Beginners

After a few days of manning, this passage redtail, trapped only four days previously, has progressed to being manned outside. Out of nervousness, she still opens her wings and beak a bit, but as long as nothing untoward happens, she sits quietly taking in the sights and sounds around her.

    It is unusual that a hawk will feed on the fist the first time it is offered food, though I have had it happen, surprisingly with a passage Cooper's Hawk and several times with peregrines and other large longwings. A positive sign is that of the hawk looking down at the meat and licking its beak with its tongue, almost like a hungry dog. This is a sign that the hawk recognizes and wants the food. I follow the routine of 20 to 30 minutes of hood training followed by 30 to 60 minutes of offering food each day until the hawk is feeding on the fist. If the hawk is not taking the food being offered, it is for the simple reason of still being

Training the Red-tailed Hawk

too heavy, and it is safe to wait another 24 hours before trying again. We can, if desired, try two sessions per day, one in the morning and one in the evening. A session of hooding and unhooding in the morning will certainly help move things along, provided our hawk is not spending the unhooded time in bating, from which a hawk learns nothing.

The hood's utility in manning is that it gradually exposes the hawk to new sights, in small doses, so the hawk learns that they are not harmful. The body language of the hawk should be the guideline to how much is enough. Some hawks, even before they are feeding on the fist, will sit unconcerned while people are moving around nearby in the house. Some hawks will even act this way outside in broad daylight. The hawk should determine how much it can be left unhooded on the fist, and at the first sign of concern, the hood should be put back on. If attempting to train a hawk without a hood, there is no luxury of suddenly being able to calm down the hawk, taking away the fearful object that made it want to bate; the result will always be a bate. Some falconers, even some who should know better, think that to man a hawk, it must be unhooded and carried about, regardless of how much it bates. They have the mistaken belief that the more the hawk sees, the tamer it will be, and that it will eventually get used to most things. However, how much damage has been done along the way to the falconer-hawk relationship and the hawk's frame of mind? It is better to introduce the new style of life as a trained hawk slowly and to carefully bring the hawk out of the hood as it becomes ready to accept new things. It will learn through seeing and accepting not to be afraid. Allowing the hawk to bate at everything that happens, believing that the hawk will eventually get used to it, will only be achieved by the wearing down of fear. Which method would make the hawk undergo the most stress? Is that good for its health?

One concern is will the hood affect the hawk's ability to cast? With the older style Dutch hoods this could be a problem but most of the more modern hoods have a wide enough beak opening that the hawk can cast through them. If there is any cause for concern however particularly if the hawk is seen to be trying to cast but cannot, the proper place for it is unhooded inside a darkened mews.

Some falconers believe that it is asking too much for a beginner to hood train the first hawk. I know a falconer who, for his first and only hawk at the time, had a hand-me-down redtail that he could not hood because it had never been hood trained and was convinced it was beyond the average beginner's ability to hood train their first hawk. When the new trapping season came around, he went out with his new apprentice, and they trapped a nice passage redtail, hooded her in the trap, and took her home. By the end of the first evening, the raw apprentice was hooding and unhooding the hawk with no problems. The falconer admitted that hooding and unhooding a freshly trapped passage redtail is really not that difficult. It is far easier than controlling a madly bating redtail that doesn't want to sit on the fist, the likely alternative if the hood is not used. Having a good supply of hoods and beginning to hood train the hawk by first hooding it at the trap will make for a smooth road ahead.

It is unwise to start a falconry career with a hand-me-down hawk. If it were perfectly trained, accepting of the hood, in good condition and taking quarry, it would be easy to learn how to handle such a hawk in the field, but if it is that good, it is unlikely any falconer will give it up. A hand-me-down hawk is usually what the old falconers called a mar-hawk, one that is badly trained and has a number of faults. These can vary from not being trained at all to being hood shy, screaming, footing, or having other aggression problems, refusing to come out of trees, or self-hunting. It will probably have broken feathers as well. The falconer passing on such a hawk will have a variety of excuses about why he or she is getting rid of it, but it basically comes down to one thing—the hawk has faults, probably instilled through bad training and will be difficult to deal with. Why start with someone else's mistake? It is better to start with a freshly trapped redtail and to remember the blank book analogy.

As Training Progresses

For training to progress, it is essential that the hawk is feeding on the fist. Each evening, we pick up the hawk, weigh it, and do some hooding practice before putting the hood to one side and offering food. Eventually the time will come when the hawk will bend down to take the food and we'll have reached our first milestone. We continue to feel the breastbone and if it is getting too sharp, a more experienced falconer can be consulted for a second opinion. If the hawk is getting too low, it can only be that not enough time is allowed for it to eat, or the chosen training room has too many distractions. Spending an hour a day in a quiet room with dim light will result in a hawk that begins to feed at some point rather than starve itself to death. The worst case I ever experienced was a passage goshawk that still would not eat after 14 days. She had put on a lot of weight on unrestricted rations while in quarantine and was obviously on the high side when I started training her. Concerned that I might have finally found a hawk that would rather starve than take the food on the fist, I put her unhooded on the bow perch in a quiet place and left some food, then watched from about 30 feet away. Within a few minutes, she jumped down and started

Training the Red-tailed Hawk

to feed. After she had taken a few mouthfuls, I went in and picked up her and the food, and she continued eating. Four weeks later, she took a wild heron as her third kill! The moral of the story is not to give up on a difficult hawk. It may well turn out to be worth the effort in the end. If there is genuine concern that the hawk is getting too low, I suggest doing what I did with the goshawk mentioned above. If the hawk starts to eat while observed from a distance, it can be allowed one or two mouthfuls before walking in to pick it up. Staying right there with the hawk should result in continued eating after a short period, the hawk's appetite having been suitably whetted.

Each day the hawk's weight and progress (or lack of it) should be logged on the weight chart or in a journal if preferred. The amount of food eaten should also be recorded. As we have already learned, this is done by either weighing our hawk before and after it has eaten, or

A newly taken up male Harris' Hawk weathering while hooded. He has one leg raised--a sign of contentment. At this stage in his training, if he were left unhooded, he would spend most of his time bating, which does him no good at all. Better to weather him hooded until he is further along in training.

Falconry: A Guide for Beginners

weighing the food before and after, then subtracting. The food can also be judged by eye, for example, half of a top half of a quail or a day-old chick. The first time the hawk feeds on the fist, we let it eat as much as it wants. In all probability, the hawk's fear will return after eating an ounce or two, and feeding will then cease. We gently clean the beak with the fingers of the hand that is ungloved and rehood the hawk. When not on the fist undergoing some manning and hood training or being fed, our hawk is left hooded on the bow perch. Being inside where there is activity that can be heard will help with manning. If not, putting a radio nearby, one that broadcasts news so that our hawk hears voices, will accomplish the same thing. By the end of the first week, our hawk will probably sit unhooded on the fist for varying amounts of time as people move slowly and predictably within view, but not so close as to cause a bate. The hood will be received well because we are still hooding and unhooding at least 20 times a day. In fact, unless things go completely backwards, our hawk is close to being hood trained. We have not actually trained the hawk to do anything, but we have instilled the idea that it is preferable to be hooded when there is something scary present. In the words of the old falconers, we have "managed" our hawk each day so it can gradually become accustomed to us, and the hood has been our greatest asset in attaining this calmness.

The Next Stage

Once our hawk takes food from the fist, we can progress to the next stage. Up until now, the only reason to stay on the fist was not being scared enough to leave, but now we can offer food as an incentive to be there. In addition to the hood, food is another tool at our disposal. After the first two feeds when I let the hawk eat as much as desired of food that is easily torn up, I make things a little more difficult at the third feed. I offer the food in a more unsettling situation in the hope that the food will keep the hawk too preoccupied to notice or care about anything else. I might also extend how long the meal lasts by introducing bony and uneasily torn food like rabbits' heads or parts of a squirrel. During this feeding time, we can begin to walk first around the house or mews, then gradually progress to outside while the hawk is feeding on the fist. Our hawk can be introduced more closely to other people, to vehicles and to anything else we want our hawk to get used to. Tough pieces of food that are difficult to tear used to keep the hawk occupied in this way are called "tirings." They are a largely underused method of prolonging a meal

> Tiring. A tough piece of food used to prolong the hawks meal, thus facilitating manning.

and thereby facilitating manning. While occupied in tearing up food, our hawk is less likely to notice its surroundings. If we can make the meal last a half hour or more as we walk around in the house, then the yard, then perhaps up and down the street, our hawk will rather quickly get used to everything it sees. If there is bating while food is on the fist, it is for one of two reasons—either we are introducing new things too quickly, or our hawk is too high in weight.

For the first week or two, if feeding on the fist goes smoothly, we aim to keep the hawk close to the weight at which it first fed on the fist. There will be an adjustment period during which the weight may fluctuate 20 to 30 grams up or down as we figure out how much food keeps our hawk level and as the parameters become set. Over the next five to seven days, we will figure out the right amount of food. We keep the hawk level as long as it takes food well and does not act overly hungry by ignoring something new in the surrounding environment to tear into the food instead. In this case, the hawk's weight can be raised. If our hawk took food well the previous day, but under the same circumstances today is less interested and perhaps bating and ignoring the food on the fist, our hawk is too high. The best thing to do is to finish the training session, put the hood on, and try again tomorrow when our hawk should be a bit lower and therefore a bit more cooperative.

The next stage after feeding quickly on the fist when food is offered is getting our hawk to jump to the fist. The way to offer food to the hawk at this stage is to hood the hawk, place the food under its feet, and take the hood off. Under no circumstances do we let the hawk see food in our bare hands. If that association is made, there will be a time when our hawk tries to foot the bare hand to get at the food. Once that happens, it can quickly become a habit, and a rather painful one at that. Hawks that foot have nearly all been taught to do it by seeing food in the bare hand or by the falconer being clumsy around the hawk's feet with that hand while the hawk is feeding, say for instance when putting the jesses back on after a flight. This habit is nearly always avoidable.

While getting a hawk accustomed to feeding on the fist, it is advantageous to show as large a piece of food as possible, but now that we want our hawk to start to fly, we cut the food into smaller pieces. For the purposes of feeding, flying to the fist, and weight control, it is useful to tear the chicks into heads, legs, and bodies. Before trying to get a hawk to jump to the fist, it should be at the stage of taking food immediately when unhooded. After offering enough to whet the appetite, a chick head for example, we put the hood back on our hawk, place the hawk on a perch, then remove the hood and hold an entire day-old chick in the fist just out of range. The arm is held out at a right angle to the direction of flight; keeping the arm in front of one's body can make the hawk too fearful to fly towards us. We hold the fist about one foot away from the hawk. Although it has fed on the fist for a few days and has flown perhaps several hundred yards to secure food in the wild, this is a very difficult psychological step for the hawk to overcome, for it is actually flying towards a human. After half a minute or so, if our hawk won't jump, we put the food just within reach but fairly high up so our hawk can reach it and snatch perhaps a small bite with its beak, but nothing more. We give the hawk a chance for a quick tug, then put the fist back to its original position. Having a taste will often give a hawk the added incentive to jump to the fist for the offered food. After another minute or so, if it still won't jump, we put the fist within reach so the hawk can step up onto it for the food. Quite often, a hawk will try to tear off the food without putting its feet onto the fist. In this situation, if the falconer relaxes the gloved hand, every time the hawk pulls at the food, the food will move towards it so that it cannot tear off a piece. The hawk will then lift up its foot to put it on the fist to hold it down, and in this way, it will step up to the fist. If the hawk does not jump, we give it only half its rations that day and try again the next day. Generally, by waiting until a hawk is taking food quickly on being unhooded, most will hop to the fist the first time, it being a natural extension of previous action. If the attempt is made too early, and the hawk refuses, we still have to give it something to eat and will be forced to move the fist toward the hawk to let it step up for the food. Our hawk just trained us that if it waits, we'll come to it. Too much of that may result in a hawk in the field that is unresponsive and difficult to recover. It is never good to wait more than 30 seconds for a hawk at this stage before picking it up without food, moving to a different perch, and trying again. If the hawk refuses a second time, rations are reduced so the hawk will be keener the following day. While it is permissible the first time the hawk is called to the fist for it to be a little slow in coming, once it has made that first jump, all subsequent attempts should be aimed at getting a quick response. Always remember, response is the key, not distance.

    My philosophy during training is that I don't care how far a hawk comes as long as it comes quickly, so I take my time building up the distance I call a hawk to the fist. If I think it will come ten yards, I may call it from five yards. Response is more important than distance. If I take a week longer than other falconers to get a hawk into the field, I know that when my hawk is sitting at the top of a tall tree on the other side of a cold river, I have confidence

Training the Red-tailed Hawk

that when it is shown the fist, or at worst, the lure, it will return. If a mother shouted "dinnertime" to a child, only allowing ten seconds for the child to get to the dinner table before removing the meal, the child would get there pretty quickly when called. A hawk actually learns this in the wild, for as soon as a rabbit or other prey animal moves, the hawk knows it had better put forth every effort to catch it because a long time might lapse before another opportunity arises. A hawk can also learn, and rather quickly, that a falconer is prepared to wait for it. That will be the hawk that stays at the top of the tree while the falconer runs around underneath producing all types of tempting food and lures, maybe even a live lure on a line, and still the hawk sits and waits, because the falconer has taught it that it can.

Introducing the dog. The dog should be under control and sitting calmly. With the hawk feeding, gradually move closer to the dog and watch the hawk's reaction. If she seems nervous or stops feeding, retreat a little way. Over the next few days move closer to the dog always taking care to avoid a bate. As she becomes more used to the dog, the dog can be allowed to move around at a distance and then closer to the hawk. She should be introduced to anything she might be afraid of in the same way. The key is to introduce all strange sights with as few bates as possible. In this way a hawk will learn to accept almost anything from dogs to large moving machinery with as little stress placed upon her as possible.

Falconry: A Guide for Beginners

When it starts to jump to the fist outside, our hawk can also start spending time unhooded, outside, on the bow perch. Because our hawk is now jumping to the fist, we can approach periodically to have it hop to the fist for a tidbit or "bechin" as it is correctly called. If we had left our hawk unhooded on the bow perch before this stage, when we approached, there would almost certainly be a bate, forcing us to pick up the hawk mid-bate to get it on to the fist. Though most hawks will bate a bit, they fairly quickly adjust to being tethered to the bow perch and will settle down. Placing the perch in view of human activity, such as people walking or cars in the distance, will help with manning. In all probability, the hawk has seen such things in the wild and won't even have much reaction. Perhaps not surprisingly, the worst hawks at this stage are actually chamber-raised and have never seen humans before. Some of them are a real hassle when first put out on a perch unhooded if enough manning has not been done from the fist. If a hawk bates a

A first year passage redtail weathering. Note how she is resting on one foot, a sure sign that she is relaxed and adjusting to her new life as a trained hawk.

[202]

lot, we either hood it up and try again when better manned or we place a sprinkler hose nearby that can be turned on from a distance so the hawk gets a shower to make its feathers wet. Once wet, a hawk will settle down to dry and generally stop bating. Anytime it is desirable for a hawk to stay put so it will become accustomed to something, soaking it with water is a useful tool and one that is under-utilized by many falconers.

Once the hawk will jump to the fist, the food can be divided into smaller and smaller pieces until only a chick leg or a head is received for coming to the fist. On the first day, only one jump for all its rations was required of our hawk. Each time the fist is raised with a piece of food in it, a whistle should be sounded so that the hawk builds up an association between the whistle and food. Later, if the hawk is out of sight, the whistle will bring her back looking for the falconer. I use a referee's whistle but any whistle can be used. A few days later, it is expected to fly up to as many as 10 times for small food pieces. In between, both the distance and the frequency of calling can be slowly increased, bearing in mind that response is the key, not distance. This training can take place in one field, but once the hawk is flying 30 yards or so, we will try other locations. Some hawks behave very well on their familiar ground, but when taken somewhere else, they show reluctance to come. This may simply be a case of being slightly overweight; taking a hawk to a new flying area should make no difference if it is at the correct weight. My practice at this stage is to take the hawk for a walk around the fields. If there are no suitable fields nearby now is as good a time as any to introduce the hawk to riding in the truck. I travel my hawks hooded on a cadge in the back of a pick-up truck. It is hooded until we reach the first suitable perch. Then I unhood it and let it take a small piece off the fist to whet its appetite. I then place it on the perch and call it a short distance, beginning the session about half the distance the hawk has come previously. After placing the hawk on the perch, I give it a second or two to settle down, sound the referee's whistle, and hold out my fist. I expect the hawk to fly promptly and eat the chick leg or head. I then move to another perch, walking if possible with the hawk unhooded most of the way, but if it shows signs of agitation, I will hood up rather than have a bate. Moving to the next perch, the process is repeated. It helps to give a hawk a minute or two to let it collect itself between flights before calling it again. In nature, the eating of many small pieces of food quickly, one after another, took place when the hawk was fed in the nest as a baby by its parents. There is a danger, a slight one for passagers, but a real possibility for captive-bred hawks, of the mind recalling this time. A reversion to nestling behavior, in the form of screaming and mantling, may follow. These habits may express themselves in only a minute or two, but they can be very difficult to eradicate once started.

Using the Creance

For very short distances of up to three feet, the leash can be used to secure the hawk, with the end being tied to the glove or wrapped firmly around the little finger. Once the hawk will instantly come a distance that equals the leash length, a creance is used. The creance is tied, using one falconer's knot, to the end of the swivel where the leash normally is. If using the tethering system, the leash and extender are removed and the creance tied to both jesses.

The creance is tied to the swivel before the leash is removed to prevent a mishap while transferring the hawk from one method of tethering to another. More creance than I expect to be needed is laid out before I unhood the hawk and place it on its perch. After unwinding the amount I need, I place the creance stick in a pocket on my jacket that has a zipper. I close the zipper almost to the end taking care not to pinch the creance. If the hawk does decide to fly off and I accidentally let go of the creance it still cannot go anywhere as the creance stick is secured inside the pocket. For short distances, as I walk away, I feed the creance between my gloved little finger and ring finger. If the hawk comes before I am ready, I already have hold of the creance. If the hawk happens to overshoot the fist, I can let the hawk down gently like playing a fish on a line. For longer distances, 20 yards or more, I walk along the creance as I go. If I hear bells ring, signifying that the hawk is coming, I put out my fist. If the hawk overshoots, I merely have to bend down to pick up the creance. In practice, once they have reached the point of instantly coming 20 yards, many hawks will start to fly before the falconer is ready to call them. To prevent this, an assistant holds the hawk on the fist, and once the falconer is at the desired spot, the assistant places the hawk on the perch.

Where open space is limited or when flying over long grass, it is useful to set up a ground line to be used instead of the usual creance. A ground line is a length of stout line, such as parachute cord, secured between two fixed points about 12 to 18 inches above the ground. In practice, the easiest way is to fix one end to a tree stump if one is available and the other to a metal spike or even a bow or block perch that can be pushed into the ground directly upwind of the stump. A ring is placed on the line before it is secured. The hawk is tied to this ring by a short length of about 6 feet of parachute cord or creance line. The hawk is placed on the stump, and the falconer walks upwind keeping the ground line just to the left while walking away from the hawk. When at the desired distance, the falconer turns, puts out a fist and calls the hawk. As the hawk flies to the falconer, it will drag the short creance along the ground line. If the hawk does try to veer off

Training the Red-tailed Hawk

to one side, it will not be able to fly more than 6 feet either side of the ground line. In this way, the hawk can be called safely in areas where, if on a normal creance, it might be able to veer off and over power lines or close to a road.

Note how the jesses are held in the reverse lock while the hawk is feeding. The leash and creance can be attached or removed while the hawk is secured in this manner.

Falconry: A Guide for Beginners

Clips on the end of a creance should not be used. They are unreliable, and they add a lot of weight to the swivel, which will swing in flight causing the swivel and clip to come into contact with the tail and possibly damage the feathers. Clips are just one indication of improperly using a creance. The way a falconer handles a hawk on a creance is even more revealing. Some falconers, mindful of the fact that the hawk is secured and cannot go anywhere, take liberties and call the hawk further than they should. When the hawk sits and waits, they don't have an appreciation of the negative lesson they are teaching. Later, as the hawk sits up in a tree taking its sweet time about coming down, they wonder why it is behaving so badly. Other falconers are oblivious to the whereabouts of the creance, and they scramble around for the end of it when the hawk flies off. Some falconers, unaware of the leg damage that can be done if a flying hawk is brought to a sudden stop, tie the end of the creance to an object so heavy the hawk can't move it. Other falconers, not realizing that a hawk drags half the creance with it no matter the distance called, place the creance stick into the ground in an effort to call the hawk a longer distance. If called

Teaching the hawk to fly short distances. Note how the arm is held out at right angles to the body so that the hawk is not flying directly towards the falconer's face.

Training the Red-tailed Hawk

50 yards, the hawk will drag 25 yards of creance. If called 80 yards, 40 yards will be dragged whether the hawk has a 100-yard creance on it (as it should if called that far) or a 50-yard creance with the stick in the ground so the hawk flies past it. Yet, another error is made by falconers who recommend tying the end of the creance to something weighted such as a drag that can bring the hawk down gently should it fly off. They don't realize that it is impossible to correctly gauge how much weight is needed to smoothly bring down the hawk because of uncontrollable variables. Who knows whether the hawk will be flying upwind or downwind when it finally needs the weight to bring it down? The size of the flying field is another factor. Although the hawk may eventually be brought down, it might not happen until it has gone over some trees or power lines. Still other falconers use a creance that is too short, saying that if the hawk will come 20 yards, it can be flown free. This is not true; I've had problems develop when the hawk is coming 40 yards on a creance, and were it not on a creance, I could well have lost the hawk.

The idea of the creance is to make the hawk think it is free to go, though after the training received, it is hoped the thought will never cross its mind. A creance is thus an insurance policy in case something goes wrong. The end not attached to the hawk should never be left unattended. Some falconers treat their creances and other gear with neglect by leaving it in the flying field where it can get lost or eaten by livestock. I have worked with falconers who have borrowed, then lost or destroyed one creance after another. When not in use, a creance should be neatly wound up in a jacket pocket or bag so it's ready at a moment's notice when needed. When a nervous hawk refuses to come into a lure, a creance can be substituted for the lure line, allowing the falconer to get further away. This might prevent a hawk from becoming lost, or the hawk can be wound up on a kill or a lure if it doesn't allow itself to be picked up.

Summary of the Daily Routine

The daily routine at this stage is to take the hawk from the mews where it has spent the night on a perch. It is put out unhooded in the weathering area on the outdoor perch. If the hawk can see plenty of activity from its perch, so much the better. If it spends too much time bating, it can be either hooded or soaked by using a garden hose sprinkler. Many hawks quickly settle down on the perch in the mews at night, and it is alright to start leaving them unhooded overnight at about the same time they learn to jump to the fist. A good test is to go in first thing in the morning to pick up the hawk without a bate

Falconry: A Guide for Beginners

for a small piece of food. If this is possible, it is okay to leave the hawk unhooded at night. If the hawk freaks out, it is better to leave it hooded until further along in training.

At training time, we pick up the hawk from the outside perch on the weathering lawn by using a bechin. The hawk, which should hop to the fist, is then hooded and taken inside to be weighed, and the leash is removed. The hood stays on as the hawk is then taken to the flying field. This replicates what will happen later when the hawk will travel hooded in the car to the hawking fields, which generally are at a greater distance. The food has been prepared beforehand and is safely tucked away out of sight in a flying vest or bag. We know by now

A passage redtail learning to fly to the fist on the creance, she was trapped only nine days previously. For small amounts of food, such as the chick leg used here, the food is held between the back of the thumb and the index finger. Note how the creance is held between the ring and little fingers of the gloved hand and then held in the ungloved hand so that should the hawk try to fly off, it can be controlled and brought to earth gently.

how much food keeps our hawk level, and so we have that amount plus a bit more. When we get to the first suitable perch, we unwind an appropriate amount of creance. We unhood our hawk as we approach the first perch, one on which the creance cannot get hooked up, and we either place the hawk on the perch or let it fly there from a short distance away. As we walk away to half the distance our hawk came yesterday, we either feed the creance through our gloved hand or walk along it, all the while listening for bells in case the hawk comes before we are ready. Once we get to the spot where we intend to call our hawk, we put a piece of meat into the hand that is gloved, stand at right angles to the hawk, blow the referee's whistle, and put our whole arm out at right angles with the fist slightly higher than the shoulder. Once the hawk flies to the fist, which should be fairly quickly, we let it eat the food and give it a second or two to make sure it knows the food is gone. Then we take the jesses, bring them into the gloved hand and out between the ring and index finger in the locked position. We can now either give our hawk a second flight from this perch or walk to another perch. By this stage, a hawk should be comfortable walking unhooded on the fist, but if it is a long way to go, it might be better to hood it. In any case, every two or three flights, we put the hood on, even if it is for a short period, so that our hawk gets used to hooding being part of the routine. Each flight, our hawk is given either the head or leg of a day-old chick or ¼ of an ounce of something bigger such as rabbit, depending on what we are feeding. Six flights for small pieces like this and then one or two more for a couple of larger pieces is enough to get a hawk trained sufficiently without its response starting to slow as its crop fills.

This daily routine continues until our hawk will fly 50 yards instantly from any perch to the fist. It is at this stage that inviting one or two friends along will allow our hawk to become accustomed to the presence of other people out in the field with us. This will pay dividends later when people want to see our fully trained hawk fly at quarry.

It is now time to introduce the recall lure. If introduced too early in training, a hawk might develop such a preference for the recall lure that it refuses to come to the fist over anything other than a very short distance. Our hawk is ready, so we introduce the recall lure by giving a couple of flights to the fist as usual. Then we place our hawk on a low perch such as a bow perch or a log. The lure is taken from the bag and dropped to one side of the falconer and a foot or so in front of the hawk. It is garnished with at least a day-old chick or an ounce of meat. Kneeling down and holding onto the lure line, we give it a little twitch if needed to get

Falconry: A Guide for Beginners

our hawk's attention, but once it sees the meat, a hawk at flying weight will jump to the lure. We hold on to the lure line, keeping it low to the ground and not letting the hawk move with it. Even if the hawk at first wants to drag the lure away, it will realize it is not going anywhere and will eat the food on it. When the food is gone, the lure will not hold any real interest, so we drop the body of a day-old chick on the ground in front of our hawk, but just out of reach. The goal is getting the hawk to let go of the lure and transfer to the chick body. We hold the line so the hawk cannot drag the lure. Pretty quickly our hawk realizes it is necessary to let go of the lure to get at the tempting chick body just lying there waiting to be eaten. As soon as the hawk opens its feet and makes the transfer, we immediately take up the lure, put it in our bag or vest, and step back a pace so as not to be towering over the hawk. Once the body of the chick is eaten, most hawks will lift up one foot, then the other, to make sure there is nothing underneath before looking around for more food. At that instant, we offer a chick leg on the fist, and the hawk hops up from the ground onto the fist. That ends the training session for the day.

A rubber inner-tube recall lure baited with a day old chick. This type of recall lure can be used with any species of hawk over 16oz in weight.

HAWK: Mariah			SPECIES: Red-tailed Hawk					SEX: F				MONTH: October 2012														
WEIGHT																										
1185																										
1180															x				x							
1175																										
1170																										
1165																										
1160														x	x											
1155				x																						
1150																		x	x							
1145												x										x	x			
1140		x	x				x				x							x							x	
1135					x	x			x	x																
1130							x	x	x																	
1125																										
1120																										
1115																										
1110	x	x																								
DATE:	6	7	8	9	10	11	12	13	14	15	16	17	18	19	20	21	22	23	24	25	26	27	28	29	30	31
FOOD:				80 grams Q	4C	3C	3C, 1B	3C, 1B, 2L	3C, 1B, 1L	4C	4C	4C	4C	4C	4C, 1B	4C, 1L	3C	3C	4C	4C	3C	7C	0	3C, 1B, 2L	3C, 1B, 2L	4C
	Trapped passage female, weighed 1225 equipped.	Ate several pieces from fingers	Ate top half of quail inside	Ate quickly in mews	Stepped up outside	Stepped up, more nervous than yesterday	Jumped leash length	8 feet to fist	10 feet to fist	20 feet to fist	50 feet to fist quickly	80 feet to fist quickly	Introduced the lure	10 ft to lure, 100 to fist	20 feet to lure, 40 yds. to fist	Switched to mornings	Rain, not flown	30 yds. fist and lure quickly	50 yds. to lure 40 yds. to fist	50 yds. instant to lure	50 yds. instant, fist and lure with dog and people	Flew free, bit slow from trees	Sunday, not flown	Several flights to fist and one to lure from trees	Followed on from tree to tree, dummy lure	Followed on from tree to tree, dummy lure

Above is the weight chart for Mariah, a passage redtail. She was trapped on the 6th October and weighed 1225 grams with hood, jesses, bells and leash. On the following day she weighed 1100 grams showing she had food inside her when she was trapped. On the first day she took a few pieces of quail meat from my fingers but would not bend down to eat. The following day, also weighing 1100 grams she bent down to take her first proper meal, at this time she was given as much as she wanted to eat. The following day she ate quickly but the amount of quail given was limited to 80 grams. On the 10th she was introduced to chicks for the first time and ate quickly. Over the next few days I figured out approximately how much day-old chick kept her weight level. It can be seen as her training progresses that the goal was to either keep her weight the same or increase it slightly as training progressed. During training a regular gorge was introduced, usually on Saturdays, followed by little or no food on Sundays. Gorging, followed by a fast, while not essential, mimics how a hawk often feeds in the wild. Note: C = whole day-old cockerel, B = body of day-old cockerel, L = leg of day-old cockerel, Q = coturnix quail.

Falconry: A Guide for Beginners

The next day, we do the same, but drop the lure about 6 feet from the hawk. Accustomed to flying 50 yards to us for food, this will be comparatively easy. The hawk should quickly jump onto the lure, remembering there will be a big meal for doing so. The next day, we try 10 feet or so, and the day after, we put a smaller amount of food on the lure such as two chick legs. We still transfer the hawk off to the body of a day-old chick. The lure flight should always be the last flight of the day. Within a week, our hawk will be flying 50 yards to the lure as well. Once coming about 20 yards, we use the whole length of lure line so that the lure is lying on the ground 4 yards to one side of us. The only thing left to do before flying our hawk free is to try a flight from the low branch of a tree. This will ascertain that our hawk will come from trees, but if training has gone according to plan, a hawk will not even have known it was on a creance.

The weight at which our hawk will fly 50 yards to the fist and lure is, at least for the time being, the flying weight. We know from the training how much food is needed to keep the hawk at that weight. We have hood trained our hawk, making it possible to travel with the hooded hawk on a perch in the car. Doing this a couple times before the first hawking trip will be useful. We have also given our hawk enough exposure to people to prevent fear of them at close range. Our hawk should be easy to pick up as flying time approaches, though there may still be some reluctance at other times. All hawks differ, and some very quickly learn to jump to the ungarnished fist at any time of day.

The detail in this chapter allows the beginner to know all the steps of training needed for a passage redtail. Many hawks are way ahead of their trainers and can be trained remarkably quickly. It is not uncommon for an experienced falconer to have a passage redtail ready to fly free in just three weeks after trapping, but it takes practice to learn to read a hawk. A beginner should take the time to learn the steps methodically before trying to take any shortcuts. To rush the training or miss something a more experienced falconer would see may result either in loss of the hawk or a regression in the stages of training. One falconer who applied for a job with my company explained on his resume how he had trained his first large longwing, a Prairie Falcon, using a revolutionary technique he developed of which he was very proud. He also noted that the Prairie was lost before he got to do any hawking with her! If he had only trained her using traditional well-tested techniques, maybe he wouldn't have lost her. The moral of the story is to refrain from trying to run before learning how to walk. By learning the basics before attempting to revolutionize the sport, a beginner will realize most of the techniques have already stood the test of time.

Training the Red-tailed Hawk

This captive-bred Red-tailed Hawk, belonging to Ronnie Moore, was 28 when the photograph was taken and was still taking quarry.

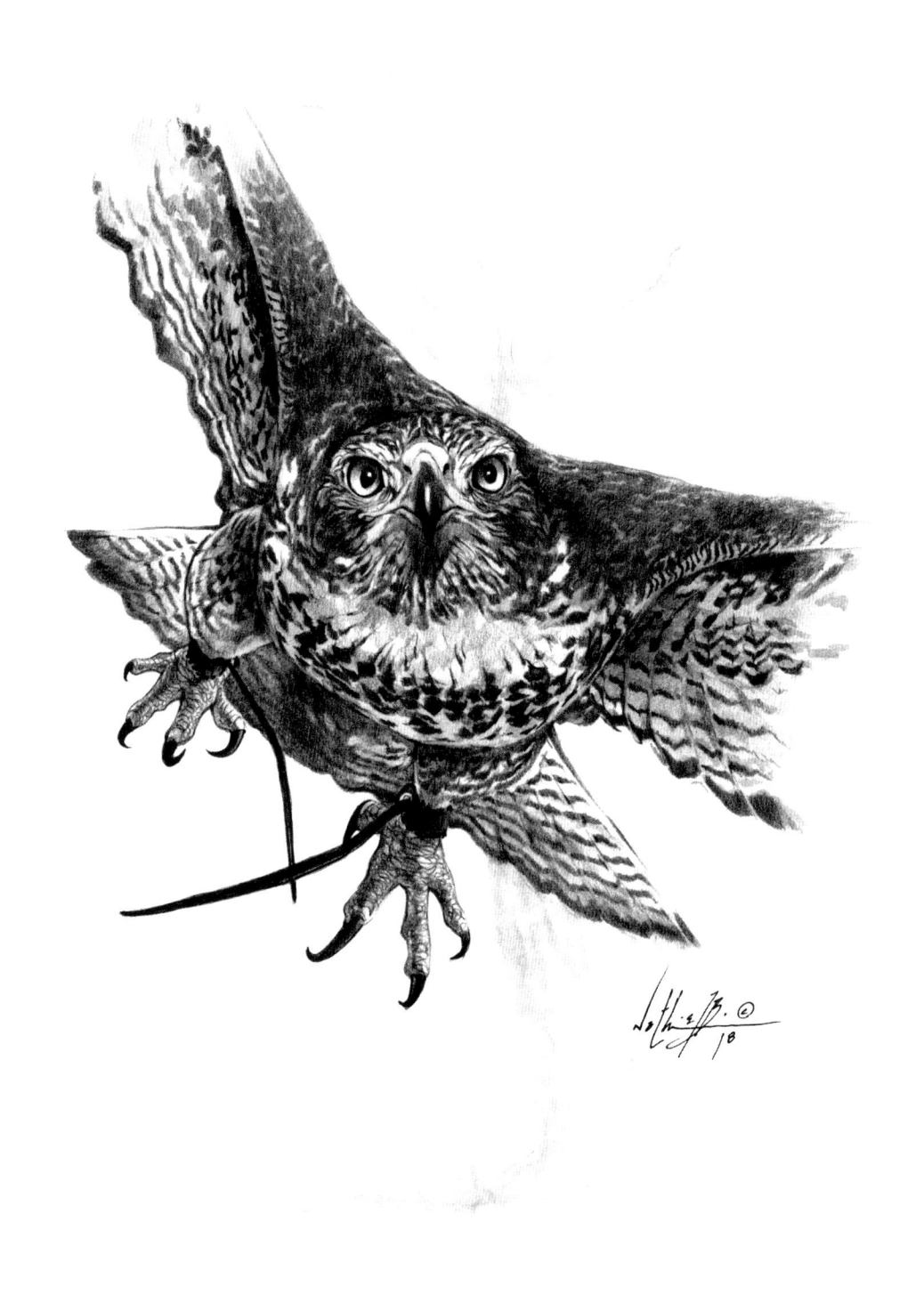

Chapter Seven

Advanced Training

At the end of the last chapter, the hawk was flying 50 yards to the fist and recall lure. During the training process, flying weight had been determined, and the hawk had become hood trained. It is now time to move on to flying free and taking the steps to ensure that the hawk is working together with me as a member of the team in the field.

On the last day or so of flying on the creance I attach the telemetry transmitter to the hawk's tail or leg, whichever method has been chosen, so it won't be unfamiliar. If I used the creance properly and the hawk has not overflown the fist or lure by being pulled up short, then she will be unaware that she wasn't free to fly away all along. Thus, flying free is more traumatic for us than for the hawk. On the day chosen, the normal procedure is followed with picking up the hawk, hooding, weighing, then going to the flying ground. She is given one flight on the creance and then hooded up. Remove the creance and wind it up so that if she needs to be followed, the creance will not be left behind. The swivel is removed and put away in the jacket or bag and one mews jess is removed. I generally start with the left leg, remove the mews jess, put it in my vest, and replace it with a flying jess. Then I do the same for the right leg, always maintaining the lock on the jess not being changed. Hawks will fly with a hood on, so a falconer must always guard against accidentally letting a hawk go free while hooded. I have twice seen this happen. One, a Lanner Falcon, hit the side of a house, crashed to the ground, and was quickly secured by the falconer running along behind. The other, a Gyrfalcon I was training, was being prepared for release by another falconer and was to be called to me over a long distance. She bated, and the other falconer accidentally let her go. She immediately started to climb, going up in circles. She probably remembered balloon training when she was required to circle up to food secured to a balloon high

Falconry: A Guide for Beginners

overhead. Because all of my hawks are trained to the whistle, I began a series of short, sharp blows on the referee's whistle. The gyr responded to the sound, coming closer until she crashed into the ground nearby where I picked her up. Another falconer I knew was not so lucky; his peregrine escaped from his fist with her hood on, flew out to sea, and was never seen again.

Flying Free and Following On

A hawk should never be flown free with mews jesses in place. Even if the hawk is only being called to the fist over a short distance, the mews jesses must be exchanged for flying jesses, or they can be removed and a loop jess or some such used. The reason for this is that if the hawk is lost, it has the best chance of survival. With mews jesses in place, the hawk will get caught up in a tree, and if the falconer does not get to it, the hawk will die.

With jesses changed, the hawk is unhooded and placed back on the perch. I generally go half the previous distance and call the hawk. The hawk has already been doing this for a period of perhaps two weeks and she is unlikely to do anything differently now that she is free. Now that we have both conquered this step it is time to move onto something that will be common in our relationship. I immediately start training to call the hawk out of trees. To do this, the hawk must be cast towards either a single or group of trees. With the jesses secured in the lock, the left arm is brought back slightly, the right foot is put toward the desired direction, and the hawk is launched toward the trees. Let go of the jesses at the end of the throw. By twisting the fist clockwise at the end, the hawk is forced to leave the fist. Though this is new, the hawk will glide up into the trees. Try to pick trees with several dead branches or with fairly well-exposed thick branches so there is an obvious target for landing. I cast the hawk at the tree from an appropriate distance so that it is an obvious target for landing, either into or across the wind. There is a bit of a knack in casting off a hawk correctly. It should leave the fist upright and just fast enough so as not to result in hanging upside-down gripping the fist. This is not the pitching of a fast ball! The hawk's head should not be snapped back as the throw is started. The fist should travel in a straight line for about 30 inches to give time for her to build up momentum. It should not move in an arc so that the hawk, upon reaching the point of being released, is hanging off the fist sideways and goes off in an uncontrolled manner. Cast a couple of times, many hawks, on the arm being moved out to one side, will leave the fist of their own accord. This is preferable.

> Cast. The act of launching a hawk off the fist.

Advanced Training

    Once in the tree, I give the hawk a minute or two to settle down. She may turn around to face me and this is a good sign. Put your fist out as normal and call the hawk back, repeating the process for as many flights as there are bechins. Sometimes, finding herself higher up in a tree, the hawk may not act as keen as when being called from posts. This is not uncommon. To make the food on the fist more appealing, waving a day old chick or larger piece of food and placing it on and off the gloved fist is permissible. Ideally, this will only need to be done until the hawk is accustomed to being called from trees, though it might be needed whenever the hawk is higher up or further away than normal. As soon as the hawk leaves the tree and is on its way, the larger piece of food can be placed back in the bag or jacket. Two or three days of this and the hawk is ready for the next step—that of teaching it to follow us from tree to tree. This is done by giving the hawk one or two flights from a tree as previous. Then, having cast the hawk back into a tree, I turn and walk away. Many hawks get to the point of anticipating the falconer and flying the instant they see the fist raised or hear the whistle. Now it is time to raise the fist slightly above your head and wave, as though waving goodbye to someone while still walking away. You can also give a whistle, not with the referee's whistle, but a mouth whistle. Many falconers call their hawks verbally by saying "come on" or similar words, but I do not. The sound of the human voice is alarming to many of the creatures I will soon be trying to catch, so I avoid talking whenever possible while in the field. The hawk should leave the tree and fly toward the falconer. I have never had one that didn't. When the hawk has covered about a third of the distance, put your fist down and keep walking while keeping your back to the hawk. Seeing nowhere to land, the hawk will fly by and into another tree. Let her settle for a minute and then call her back to the fist for a bechin and then try another follow-on flight. It is tempting at this point in training simply to start hawking. However, at least with passage redtails, if taken hawking too soon after flying free, they quickly begin self-hunting because the habit of following from tree to tree has not been established. The result is that as soon as the hawk is released, it quickly goes off on its own, paying very little attention to the falconer below. Once this habit is established it can be very difficult to break and the falconer ends up being nothing more than a means of transport for the hawk to the field. Once there, the hawk goes off on its own as the falconer does his best to follow. Such a hawk cannot be considered trained, even if the falconer is able to recover it at the end of each outing. Another issue that may become relevant at this point is that, based on their experience in the wild,

Falconry: A Guide for Beginners

some passage hawks have definite preferences on what they will and will not chase. For instance, not all passage redtails view squirrels as potential prey and may not look for or notice them. Therefore, it is preferable to have a week or two of following-on flights with some advanced lure work, both to reinforce the bond between us and to make sure we are both chasing the same quarry.

> Lure. 1) A "recall lure" may be any object that the hawk has been taught to associate with food. 2) A "dummy lure" is an object made to resemble a type of quarry that the falconer wishes the hawk to chase.

During this period of training, the lure is only used to recall every fourth day or so, and always as the last flight. I want the hawk to remember what it is without thinking that by waiting long enough, the lure will be produced; that might cause a hawk to refuse the fist. The recall lure needs to be familiar, but its purpose is for use in situations when the hawk will not come to the fist or is lost. The recall lure, being swung around on the lure line, is more visible and thus likely to be seen from longer distances by a hawk that has wandered off. Also, because it offers a bigger reward than the fist does, a hawk is more likely to come to it over very long distances. It is also attractive in the event the hawk has caught a mouse or other prey and is ignoring the fist because of losing the edge from its appetite.

Dummy Lure

I now introduce the hawk to the dummy lure. If cottontail rabbits are to be the main quarry, a small rabbit lure is used. If jackrabbits are to be the quarry, a larger rabbit lure is preferable. For squirrels, it will pay to use a squirrel lure complete with a bushy tail. If flying a Harris' Hawk on birds such as pheasants, a dummy pheasant, like the ones available for gun dog training, can be used. Many of the books suggest attaching the dummy lure to the lure line and running along with it trailing behind. But when was the last time anyone has seen a rabbit running along four yards behind a person? Rabbits and pretty much everything else a hawk is trying to catch will be moving away from the falconer, not following, so it is better to attach the dummy lure to the creance and have someone else pull it. All 50 yards of creance can be used and by running it around a tree or through a line of bushes there is no connection between the lure and the person pulling it. The object of the exercise of course is to teach the hawk to chase and catch the type of quarry that will soon be sought in earnest. The more realistic the training, the smoother will be the transition to the real thing.

Advanced Training

Lure Machine

Bagged quarry, or baggies as they are more commonly known, are live animals released so that the hawk has a very good to excellent chance of catching them. They are useful for introducing the hawk to a particular type of quarry. For instance, a falconer may hide a rabbit under a box, then approach and pull a cord so the rabbit is revealed. The rabbit may run away or just sit there. Some falconers will use any kind of bagged quarry they can find, even resorting to buying a rabbit from a pet shop. To ensure capture, the baggie may be tethered. I find the use of bagged quarry, especially for training broadwings and shortwings, to be distasteful. If the dummy lure is used properly, bagged quarry is unnecessary. A young hawk that has been flown only to the fist and recall lure and is then taken out and briefly shown a live wild rabbit that is seen as a brown piece of fur running away will probably not even recognize such a creature as food and will likely not chase it.

A Harris' Hawk closing in on a wing lure pulled by the lure machine. A lightweight lure, such as the pair of duck wings used here, can be pulled at speeds faster than the hawk can fly, which really gives the hawk a good work out.

[219]

Falconry: A Guide for Beginners

Some falconers will claim such a hawk needs a baggie to get it going, yet bagged quarry rarely if ever behaves like a wild animal. However, a hawk that is trained and flown for a week or two to a thoughtfully used dummy lure will recognize the same glimpse of brown fur moving away from it as food and will give chase. If those falconers who use bagged quarry would make proper use of dummy lures, they would understand that baggies are not really necessary. Properly used, a lifelike dummy lure not only negates any need for bagged quarry, but generally also leads to a better-conditioned hawk, both mentally and physically. It is now that the lure machine is truly useful, for it will pull a rabbit lure in a zigzag course over several hundred yards in a very lifelike manner. Though it requires some time to set up, if lifelike enough, hawks flown to it do not hesitate for one second when they see the real thing. This also means that on days when hawking is not possible, the hawk can still be given lifelike flights to keep in tip top condition and remain fired up for the next real opportunity.

It is normally not necessary to introduce a passage hawk to a lifelike dummy lure in the same manner as the recall lure, though it is advisable to give a hawk a couple of very easy catches at first to build up confidence. For the first few flights, I ask someone to pull the lure out of cover about 10 yards in front of my hawk, slowly crossing my path and the hawk's view as it sits on the fist. If the hawk takes a good look at it, but doesn't give chase, the lure is allowed to continue into more cover so that in essence, it gets away because the hawk did not chase it. I then set the whole thing up again and try at a shorter distance, making sure that this time the hawk can see food on the lure. Once the hawk is on the lure, the lure is tugged to get the hawk used to the struggle it will have with a live animal. If the hawk grabs any other part of the lure except the head end, tugging continues until the hawk transfers its feet to the head end. This will pay dividends when the hawk takes quarry because it will know that grasping the head allows control of prey. A hawk that hangs on to the back of a rabbit will get tugged around and possibly lose its grip, while one that tries this with a squirrel is vulnerable to being bitten. From easy short flights, I can progress to more difficult flights of a longer distance. The goal is to get a hawk to look away from me as I walk along with her on the fist or as she is following in trees. I want the hawk to look at the area where I am using the beating stick or where the dog is working. If no lure machine is available and I am relying on someone to pull the lure on the end of a creance, it is time to be creative and not let the hawk discover that the lure is associated with humans in any way. The recall lure should be associated with humans, but the dummy lure should

Advanced Training

not. For a hawk that will be given flights at squirrels, the creance is thrown over an exposed branch, and the lure is pulled up the trunk of the tree so the hawk will see squirrels using trees to escape. Being creative with the use of dummy lures will benefit a hawk by making it far more prepared for the next step.

A hawk is transferred off the dummy lure in exactly the same way I taught it to leave the recall lure—I drop a day-old chick or similar-sized piece of meat just to one side so that the hawk must let go of the lure to reach it. The hawk cannot drag the lure because I either hold it with the gloved hand, covering most of it, or I keep a foot on the lure line. Some falconers transfer a hawk onto the fist and off the lure or a kill by holding a fairly large piece of food in the fist. Then, by covering the kill or lure, they persuade the hawk to lift up one foot, then the other. I use this method with my longwings, but broadwings treated like this nearly always end up damaging tail feathers and mantling because they are usually more possessive over their kills than longwings are.

Captive-bred Harris' Hawks will generally, once they are flying free and know what the recall lure is, chase anything that moves. Introducing them to the dummy lure is normally as simple as giving

Immature passage redtail about to bind to a dead squirrel pulled by the lure machine. Several days of flights like this prior to hawking will greatly increase the changces of the hawk chasing the first squirrel it sees and will help the hawk to realize the falconer will assist it in finding quarry to chase. For times when quarry is scarce, flights to the lure machine will help keep the hawk keen on quarry.

[221]

Falconry: A Guide for Beginners

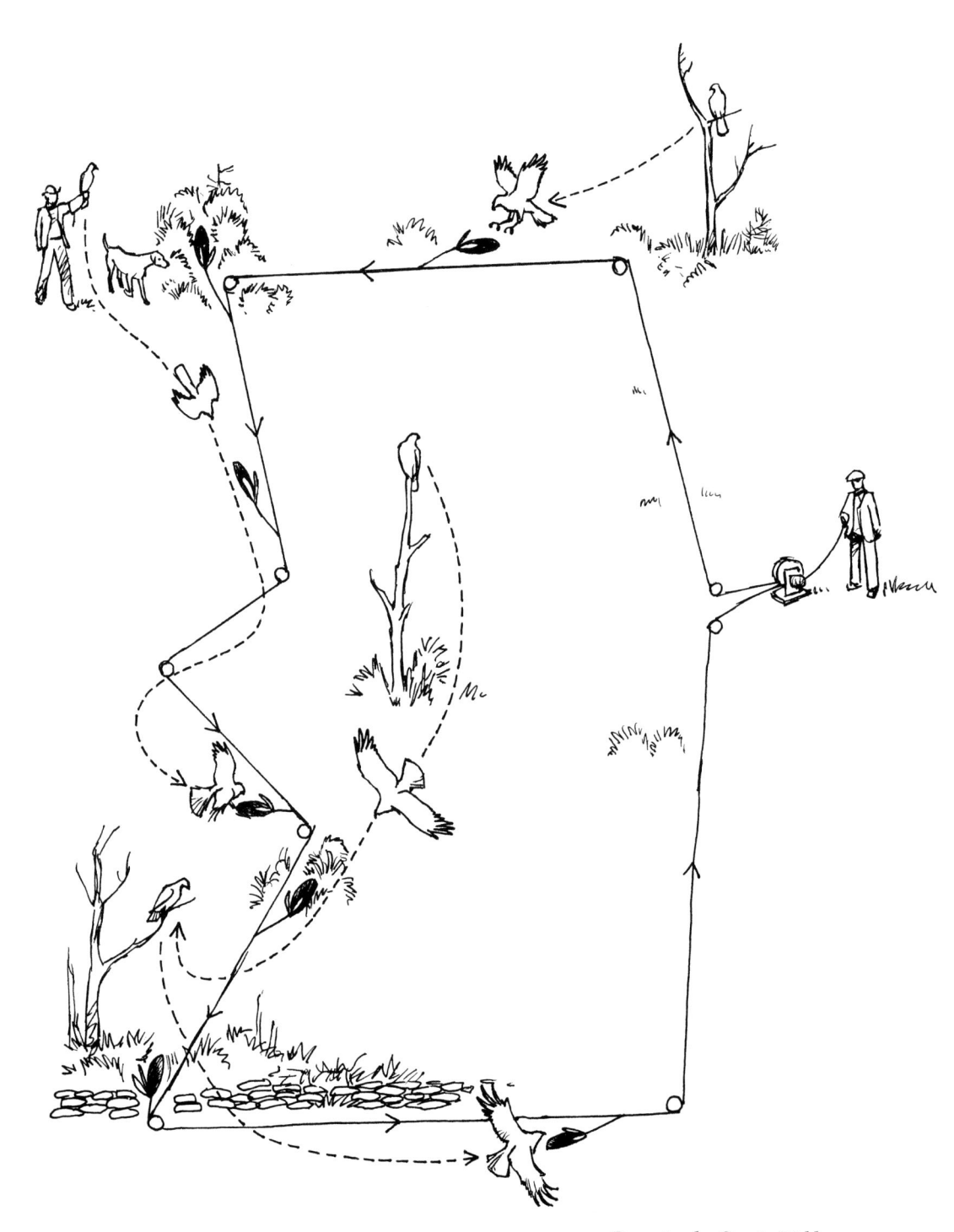

Drawing by Carrie Webber.

Advanced Training

them one or two easy flights that are each followed by a reward. Soon the hawks will be zooming through the trees in an effort to get at the lure pulled by the lure machine or dragged on the end of a creance. It is worthwhile to use different types of dummy birds as well as fake rabbits for Harris' Hawks. They are more suited to taking bird species than redtails are, so by doing this, Harris' Hawks become more likely to chase any bird they see. Even if they can't catch such quarry, they are still provided a flight. I expect my Harris' Hawks to chase almost any suitably sized bird that appears close to them when we are out hawking, and I find that the use of different types of lures definitely helps.

I am fond of using the lure machine. With a bit of ingenuity and thought, I can set up courses that drag the lure through the woods at high speed, dodging around trees and under or over fallen logs. Hawks become very adept at taking the lure while flying almost flat out, and they really enjoy this sort of flying. It's far more satisfying for them than simply following from tree to tree. It's a good time for several falconers to get together and have some fun flying one hawk after another, not in competition, for falconry should never be competitive, but with everyone helping each other improve their hawks' flying skills. In the accompanying diagram are a couple different ideas for flights that utilize the hawk's flying from trees, from the falconer's fist, over a pointing dog, and in other situations. Using the imagination to conjure up new courses will ultimately allow a hawk to benefit.

When a hawk is flying the dummy lure with enthusiasm, there is nothing more to be done than to go hawking. The hawk is now trained, though not yet made. If I have done my job, the hawk will be good to the hood and still in the same feather condition as when acquired. I will know the flying weight and the amount of food that keeps the hawk level. We will have gotten to know each other pretty well. A conscientious falconer treasures a hawk as a friend and hawking partner and plans to spend a lot of time with it. A hawk is not a burden, but rather the highlight of a falconer's day as he or she rushes home from work to set out for the hawking fields.

Fitness Work

For many falconers, as the season progresses and the days get shorter, flying the hawk at quarry every day becomes difficult. Hawks flown at quarry only two or three times a week are obviously not going to be as fit and productive as hawks flown more often but there are a couple of things the falconer can do to maintain or increase fitness in a hawk that cannot be flown often enough. The first and most simple way to get some exercise for the hawk, assuming there is a little daylight available, is to repeatedly cast the hawk into trees and call it back to the fist for a small reward, perhaps ending with a call to the recall lure for a larger reward. Even this simple exercise is better than not being flown at all. It will also have the benefit of increasing the response of the hawk when she is taken out hawking as many hawks will, when flown at quarry often, especially if they are regularly successful, become a little slow at the recall. Being flown to the fist from trees on days when she can't be taken hawking will help in this regard when she is out hawking. If I do this kind of exercise I prefer to pick an area where there is little chance of the hawk seeing quarry and I try to always use the same place so that the hawk gets used to this place as an exercise only area. If daylight is not available hawks can often be given some exercise in this way in areas where floodlights are being used, perhaps to illuminate a ball field for instance. The second way to exercise the hawk, if more time is available, is to set up a series of flights to the lure machine, perhaps increasing the effort required by calling the hawk uphill to the lure so that the effort she puts in is more than if she is simply allowed to glide out of a tree to the lure. Flights to the lure machine will cause the hawk to expend more effort than simply being called to the fist out of trees. The third method is to teach the hawk to do jump ups. There are various methods to do this but the following is the method I use. The high ring perch is used with an additional section inserted so that the top of the perch is some ten feet above the ground. The hawk is tied with perhaps a slightly longer leash to the ring of the perch, and then I place her on the ground and stand slightly to one side as she flies up to the perch. Once there I call her down to a small piece of food on the fist, then place her back on the ground and repeat. The number of flights is gauged depending on the hawk's fitness or lack thereof but my aim is to build up to 40 or 50 flights per session. Some falconers place the hawk on the ground then call the hawk to their fist high above their head, often standing on a step ladder to do so. My thinking is by placing the hawk on the ground and asking her to fly up to the perch and then rewarding her for coming down to the fist, her desire to quickly get back up into the trees will be increased. She is learning desirable traits that I want her to use while we are out hawking.

Advanced Training

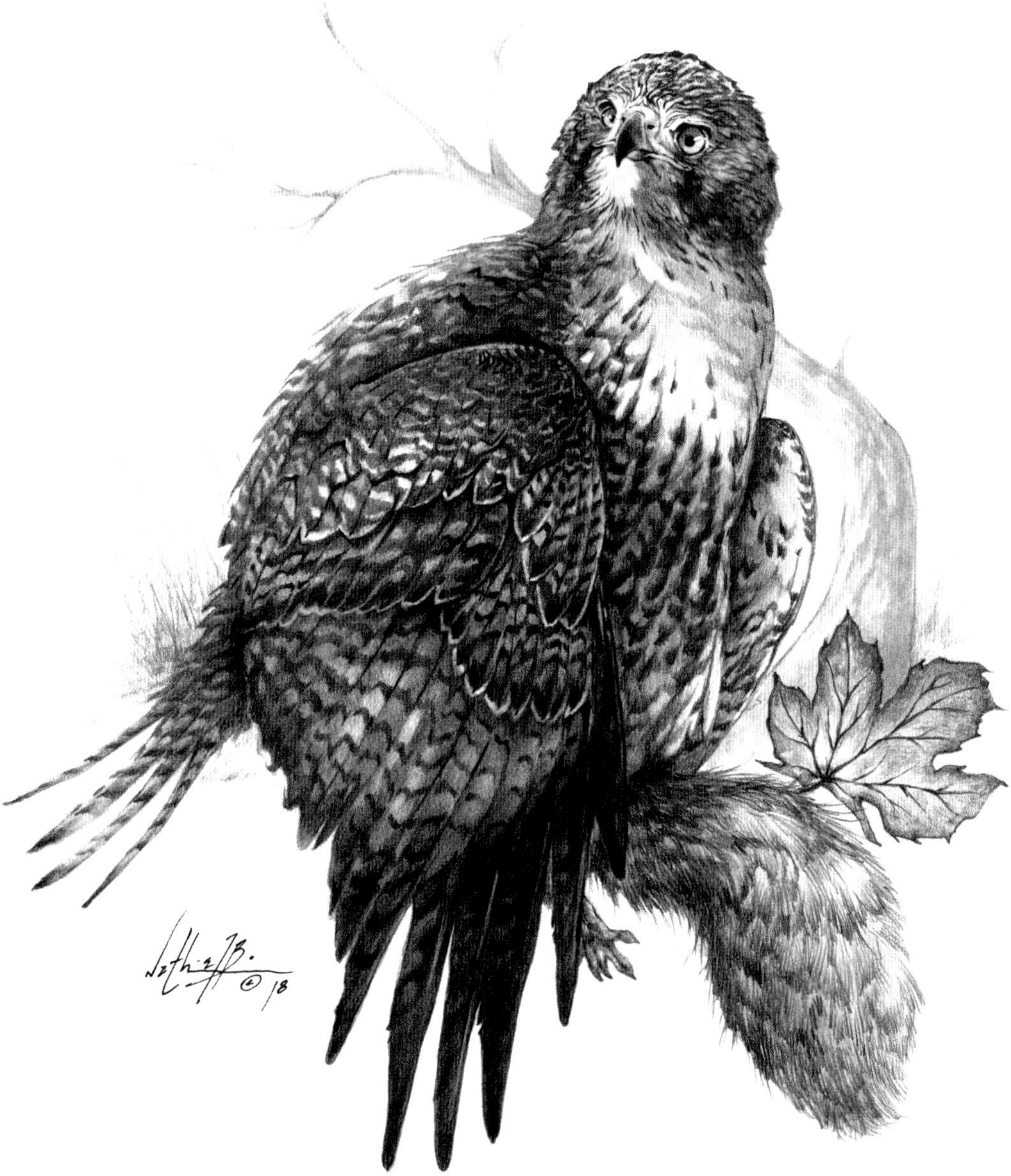

Chapter Eight

Hawking

Once the hawk is responding well from various perches to the fist and the recall and dummy lures, there should be no time wasted in getting out to fly at quarry because delays may cause a hawk to become fist or lure bound. The quarry most suitable for regular flights with passage Red-tailed Hawks includes cottontail rabbits (rabbits), jackrabbits (jacks) and the various species of squirrels. While redtails will occasionally take birds and other mammals as well as snakes, none of these quarries can be relied on to provide regular flights. The availability of rabbits, jacks, and squirrels varies with location. The falconer will need to scout his or her own particular area to find out what quarry is available, but at least one of the quarries mentioned here is generally common enough in any given area of the U.S. to make flying a redtail worthwhile. This is true not just for someone new to the sport, but also for any other falconer looking to fly a hawk at quarry. It is why, after flying hawks for over 40 years, I still choose to fly passage redtails at squirrels. They are quite simply one of the commonest quarry species I have available and the passage redtail is the ideal hawk to fly at them. I can hawk on most days, finding quarry literally right out my back door and in the surrounding woods. On most days, my hawking takes up less than two hours per day, often a lot less. That allows me to hold down a full time job and still have time to spend with my family.

> Slip. A chance to chase quarry. It is the falconers' responsibility to provide his hawk with regular slips at quarry. A good slip will result in a fair opportunity to take quarry while a bad slip is the opposite and may result in a miss or even a lost hawk. A hawk is "slipped" at quarry when released to chase it.

Flying a hawk at quarry requires land where the hawk can be flown and quarry that is available in sufficient numbers that slips can be found on each hawking excursion. While that may and should appear obvious, good falconers tend to be those who have access to enough land holding sufficient amounts of quarry. They also have time to fly their hawks at least four times a week, preferably more, and the enthusiasm to do so. Permission to use land should always be obtained. Falconry is a minority field sport, and we should all work hard to maintain a good reputation. Poaching, leaving gates open, or damaging fences by climbing over them are careless actions that do not leave an impression worthy of respect. The landowners should be familiar with the falconers' vehicles and what it is they intend to do. Most landowners are very receptive to falconers, especially if they are flying at rabbits and squirrels. It is best to find out in advance which landowners want to be notified of your presence and which will let falconers come and go as they please. Landowners should be asked if they'd like notification of friends or dogs accompanying the falconer and if there are certain times when hawking will not be permitted. In upstate New York where I live, we are sometimes asked not to hawk in particular areas during the deer season so that we do not disturb those hunting for deer. Falconers should be mindful that they may be sharing access to land with others and thus remember to be courteous to them. Safety is also an important factor and the appropriate amount of hunter orange should be worn when out and about during deer season.

Some folks with no hunting experience have no idea about what is involved in getting close to wild animals. They walk through the woods and fields talking loudly and wonder why they don't see much wildlife. To hawk successfully, the falconer first has to get the hawk into a position where it can have a good chance of catching quarry. If the quarry has been scared away long before it can be approached, it's not a surprise if a passage hawk goes off hawking by itself. To be a useful partner to the hawk, the falconer has to show that slips will be provided. A slip is an opportunity for a hawk to chase quarry. As the falconer walks through an open field or pasture or moves through the woods with the hawk following along in the trees, a lookout is kept for places where rabbits might hide. Clumps of bushes, dry river beds, and any type of cover that might hold a rabbit should be investigated by approaching quietly. With the hawk either on the fist or in a good position in a tree nearby, the hawking stick is poked into the cover and routed about to make anything in there want to leave. As quarry is flushed, the traditional falconer's cry of "hey, hey, hey" is given to alert the hawk that something is on the move. While walking along, unless the falconer needs the hawk to follow or come to the fist, as little noise as possible should be made. It will not take long to recognize the type of cover the rabbits of the area utilize, and with this recognition, successes will increase.

Hawking

If the majority of hawking is done in open fields, it is useful to teach the hawk to fly from an elevated T perch that is carried along. Such a perch can easily be made by utilizing a painter's pole with a painting roller on top secured so that it doesn't rotate. Some of these poles are extendable up to 20 feet or so. From up on top, the hawk gets a much better view of the surrounding area compared to simply being carried along on the fist. With the added height, which can be converted into speed, the hawk gets a better start at quarry when it flushes. The hawk is taught to fly to the T-perch by the falconer's placing of bechins on it, and once it is known that quarry may be flushed while on the perch, the hawk quickly learns to ride the pole and even to return to it without food after an unsuccessful flight.

> Flush. Not really a falconry term, but falconers use it a lot. To flush quarry is to make it fly or run so that the trained hawk has a chance of catching it.

Mariah on a cottontail rabbit.

Falconry: A Guide for Beginners

If other people are out with a falconer hawking rabbits, they should form a line about five yards apart with the falconer in the center. They should watch for cues and move only when the falconer does, stopping when he or she calls the hawk back to the fist. Nothing is more annoying to me than to have beaters who go it alone, flush quarry when the hawk is out of position, then look up to see where it is. A falconer should give a prep talk at the beginning so everyone knows what to expect. I, for one, dislike having to give a running commentary or answer questions while hawking; I simply want to dedicate all my faculties to serving the hawks and getting the best chance for good slips. It is hard to do that when bombarded with questions, many of which have nothing to do with the job at hand. It must be remembered that we are out there to serve the hawk, not the other way around. Eventually, a rabbit will flush and the hawk, if trained properly, will give chase. It may or may not be successful. If the quarry puts in ahead of the hawk, it will likely swoop up into the air, making its mark as the old falconers would say, and then perch nearby. The falconer must get over there as quickly as possible and try to rout the rabbit back out. A hawk will quickly learn to appreciate this action of the falconer's, strengthening the bond between falconer and hawk. The goal should be at least half a dozen slips per day for a broadwing. Any less than that, and a hawk may not have opportunities for success often enough to make hawking worthwhile.

Dogs have been used for hawking for centuries, and many sporting breeds were first utilized with hawks long before guns were invented. Every falconer has a view on what constitutes a good hawking dog, but for broadwings such as the redtail and Harris' Hawk, the types can be divided into two groups, those which point and those which do not. Of those which point, the German shorthaired pointer (GSP), German wirehaired pointer, or the Vizsla are good candidates if they are trained correctly.

The wider ranging English pointers and the various breeds of setters are generally better suited to more open country and are thus often the preferred breed of those flying longwings at game birds such as grouse, partridge and pheasant. Of those which do not point, the spaniels, Labrador retrievers, and others including the dachshunds have all been used successfully. After seeing many different breeds worked in the field, I am convinced that the type of dog is almost of secondary importance to the ability of the dog trainer. I have even seen German Shepherds work well with hawks when in the right hands, yet other falconers will get a perfectly capable breed like a GSP and make nothing of it because they don't put in the time and effort to train it properly.

Hawking

To find rabbits, a dog needs to work cover thoroughly and at a speed and range that allows the falconer and hawk to keep up. A dog which points is useful, as it allows the falconer to get the hawk into position prior to the flush, but it is not as important when hawking rabbits as it is when pheasants or other game birds are being pursued. In those cases, a much closer slip is preferred, especially on the second flush. Though it may seem a dog is not needed for squirrel hawking, they do come in handy. If a squirrel can get to the woodland floor, it will run straight for either a tree with a hole in it or some ground cover in which it knows it is safe. A squirrel will be more reluctant to do that if there is a dog waiting at the base of the tree and will more likely try to escape the hawk by moving from tree to tree through the branches, thus prolonging the flight and giving more chances of being

Alistair McEwan gets ready to slip his male goshawk at a pheasant pointed by his German shorthaired pointer. A pointer, such as the GSP, gives the falconer a chance to get his hawk into an advantageous position.

Falconry: A Guide for Beginners

caught. Hollie, my lab, will also force squirrels up into a tree and bark at them. This acts as a magnet to the hawk who may have gone off chasing something else. Hollie will also run to the site of the kill and stand nearby, which both helps me locate my hawk and keeps it safe from any other predators that are around. The bond between dog and hawk is so strong that when the hawk is out weathering, Hollie will lie nearby, keeping her feathered friend company.

It is in hawking squirrels that the passage Red-tailed Hawk really comes into its own. No other hawk is as well matched for this difficult, yet abundant quarry. I caught my first squirrel with a goshawk in 1980, and it took a month on antibiotics for her to recover from the bite the squirrel inflicted upon her. I caught a lot more with several different female Harris' Hawks through the 1980s and 1990s, but eventually gave up as one after another, each hawk was temporarily put out of action by bites. The passage redtail, however, is built differently from other species because it encounters and preys on squirrels in the wild and has evolved to be able to deal with bites. Many passage redtails when trapped have bites and small scars on their feet, most of which have healed up. For some reason, whether it is antibodies or having more meat on their feet, they are able to withstand bites much better than any other species. We are fortunate to have a species capable of taking squirrels safely because the flights are, to me at least, one of the most exciting available for broadwings or shortwings. Flights will often last ten or more minutes as both squirrel and hawk maneuver for position. Finally, the squirrel makes it to a refuge such as a hole from which it can't be evicted or the hawk is successful; I have never had a hawk give up if the squirrel was still visible. In squirrel hawking, it is a real battle of wits and strategy played out in the tree tops. One can witness both species working to their full potential in a battle that takes place between these same two species all the time in woods and forests in the wild across North America.

It is usual for the hawk to follow the falconer moving along in the field trying to flush quarry, but in squirrel hawking, the hawk often moves ahead. High up in the trees, the smallest movement of a squirrel can be spotted from a surprising distance. Because of this, my own approach, which may differ from some other squirrel hawkers, is to walk slowly through the woods gently tapping a tree with the beating stick, an old ski pole, every 20 yards or so. If there is nothing moving, the hawk will keep up with me but as soon as it sees something, more often something spooked by our approach, it sets off, and the flight begins. The dog follows closely and if close enough when the hawk takes stand, she will take position underneath the tree and wait to see what happens next. If she did not see the hawk land, she stops and listens for bells before resuming the search to home in on the action. Often, although the hawk spotted the squirrel and thus moved closer, the squirrel will freeze and use a tree branch to hide itself from the hawk. If this were a wild hawk, the ruse may work, but this hawk is trained. It is our job to make the squirrel move so that the hawk can see it and get a shot at it. The squirrel meanwhile tries to figure out who is the more dangerous; if the hawk did not get close on the first flight or is still some distance away, we, the big scary person and dog on the ground represent the greater danger and so the squirrel will move to hide itself from us and in thus doing will show itself to the hawk. Passage redtails are very deliberate in their attacks; they are not reckless in the same way that goshawks and even Harris' Hawks can be. They have encountered squirrels before, know that squirrels can bite, and know they must get a good shot at the squirrel's head if it is to be taken safely. It is partly for this reason that it is a mistake to fly a

Mariah's first squirrel. Note the grip she has on the head of her quarry.

Falconry: A Guide for Beginners

redtail that is low in condition or overly keen, since the hawk may, in its desperation, take the squirrel in a manner that is more likely than not to result in a bite. I like to fly squirrel hawks as high in condition as I can, but consistent with obedience because I want the hawk to use its cunning in taking a squirrel and not be so desperate to eat that it throws caution to the wind and plows into the squirrel when it would have been better to wait for a clearer shot.

Once the squirrel is on the move, the hawk will select its shots. If it misses or the squirrel avoids the attack, it will swing up into another tree nearby and seek to regain the height advantage, often moving from tree to tree to do so. The squirrel, from the moment it first knew it was being pursued, will have been coming up with a plan to get to a hole. It lives in these woods and knows each tree and escape hole intimately and will want to use both to advantage. While it may seem obvious that a squirrel is happier in the trees, as often as not, it will prefer to use the ground to put distance between itself and the hawk. If the squirrel can get to a nearby tree by jumping from one tree to another, it will. However, the squirrel often seems to prefer making the dash on the ground, and once there, it will pass right by the falconer and the dog in an effort to get to its safe haven. As it goes in, it will often let out a small chatter which sounds to me like it is laughing at us, or maybe it is saying something unprintable! It is therefore the falconer's job to try to keep the squirrel up the trees for as long as possible. This doesn't guarantee it will be caught, but at least it keeps the flight going.

Some flights start with the hawk launching an attack on a squirrel it has seen on the ground at some distance through the woods. It is here that quietness pays off. Thrashing through the woods banging every tree in sight will rarely result in such slips as the squirrels will have immediately moved into the safety of holes. I rarely make a lot of noise unless it is after the flight has started; this is to prevent the squirrel from coming down onto the ground. If by some chance we have been out a while and have seen nothing, noise might help, but generally the squirrels are holed up because of inclement weather, and making lots of noise will not dislodge them. Sometimes squirrels can be flushed from their dreys. A drey is the name given to the collection of sticks squirrels use as a home. Dreys are often built in trees that have vines running up them. Shaking the vines violently will sometimes cause a squirrel to leave the drey so the flight can begin. Some hawks, if they see a squirrel go into a drey during the course of a flight, will go over and rip the drey apart trying to persuade the squirrel to leave. Others, and they are a minority, methodically pounce on every drey they come across hoping to find someone at home. Scruff, my male

Hawking

Harris' Hawk would do this until I broke him of the habit by calling him away for food and then taking my fist away before he could get there. He figured out fairly quickly it was an unprofitable enterprise, and it didn't diminish his willingness to come to the fist at other times. Some squirrel hawkers carry slingshots and marbles for firing at dreys and stationary squirrels in an effort to flush them. If the number of squirrels in an area is limited, this might be a worthwhile practice. Other falconers go even further and carry tree climbing spikes and smoke bombs to attempt flushing of squirrels from refuge holes. I have not found it necessary in my part of the world to resort to such tactics to find flights, but if other local falconers need to make use of such implements, they are worth a try.

In the belief that it will cut down on the risk of squirrel bites to the legs and toes, some falconers equip their hawks with wider anklets that include leather strips running across the top of the hawk's toes. Others believe this is not necessary, and I fall into the

By allowing the hawk to follow from tree to tree she will see much more quarry than if carried around on the fist. She's also in a better position to launch an attack on anything she sees.

Falconry: A Guide for Beginners

latter camp. One thing I am sure of is that hawks flown at squirrels should not have jesses of any kind in the anklets while flown, for it is not uncommon in the heat of the kill for a hawk to be found holding onto its own jess along with the squirrel, unable to move the foot to which the jess belongs. A hawk must be able to move its feet freely if it is to securely and safely deal with its prey. Another consideration is that of making in. Some squirrel hawkers believe the falconer should get there as soon as possible to take hold of the squirrel and prevent its biting the hawk. Because Red-tailed Hawks routinely take squirrels in the wild and are accustomed to dealing with them on their own and because of observing hawk behavior on a squirrel kill, I do not consider this to be necessarily the best approach. Observing a hawk on a squirrel in the moments just after the catch reveals the hawk is very intent on getting and securing a grip on the head of the prey. If approached quickly, the hawk will likely transfer at least some attention to the falconer, and it is during that inattention that a bite often results. My practice therefore is to let the hawk come to the ground with the squirrel and move in deliberately, but with no great haste. I expect the hawk to have both feet on the head and/or neck and upper chest area. I then squeeze the squirrel around its chest cavity to kill it and let the hawk relax before trading it off for a day old chick or some other suitable item of food. A sharpened screwdriver thrust into the head can also be used to quickly kill quarry. For birds, especially large ones, I have found a pair of electrical wire strippers very effective for severing a vertebrae. The wire strippers resemble the tooth on a longwing's beak and are very efficient. Care must be taken in either case to avoid damaging the hawk's toes.

> Make in. A falconer makes in to a hawk when he carefully approaches her on the lure or quarry.

As mentioned, I do not feed any hawks on the kill, though I do feed them at the site of the kill. To reiterate the reasons, the first is to prevent transmission of disease; the second is so that I can accurately keep track of the hawk's food intake and therefore weight and health; the third is to prevent the feeling in the hawk's mind, no matter how well it is done, that it has been robbed by being persuaded to let go of a large food item. While holding onto the quarry with the gloved hand, I drop the chick to one side, slightly out of reach, just as I did during training to the lure, and the hawk will release the quarry no matter how much larger it is and transfer over to the chick. I pick up the quarry and turn away from the hawk so that she cannot see it and put it in my jacket, at the same time stepping back from the site of the kill so I am not towering over the hawk. By the time the hawk has finished the chick at the site of the kill, another chick awaits on my fist. Often, my hawk will want to lift up both feet to check that there is nothing underneath, will then jump up to the fist, and will feed on my fist as I walk away from the area. In the hawk's mind, it has caught something and eaten it, not caring that it wasn't the squirrel or rabbit. If I intend to fly my hawk again, I use only a chick body to call it off the kill and then a chick leg or head to call the hawk up to the fist. When ready, the hawk will leave the fist and fly up into a tree, and hawking can resume.

Once the hawk has made a dozen or so kills, the time has come for double kills if so inclined. My general policy is to go for a second kill only if the first flight was an easy one and the likelihood of a second kill is high. I rarely do it if I am hawking alone, though if I have guests out and they want to see more flights, I do it for them, not for the hawk. I do not want to end the day having to toss out the first kill as a reward because the hawk has failed to make a second kill. I consider such an ending a failure on my part due to my own greediness or to succumbing to the wishes of others whose interests do not lie with the hawk. Falconry is not about racking up large numbers of kills or taking more quarry than other falconers; it is about bringing the best out of each individual hawk and about the falconer's making a commitment to each hawk to play his or her role as partner. While multiple kills are not unacceptable, if the hawk has had a few good flights and then taken quarry, I call it a day and look forward to the next day. After a particularly good effort, regardless of how well made the hawk is or who is out hawking, it is always nice to feed up and relax and relive the flight in one's mind. As Nick Fox so rightly says, why follow champagne with beer?!

> Made. A hawk is said to be "made" when there is no doubt that it will fly a particular quarry. This generally requires at least 10 kills. For instance, a hawk is said to be "made" to rabbits when it will chase them without hesitation.

The more time spent in the field exposing a hawk to quarry, flushing suitable quarry for it, and providing slips, the better the bond the hawk will have with the falconer. Some hawks make their first kill very quickly. On rare occasions, it can happen on the first ever flight at quarry, though personally I've had that happen only twice. Once was with Star, a Eurasian Sparrowhawk that took a blackbird on her first flight, and the second time was with Bingo, my black musket who took a dove inside a barn on his first flight. With other hawks, several weeks might be spent in the field chasing quarry before they finally catch something. Scruff took three weeks of daily flying before he finally caught a moorhen, yet still went on to kill over 50 head in his first season. Mariah, the redtail featured in this book, had her first flight 28 days after being trapped and caught her first squirrel two outings later.

HAWK: Mariah				SPECIES: Red-tailed Hawk					SEX: F					MONTH: November 2012															
WEIGHT																													
1185			x																										
1180																													
1175					x			x																		x	x		
1170																													
1165															x		x	x	x						x				
1160	x	x		x			x	x				x						x											x
1155		x			x				x	x		x		x															
1150				x							x																		
1145																													
1140																													
1135																													
1130																													
1125																													
1120																													
1115																													
1110																													
DATE:	1	2	3	4	5	6	7	8	9	10	11	12	13	14	15	16	17	18	19	20	21	22	23	24	25	26	27	28	29
FOOD:	4C	4C	7C	0	4C	5C	2C	4C	3C 1B 2L	8C	0	2C	4C	4C	4C 4L	4C	1Q	0	4C	4C	4C	4C	4C	8C	0	4C	3C	4C	4C

Notes by date:
1. Follow on through trees. Dummy lure.
2. Follow on and dummy lure work.
3. Chased first squirrel but it got to a hole.
4. Day off, fasting.
5. One squirrel, good flight.
6. Two good squirrel flights.
7. Too high, not flown.
8. One squirrel.
9. Several flights.
10. No slips, followed well, used dummy lure.
11. Sunday, not flown, not weighed.
12. Still overweight, not flown.
13. One squirrel.
14. Followed well, couple flights.
15. Saw nothing, used dummy lure.
16. One rabbit.
17. High winds, not flown.
18. Sunday, not flown, not weighed.
19. One squirrel.
20. Flew well, no slips, used dummy lure.
21. One rabbit.
22. One squirrel, okay at higher weight.
23. No slips, followed well.
24. One squirrel.
25. Sunday, not flown, not weighed.
26. One rabbit, okay at higher weight.
27. Too independent, called her down.
28. Better, one squirrel.
29. Heavy rain, not flown.

Mariah's weight chart for November 2012. The falconer can try increasing the hawk's weight periodically but must be careful t are no adverse reactions. When Mariah's weight was first increased following a gorge and fast on 26th she flew well the first c then, even though at the same weight, the next day she began to get a little independent so her weight was brought down by 10 grams. Unwanted behavior learned while being flown overweight will not necessarily be corrected if the weight is reduced back where the hawk was performing well, so care must be taken when increasing the weight to make sure such behaviors do not bec a habit. If she becomes independent, get her down quickly and stop flying before the unwanted behavior becomes the norm. Note: C = whole day-old cockerel, B = body of day-old cockerel, L = leg of day-old cockerel, Q = coturnix quail.

Hawking

When the hawk is taking quarry, it is time to try putting the hawk loose into the mews at home. Some hawks take to this quite well, but many others bounce around the mews and crash against the window. If so, the hawk can be kept tethered while in the mews and put out onto the perch on the weathering lawn during the day. For such a hawk, it may be worth trying again later in the season, though some hawks never learn to settle down in the mews if left unsecured.

At the end of the season, which may be determined by a state's fish and game department, it is time to feed the hawk up. I never fly a hawk at quarry after March 20, the first day of spring, but that is a personal preference. I do not like killing animals that may be pregnant, nesting, or have young to rear. Because wild hawks do it, some falconers claim we can too, but wild hawks must kill to live; my trained hawk and I do not. On the final day of the season and for the next week or so, the hawk is given double rations. There is a choice with a passage redtail about whether to release it or molt it out for the next season. That choice is entirely up to the individual falconer, and there is nothing wrong with either decision. If it is decided to release the hawk, it is fed up as high in weight as it will go. Hopefully the hawk will start to bate away upon the falconer's approach because it is desirable for it to get a little wild before being released. A place as remote as possible should be chosen so there will be little chance of human contact, at least for the first week or two. When the day arrives, the hawk's bells and anklets are cut off, and the hawk is released with best wishes for its future. Who knows? Maybe one day, one of its offspring will be trapped and flown.

If it is decided to keep a redtail, there are two ways to molt it out. The first is to turn it loose into the mews, leaving it entirely alone until the end of the molt, which will not be until at least the following September. The second method and the one I prefer for redtails, though not necessarily other species, is to continue to handle the hawk each day, putting it outside to weather and bringing it back in at night. In this way, the hawk remains somewhat tame, and it is an easy exercise to reduce its weight at the end of the molt, bringing it back into flying condition. If using this method, the hawk must be hooded at least once a day. One of my tiercels was made hood shy when left with someone who didn't hood him for the entire six months of the molt and then wondered why the hawk wouldn't take the hood when it came time to fly him again! While molting, a hawk should be fed a variety of food. Many a hawk has eaten nothing more than quarry caught the previous season, which has been frozen, thus killing any disease it might contain. I do not feed my hawks too high during the

Falconry: A Guide for Beginners

summer molt because it is only extra weight that must be removed in the early fall, but I allow them to creep up by about 200 to 250 grams for a hawk the size of a redtail. Once the molt is complete, the hawk is put onto small rations, perhaps only two legs from a day old chick until signs of wanting to fly to the fist are shown. The hawk is then put through a short refresher course, and hawking can begin again. An intermewed redtail, like any other intermewed hawk that has had a successful first season, is a delight to work with. It knows the game and what the falconer is doing to help find quarry. With a brand new set of feathers, a hawk is normally more efficient than in its first year. Many hawks will fly at a higher weight in their second season, but a falconer must always look for the subtle signs that the hawk is not really on flying weight. If too much quarry is missed at the last second, if the hawk is a bit slow in coming back to the fist or flies a little wider than usual, especially in new areas, it may need slight reducing to be brought back on form.

Hawking

*Mariah, passage redtail with a fox squirrel and grey squirrel she has just taken.
This photograph was taken two months to the day after she was trapped.*

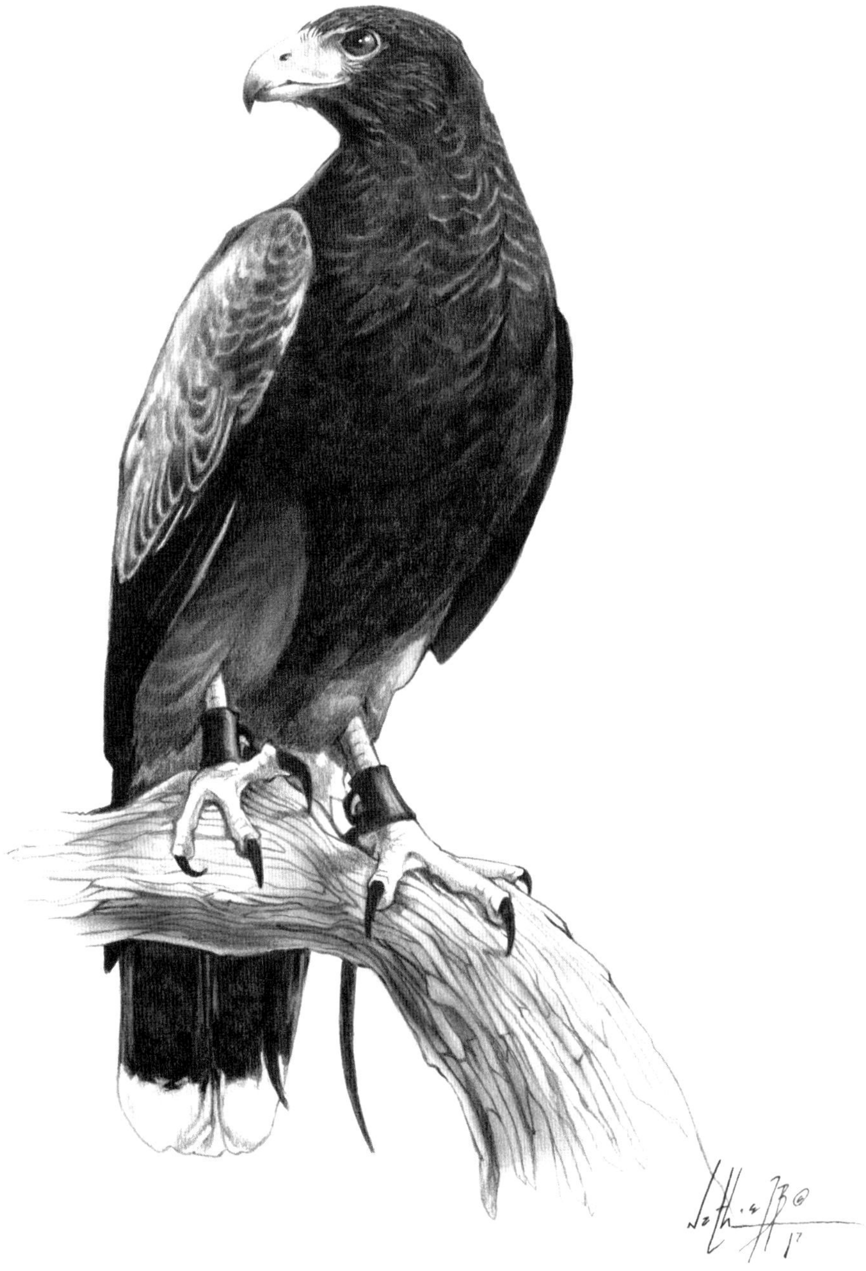

Chapter Nine

The Harris' Hawk

The Harris' Hawk is found in the southwestern United States in Texas, Arizona, and parts of southern California and New Mexico. It is unique as a raptor species in that individual's band together to hunt cooperatively. They are often comprised of family groups; it is not unusual for young from a previous year to assist in raising the young born in later years. First flown for falconry as recently as the 1960s, the Harris' Hawk is now the most commonly flown of the broadwings and shortwings, both in the U.S. and Europe, and is possibly the most commonly flown of all raptor species in those areas. Falconers are allowed to take a passage Harris' Hawk in Texas and Arizona, and many individuals of this species are produced by breeders each year, making them readily available for anyone wanting to fly one.

The Harris' Hawk offers many advantages to a beginner. It is possibly one of the easiest species to train to come to the fist. It can, if introduced properly, be flown with others of its own kind, making it possible for a beginner's hawk to be flown in company with a more experienced hawk flown by another falconer. Both the hawk and the beginner learn quickly in this way.

An opinion occasionally voiced by American falconers is that it is important for the beginner to start by trapping his or her own hawk. In theory, this teaches the new falconer the art of trapping, which many in the sport feel all falconers should know. Because trapping a hawk requires effort on the part of the beginner, it shows determination, a quality important for any falconer to have. In essence, writing a check to buy a captive-bred hawk is seen as too easy and showing no real commitment. My view ignores the theory of someone becoming a good falconer because of starting a certain way. I have seen and met hundreds of falconers of varying degrees of ability. How they started

Falconry: A Guide for Beginners

seems to have no real influence on how they turn out, so I focus on the practicalities of what is needed by the beginner. The passage redtail and the passage or captive-bred Harris' Hawk all meet those needs. Of course, if one lives and hawks in a country where redtails do not exist in the wild, all of this is moot. In such a case, the captive-bred Harris' Hawk is, in my opinion, the best hawk for the novice falconer. One point that is worth noting is that young, captive-bred Harris' Hawks bones take a while to develop and harden. For this reason care should be taken not to let them bate too much from a perch to which they are tethered. If the new hawk is bating a lot it can either be hooded or the cause of the bating, people passing too close, etc. should be removed until it is further along in the manning process. Avoid putting the new hawk in a transport box to stop it bating. I know of more than one young Harris' Hawk that has broken a leg while crashing around a transport box into which it was placed and one which died under the same circumstances. Transport boxes, if used, should be introduced carefully further along in training when the hawk is calmer and more willing to accept new things.

   The training of a captive-bred or passage Harris' Hawk does not differ significantly from the techniques laid out in this book for a passage redtail, although once a Harris' Hawk is feeding on the fist, the whole thing is generally a bit easier. That is the reasoning for writing this book with the passage redtail in mind. In short, anyone who can train a passage redtail should have no problems with a Harris' Hawk. While some falconers take a more lackadaisical approach to training and flying Harris' Hawks, especially if flying them in groups as is commonly done, it is still important for the beginner to proceed conscientiously through the steps in this book. I train my own Harris' Hawks this way. Other falconers do not use the hood with Harris' Hawks, preferring the transport box instead. Or they introduce a young Harris' Hawk with little training to a team of made Harris' Hawks, then let the young hawk learn by following its elders. I prefer and require more discipline in my falconry. Because I like to feed my hawks up at the site of the kill and then walk back to the car, I must carry the hawk on the fist. If not hood trained, there will be a lot of bates along the way. While the Harris' Hawk is very forgiving, I do not like to carry a bating hawk for what could be miles, upsetting both it and me and spoiling the memory of the flights we've enjoyed. While I have flown groups of up to nine Harris' Hawks together at a time, I feel that two good hawks, one of each sex, brings out the best in both the individual hawk and the quarry we are trying to catch. I find it difficult to appreciate each hawk when lots of them are being flown, and I think it takes unfair

The Harris' Hawk

advantage of the quarry. Though some falconers claim the hawks fly this way in nature, wild hawks do not have human beaters working for them. However, everyone has personal preferences, thus I would not be too unbending once a beginner has learned to train a hawk from start to finish.

Compared to other species, the Harris' Hawk is generally quick to train once the point is reached when it is jumping to the fist for food. Males especially can be a bit nervous in the early stages, needing some persuasion to feed on the fist, but as long as time is spent each day, they will eventually feed. The worst one I had in this regard was Scruff, a male I trained in 1983 who later turned into the best Harris' Hawk I have ever flown or have seen flown, so a beginner should not be discouraged by initial difficulty. I have had plenty of other Harris' Hawks that fed on the fist the first day and were ready to fly free less than 10 days later. Because of the speed at which they train, it is important to go methodically through the various steps, especially hooding. While still on a creance, many Harris' Hawks will start to follow the falconer before he or she reaches the distance at which the hawk will be called. To correct this, it is useful to teach a Harris' Hawk to fly back to the perch so that while doing so, the falconer can turn and run in the opposite direction while looking over a shoulder and still handling the creance. A better alternative is asking a helper to hold the hawk until the falconer is ready to call it, then having the helper place the hawk on the perch prior to being called off. Of course, if a hawk is following that well, it is really ready to be flown free.

Introduction to the lure generally poses few problems. I have frequently had a Harris' Hawk immediately attack a recall lure the first time it was dropped a few feet away, even when ungarnished. Some falconers dispense with lure training, but I do not. The lure is useful if the hawk is lost and is a tool for exercising the hawk and teaching it how to chase and how to foot objects while travelling at speed. Furthermore, hawks enjoy it. On days when a hawk is not flown at quarry, it is far better exercise to fly the lure machine than just to be called to the fist several times. I usually fly my hawks every day and have not had need to experiment with night flying, at least for conditioning purposes, but a number of my colleagues exercise their Harris' Hawks in areas with street lights or in parks or ball fields with flood lighting. A Harris' Hawk can be kept very fit this way by using the lure machine. It doesn't take much lighting for them to see what is taking place. Wires and fences are harder for both hawks and humans to see at night, so the selected area must be carefully chosen to prevent accidents.

Falconry: A Guide for Beginners

Harris' Hawks will take a far wider variety of quarry than trained redtails. They are quicker off the mark, often quicker on the turn, and are capable of learning techniques enabling them to take game birds such as pheasants, partridge, quail and ducks that are beyond the ability of most redtails. They are not built to punch through thick brush in the same way redtails do, but I have seen them take quarry in places so tight they could not even open their wings. They tend to follow the falconer with a bit more attention than the average redtail, which I suspect stems from the habit of hunting in packs in the wild. This pack mentality quickly leads them to treat falconers and dogs as part of the group, and where the ground crew goes, they will eagerly follow.

Harris' Hawks are not as suitable for flying at squirrels as redtails, which have thicker toes with more flesh on them. The Harris' Hawk is easily agile enough to take squirrels, but seems to get bitten more often, and the bites do not heal as well. For this reason, if squirrels are going to be the main quarry, the redtail is the hawk of choice. Where the Harris' Hawk excels is in its versatility at taking a wide range of quarry in the field. The Harris' Hawks I have trained and flown over the years have collectively taken in excess of 50 different species of quarry, ranging from mice up to jackrabbits, hares and even a young deer, and birds from tiny sparrows up to pheasants and ducks. My colleagues in upstate New York have taken turkeys with their Harris' Hawks. Canada Geese, Brant and Snow Geese are other species that could likely be taken. Unless these large quarry—jackrabbits, hares, geese or turkeys—will be chased on a sizeable portion of the flights, I have a slight preference for the male Harris' Hawk. The male, however, needs more finesse in handling and weight control than the female. A male that takes pheasant or mallard-sized birds is really flying at the upper limits of capability, and if not in tip top form and at the correct flying weight, he may refuse or be reluctant to bind to such quarries. A female, carrying more weight and having bigger feet, does not have to be quite so finely tuned. I have seen males refuse the larger quarries when only ¼ ounce over flying weight, and while not all of them are like that, the majority are. Even Scruff, in his first season, only took two English rabbits before he refused to bind to them. In his second season, he figured out how to get them by the head, and from then on, he never refused. However, I have seen males that would not bind to a fully-grown English rabbit or black-tailed jackrabbit unless conditions were exactly in their favor and they were precisely on flying weight. It is therefore wise to go for a female for a first hawk so the beginner has more room for error in controlling the flying weight.

The Harris' Hawk

When hawking, I allow the Harris' Hawk complete freedom once the flying ground is reached. Having weighed the hawk and hooded it for the ride to the flying ground, upon arrival, the jesses are removed, and the hawk is unhooded and allowed to fly into the trees of the area it will fly over. I do not use flying jesses with Harris' Hawks, but fly them with only the anklets and bells on. If the area is an open field, I use a T-perch or allow the hawk to ride on the fist unhooded, but I prefer to see hawks flying and usually fly in areas where they can get into the trees. Once settled in the trees, beating commences, and it is my job and the dog's to flush quarry for the hawk. It is rare with a Harris' Hawk that I am looking for a certain species of quarry as is often the case with a redtail or other trained hawk. I encourage my Harris' Hawks to chase anything that moves by actively reflushing any legitimate prey species that has been put in to cover.

By teaching the hawk to utilize a T perch, she is given an added height advantage while walking through tall cover. T perches can be made by modifying extendable paint rollers by adding Astroturf to the roller and securing it so it no longer rotates.

Falconry: A Guide for Beginners

Many falconers, not just beginners, have problems with finding the Harris' Hawk's flying weight. Harris' Hawks have a wider response weight than almost any other hawk. I had one female who would fly perfectly well to the fist and lure at 42 ounces, though her proper flying weight was 33 ounces. As her weight increased above that level, her willingness to take quarry diminished accordingly. She would still chase and catch quarry on easy flights, and she was very responsive back to the fist, but she lacked the necessary incentive to bind to quarry or make real effort if the flight appeared at all difficult. Many Harris' Hawks will fly easy quarry at one weight, but refuse to try for more difficult quarry. The falconer often doesn't notice such behavior or doesn't care. A large number of Harris' Hawks are thus not flown to their full potential.

In my experience, when a Harris' Hawk is flown at difficult quarry and is required to exert itself, it needs to be kept within ¼ ounce of its flying weight or there will be a difference in willingness to perform its best. Again, Scruff can clarify a point. He first flew free at 22 ounces. Because it is normal for a captive-bred hawk to

Scruff, my male Harris' Hawk on a French partridge he took. The German shorthaired pointer is about as perfect a companion as a Harris' Hawk flown at game birds can have. It is essential if the hawk is to be served after putting in a pheasant, partridge or quail following a long distance first flight.

increase in flying weight during its first year as it puts on muscle, I accordingly increased Scruff's weight to as high as 23½ ounces during his first season. At this higher weight however, he tended to be very wide-ranging in the field and would take on quarry at distances well in excess of 400 yards. The problem was that he was all over the place and rarely waited around for the beaters and dogs down below to flush quarry for him. Although trained, he was, in essence, out of control. A weight reduction back to 22½ ounces brought him under control. At this weight he was strong, fit, would not refuse any quarry with which he was familiar (a sure sign that a hawk is at flying weight) and paid attention to what we were doing down below. If his weight varied either up or down by as little as ¼ ounce, his performance would change. At a lower weight, he was too keen on what we were doing; he perched lower in trees or would come and land by me in the hope of getting a tidbit. At ¼ ounce higher, he would not pull out all the stops on difficult flights even though he would still take quarry. One of my goals when flying a trained hawk is to bring out the best that the individual has to offer. That simply cannot be done if a falconer is lax about weight management. Unfortunately, the Harris' Hawk lends itself to that approach.

While rabbits are the quarry flown by most falconers with Harris' Hawks, they can be trained in techniques allowing them to bring many other quarry species to bag. In England and Scotland, I hawked a lot at pheasants with my Harris' Hawks. Pheasants can be caught by almost any Harris' Hawk on an occasional basis, but to catch them regularly, the hawk needs to fly them into cover and wait for the falconer to come up and reflush the pheasant. The techniques outlined next will work for pheasants, quail, and also partridge and some other game birds.

Harris' Hawks lack the initial speed of accipiters off the fist, and unless a very close slip is given, they are rarely successful at taking pheasants on the rise unless they can close the gap, perhaps when the pheasant is struggling to break through cover. For Harris' Hawks to take pheasants on more than a chance basis, certain protocol is needed to prepare the hawk for the flight, to set up the flight, and to manage it once it starts. To catch a pheasant that outflies the hawk on the initial flush, the hawk needs to follow the pheasant and mark it closely as it puts in. It then needs to wait nearby, preferably up in a tree or on a pole, not poking around on the ground, until the falconer comes and reflushes the pheasant. The hawk needs to learn this through experience that is given by the falconer.

Falconry: A Guide for Beginners

Though especially true for pheasants, to take quarry regularly, a hawk needs to be fit. It is important therefore that a hawk be flown as often as possible. There is a huge difference between a hawk given two or more hours of flying a day and one that is only flown on weekends. The oft flown hawk learns how to use the wind, to select the best branches for landing, to convert height into speed, and to employ many other useful tricks that take the weekend hawk years to develop, if ever. Even among hawks free flown, there is a natural difference among individuals; some excel in other areas, making up for what they lack in flying style. A hawk frequently flown from a T-pole must be carefully observed. Though it still gets plenty of exercise, it might also clamp itself to the pole and stay there for extended periods while the falconer is the one who does all the work and becomes fit.

Once at the flying field, the hawk is unhooded and allowed to fly up into the trees if there are any. At no time should the hawk be restrained from flying. I have seen falconers hold back a bating Harris' Hawk as a pheasant flushes 100 yards away in the belief that the hawk can't catch it. Though it may not be caught on the first flight, such a pheasant has a chance of being caught if the hawk is taught properly and works hard. If repeatedly held back, the hawk will soon cease to chase pheasants at all, even those up close. If not prepared to let a hawk chase, it should remain hooded to prevent disappointment. If taking a hawk to areas where pheasants are found, there will eventually be an opportunity for that first flight. How this and other flights early in the hawk's career are managed will determine if the hawk turns into one that takes on a pheasant already in flight 100 yards away and brings that pheasant to bag.

Most Harris' Hawks, assuming they are in flying condition, will chase the first pheasant they see. There is something about the wingbeat of a game bird that gets hawks excited. Quite often, what the falconer first sees is the pheasant in flight with the hawk trailing behind. The falconer should follow the flight and watch where the pheasant puts in. When the hawk quits, which it probably will, the falconer goes to the place where the pheasant landed, and the hawk follows. It is important in this and subsequent flights to get to the spot as quickly as possible. Later on, when the hawk starts to mark the pheasant, it will be reluctant to move with the hawk positioned above. But before this stage is reached, a pheasant will run after it lands. It may well be dozens of yards away if a falconer doesn't arrive quickly enough to put the hawk into a tree to hold the pheasant down. Even if the falconer is quick, many hawks, after a period of time, will leave the pheasant they put in and go off to look for something else. As a hawk makes progress and grows confident that the falconers will come up and reflush, it may wait longer, but even the best of them won't wait forever. If possible, a hawk should not be rewarded with food at any time during the flight. It needs to learn that once a pheasant is flushed, all attention should be devoted to its catch. It is a mistake to reward a hawk for a "nice flight" when the hawk actually gave up. Hawks don't appreciate what is aesthetically pleasing to a falconer. If rewarded for quitting, turning round, and coming back, the hawk will soon give up whenever the flushed pheasant looks like it might require some effort to catch.

A very common mistake is to continue beating in the area where a pheasant flushed in the hope that the hawk will come back to rejoin the hawking party. The hawk will normally do exactly that, but in subsequent flights, each pheasant will be chased for a shorter distance until finally the hawk tries only for the very easy pheasants that flush nearby or appear at a disadvantage. When a falconer arrives where the pheasant put in, a genuine effort to find it should be made. On the first flush, beaters alone are normally enough to make a pheasant fly, but on the reflush, a dog is almost essential. I prefer a German shorthaired pointer, but any dog that points and goes into thick cover will suffice. Even a spaniel will do, but quite often either the falconer or hawk has not marked the pheasant very accurately or the pheasant has moved. In this case, a point will provide time to reposition the hawk whereas a spaniel will flush without giving such a luxury.

If this procedure is followed every time, the hawk will still try very hard on the initial flush, but if unsuccessful, will follow the pheasant until it puts in and wait for the falconer to appear to reflush it. It is now that the score will start to add up. Furthermore, as the season progresses and easy slips become a thing of the past, the falconer will still have a pheasant-catching hawk. Such a hawk will think nothing of flying a pheasant that was flushed 100 or more yards away into cover over distances greater than ¼ of a mile. This is pheasant hawking with Harris' Hawks at its best.

The free flight method involves 1) teaching the hawk that each pheasant or other quarry should be given 100% effort, 2) hooding the hawk when not flying it, and 3) keeping the hawk at the right weight. This method will have a positive result—a very intense hawk that will always give its best when in the field. Hawks thus treated will try for all sorts of quarry in any situation. It's as though removing the hood is an invitation to the hawk to go out and give its best. It will be necessary to hood the hawk to allow the falconer and the field an occasional breather. A Harris' Hawk thus flown is vastly different than one flown only on weekends with little attention paid to weight control or working hard for its food. Once a falconer has flown or seen a Harris' Hawk capable of such flights, all desire to settle for anything less will be lost.

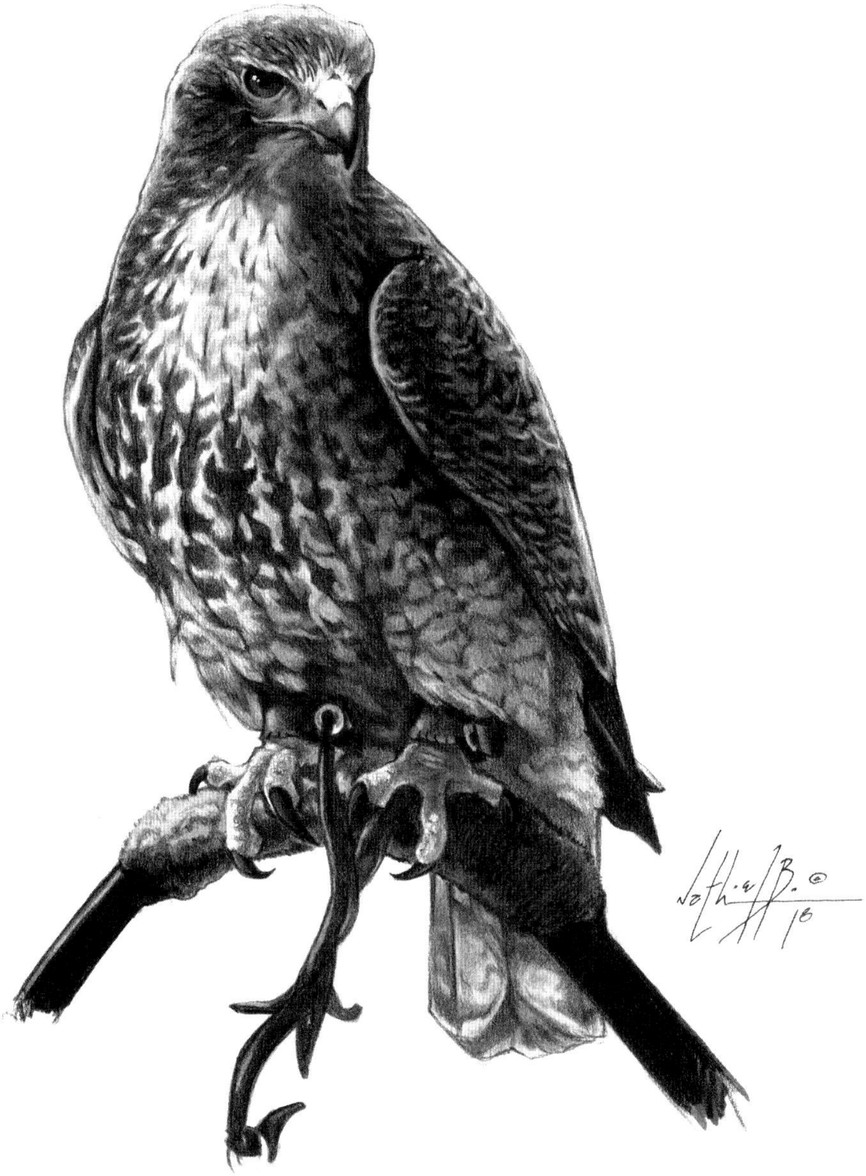

Chapter Ten

Wrapping Up

Daily and Weekly Routines

    A hawk in the care of a falconer relies upon him or her for its safety and well-being. Each time the falconer handles the hawk he should take a good look at its overall appearance. Is anything untoward? Are the feathers a little more fluffed than normal, is there any sign of weakness in the hawk's bates, or is breathing unduly labored? Anything different from the norm is cause for concern. A falconer must become accustomed to checking mutes to see if they seem runny or if there is any lime green tinge to them (a sign of Aspergillosis.) At the first sign of a hawk being unwell, the falconer should check with a vet and other local falconers. Waiting is unwise, for hawks, being relatively small creatures, have little reserve to fall upon if something affects their appetites and their willingness or ability to eat. A falconer should have in mind a local vet prior to getting a hawk so that when the situation arrives, time is not wasted. Using the same vet as other falconers in the area allows the vet to build up a broader knowledge base from the hawks seen.

    The equipment on the hawk should be checked each time it is handled. If the jesses look worn in any way, they should be changed immediately. When making equipment, it is always wise to make and buy spares. One of my employees once changed only one jess on one of my hawks. When I picked up the hawk, I found the new jess to be an inch shorter than the other one. When the hawk bated, the leg with the short jess took up more than its fair share of the shock at the end of the bate. Such laziness has no place in falconry. If jesses need changing, they should both be changed. Knots and buttons, if any, on leashes and jesses should be checked for signs of wear so they can be changed at the least indication for concern. Cracked bells will cause cuts and abrasions if they come into contact with a hawk's foot. Loose bewits will allow bells to hit the perch and will facilitate cracking of the bells. Changing the bewits and bells is necessary if these deficiencies are noticed.

Faulty equipment does not include only what is worn by the hawk. I've seen rusty bow perches that can cut and infect a hawk's feet, broken rings that will allow the hawk's escape, lightweight perches at field meets that can easily be dragged over by the hawk to result in killing the neighboring hawk, and short spikes that are pulled out of the ground so the perch is dragged along, also sometimes killing neighboring hawks. Many hawks in the U.S. are killed after being put out to weather unprotected. A falconer who values a hawk will build a properly protected facility. Not only will it keep the hawk from attack, but should some part of the equipment malfunction, the hawk will be safe inside the weathering area upon the falconer's return.

Hawks in captivity will at some point require coping of beaks and talons. Another falconer, one who is experienced in coping, should be asked to help with a new falconer's first coping attempt. If feathers need repair, the process of imping is used. This is a fairly simple process that can be practiced on any kind of feather before trying it out on a hawk. Prevention of feather injury in the first place is far preferable however. Many, if not most, broken feathers are the result of bad handling, bad training, or faulty equipment. A mews that is too small can result in feathers that contact walls. Transport boxes, weathering areas that are too small, teaching a hawk to mantle over its kills or the lure, and rough handling in confined spaces or near hard objects are all causes of broken or bent feathers. I cringe when I see a falconer handling a hawk in a rough manner. When treated kindly, feathers may never need to be imped.

For clear instructions on imping and coping please refer to the author's chapters in *North American Falconry and Hunting Hawks* by Beebe and Webster published by Western Sporting.

Field Etiquette

When out hawking with a falconer, there are some things that guests should keep in mind to avoid being nothing more than a nuisance. The falconer will likely be preoccupied with doing right by his hawk in preparation for the upcoming event. He may well have a lot of questions he is asking himself and probably some doubts about whether the hawk's weight is right, whether it will perform in front of others, what will happen if something upsets it and causes it to fly

Wrapping Up

away. Now is not the time to bombard the falconer with questions about which type of hawk is best for a beginner, what type of dog would be recommended, or why the falconer isn't doing everything exactly the same as other falconers the guest may have accompanied. Those questions should be saved for a time when the falconer is not concentrating on the hawk and can better concentrate on the answers and any discussion they are sure to provoke.

It is important not to do anything that will upset the hawk. Many hawks, even ones that are well manned, are fearful of people they don't recognize and so keep a respectful distance and especially do not walk behind the hawk. If a hawk is upset by something at the start of the day, it is not likely to fly its best and may decide it would be better off somewhere else. One's eyes should be averted if a hawk looks directly at a guest; staring, to a wild animal expresses aggression or fear. Avoid walking up to the hawk to examine its equipment or to get a closer look or a photograph, it must be remembered that guests are present to observe, not to upset the proceedings. On no account, ever, should anyone try to touch a trained hawk without asking the falconer first, and don't be surprised if he denies the request. Just because a pet dog likes being stroked does not indicate that a hawk might appreciate the same token of affection.

Prior to setting off the falconer should brief guests out on what to expect. If the guests are to actively participate in beating then they need to be given instructions on when to beat, how to stay in a line, etc. so that they are not flushing quarry when the hawk is out of position. If a group of falconers are taking it in turn to fly their hawks, such as a field meeting, it is helpful if those who are awaiting their turn, spend some time with guests explaining what is going on. Once flying has begun it should be remembered the falconer, hopefully anyway, knows what he is doing and knows his hawk. Just because the falconer may need to call his hawk more than once does not mean it will come faster if others join in on the calling. If the falconer is waving a glove to attract the hawk's attention, that is not an invitation for others to do the same. If the hawk is ignoring the falconer, it is not likely to pay any more attention to someone else who may only distract it even more by confusing it. The same applies to the falconer's dog if one is present. When I am dealing with a dog that has for the moment forgotten its training and is intent only on embarrassing me, nothing is more infuriating than to hear other people repeating my commands in the belief that the dog will somehow listen to them even though it is ignoring me.

[255]

Falconry: A Guide for Beginners

For the falconers doing the actual flying, especially if they have not hawked together before, some basic ground rules should be agreed upon before setting out. Depending on the species of hawk being flown and the type of quarry being pursued different rules might apply. With Harris' Hawks that have previously been flown together and are known not to crab, i.e.: try and catch or fight each other, then often the falconers elect to fly them all together. If this is the case then the slowest hawk, or falconer, sets the speed of the advancing group. It is very rude and selfish (but I have seen it happen more often than I care to remember) if one or two falconers, perhaps flying more experienced hawks, head off on their own taking in all the ground that should have been flown by all the members of the group and ruining the chances for others hawks. When out in a group, the purpose should be to work together for the benefit of all the hawks.

When short and broadwings other than Harris' Hawks are flown it is safer to fly them separately to avoid crabbing and the disastrous results that can come from it. It should be firmly established whose turn it is to slip their hawk next and all the other hawks must be restrained, even if the hawk whose turn it is refuses the slip. Once a flight commences everyone should stand still. If the flight goes a distance and the falconer needs to follow the hawk to recover it, the rest of the party should await his return so that they do not move over fresh ground possibly flushing quarry and wasting slips. Two way radios are useful in such circumstances so that the falconer whose hawk has gone off can radio back when she is recovered and hawking can recommence with the next hawk.

While everyone hopes their hawk will perform well when others are out, that is not always the case. Often, having guests out proves too much for a hawk which normally flies with just the falconer and perhaps his dog as company. I suspect the nervousness we feel as falconers, for we all want our hawk to fly well in front of others, in some way gets transmitted to the hawk and even the most reliable hawk can be put off stride. The more a hawk is flown with other people the better it will become under such circumstances but for the first few attempts a wise falconer will not try his hawk beyond what he thinks it will tolerate. Thus for the first few outings with other people it is wise to take only one or two people along with you and by choice, choose other falconers who know, or should know, how to behave around a trained hawk and what to expect. I admit, that as I get older, the number of people on my mental black list of who I will not take out hawking grows longer each year. There is nothing worse than having a perfectly good hawking day ruined and a hawk upset by the actions

Wrapping Up

of someone who should know better. I will keep the list short of things that grate on my nerves but upsetting the hawk by walking close behind it, flushing quarry when the hawk is nowhere close, making so much noise that all the quarry disappears long before we get in range and, by far the worst, telling me what I am doing wrong are all on there. Guests get a free ride once or twice until they know better but repeat offenders are quietly avoided for future hawking trips.

If things are not going the way the falconer planned, guests would be wise not to offer advice or suggestions. Other falconers out with any experience will remember the same sorts of situations and recall that it takes time, often later when things have calmed down, to reflect quietly on what went wrong and how to put it right for the next time. They will sympathize with the falconer and keep opinions to themselves unless asked for them.

Recovering Lost Hawks

Many hawks are lost in ways that could have and should have been prevented. Generally, when a hawk is lost, some of the blame at least lies with the falconer. This happens when hawks are flown overweight, without telemetry or close to roads or rivers that are difficult to cross. One hawk, flown very low in weight, failed to get across a wide river and ran out of energy half way across. As it floated downstream, a Bald Eagle snatched it off the water and flew off with it. Many mishaps can be prevented by the hawk being obedient in the field. A hawk that returns quickly to the falconer when called can be taken out of the air before danger develops. If an eagle appears, the hawk is called down. If it is getting late and Great Horned Owls start moving, it is time to get the hawk down and to go home.

Regardless of how well trained the hawk is and how disciplined the falconer, the time will come when the hawk is lost. How to look for it varies somewhat depending on the species of hawk, weather and the circumstances under which it was lost. Assuming the hawk is flown with telemetry, which all hawks regardless of species should be, then one starts by following the signal as outlined in chapter three. Remember, height is your most important consideration if you lose the signal. If there is reason to suspect the telemetry has failed or the hawk has been lost from the mews or weathering yard through some sort of equipment malfunction then you have to do it the hard way and that means getting nature to help you. Crows, jays, blackbirds, starlings and other species of birds will mob hawks and let out alarm cries if one is close by. One must learn to listen for and follow such calls. Even birds in flight should be watched. I was looking once for a lost Ferruginous

Falconry: A Guide for Beginners

Hawk and happened to see a passing Seagull pause and make one small circle over a particular spot in a field, the ferruginous was right underneath where it circled.

It has been stated a number of times that hawks generally go downwind but in my experience that is not always the case unless the wind is particularly strong, and even then they sometimes just get out of the wind by flying low and go in a different direction. During the migration, if that is why they have flown away, they may travel with the wind but at other times of year unless you have good reason to think that they went downwind, don't spend all your time looking in that direction.

Longwings will generally fly far farther than shortwings and shortwings generally fly farther than broadwings. While broadwings and longwings do not typically try and hide themselves and may well sit out on exposed branches or on the top of buildings, shortwings will rarely sit so exposed. One can be within a few yards of a shortwing and yet walk right past it. Because telemetry sometimes fails and because hawks can be lost from the mews and weathering yard, all trained hawks should wear bells, even when they are not being flown. Shortwings and broadwings should wear tail bells as well as leg bells as even when sitting still, it is hard for them to keep the tail bell silent indefinitely.

Do not give up too quickly looking for a lost hawk. If she has killed and is feeding up she may well take an hour or more and then, especially if it is getting late, she will fly up into a tree or look for some other safe place to spend the night. I have been frustrated on more than one occasion to receive a phone call from a falconer saying they have lost their hawk and are now sitting at home licking their wounds when there is still daylight left. The best chance of finding the hawk is the day she was lost so do not give up until nightfall. If the hawk is found but refuses to return, tying the lure to the creance or using a dead animal that she is familiar with may persuade her to come down. If that fails, throwing the lure on a creance over a branch near her if she is in a tree and pulling the lure up to her level may make her come over to it. If she grabs it she can either be pulled with the lure out of the tree or if she refuses, just keep tugging at it and when she tries to fly away with it lower both her and the lure down. The surest method of getting a longwing which is refusing to come down out of a tree or off a building, etc. is to let it watch another hawk of the same or similar species eat. Longwings can be very jealous of another hawk feeding so flying another similar sized longwing nearby, even if it is only on a creance and over a short distance, can bring down hawk that is refusing even live lures. Such a method is not safe with other species. Sometimes however, one just has to wait the hawk out and that may

Wrapping Up

take some time. As long as the hawk stays nearby it will, eventually, get hungry enough to return but it may by that stage be so nervous that the usual lure line will bring it too close to the falconer. It is for that reason that a creance should always be kept handy so the falconer can toss the lure some distance away from him allowing a nervous hawk to land on it.

One can almost predict that some hawks will be lost because of the manner in which they were trained and flown. Many falconers resort to live lures believing either that it makes for a better hawk or that hawks cannot be trained without them. One falconer flying a tiercel I bred used such a tactic. When the pigeon he served for the hawk escaped under a railroad car, the hawk remained airborne, but the falconer had no way of calling it back. It eventually got bored, flew away, and was picked up the next day as a carcass that had been eaten by an eagle. The eagle alone didn't kill that hawk. When I talked to the falconer about what he thought went wrong, his feeling was that the hawk's loss could not have been prevented! Perhaps if he had trained the hawk better, it would, as its brother is, still be alive and going strong.

Saker Falcons are notorious for getting lost, especially in their first year. I have seen sakers so tame that nothing can make them bate from their perches or the fist, yet they become so upset in the field that they fly away as if they are wild hawks. Two of our Saker Falcons were out for three days under constant pursuit by us. One came back only when I flew its brother to the lure on a creance and he got jealous and came down and joined in. The second got so afraid of the falconer following it, that it flew away at the sight of the car she was driving! I got that hawk back, when purely out of luck, it landed on a fence post near an embankment. I was able to creep out of sight along the embankment and when close, I threw a pigeon on a line over the bank, and the hawk came straight to it. She allowed me to pick her up without any bother even though I'd never handled her before, but the moment she saw the falconer who had lost her approaching in the distance, she bated in a mad panic. Fortunately I had secured her at that point. That hawk went on to become one of the tamest, most reliable, and well liked hawks we ever flew.

When a hawk is inevitably lost and cannot be found, it is time to learn from the experience by taking a hard look at one's practices to discern if anything might have been done differently. I have lost, never to be recovered alive, five hawks in over 40 years of flying hawks and the number of individuals I have flown now numbers in the several hundred. The second hawk I ever owned, a haggard male European Kestrel, was the first one I lost. I'd had him six weeks, and although he

Falconry: A Guide for Beginners

was ¼ ounce overweight, some friends had come to see him fly. Like an idiot, I flew him. I never got him back, though I did find him breeding weeks later near the place I lost him, still with his bell attached. The second loss was a Prairie Falcon that I flew in a wind that was too high. The transmitter she wore was unreliable, and we never did get a signal. I never heard of her again, and I now always fly longwings with two transmitters. The third hawk I lost was a male gyr-barbary hybrid that spent the night out the first time he was flown free. Again, guests had come along to see him fly, and I had weakened to their pleas and flown him free when I knew I shouldn't have. At sunrise the next morning, he flew across a lonely desert road to be hit by a truck that was probably the only moving vehicle within 20 miles. I picked up his limp body seconds after he had been hit, as the sound of the truck disappeared into the distance. Perhaps it is not fair to call this one a loss as I would have got him back eventually if he hadn't been killed. The fourth loss was another male gyr-barbary hybrid that I trained in the high desert and did not acclimate to the new area to which I had relocated, an area much warmer with much more quarry available. The hawk went up on the soar the first time he was released and went over a mountain range. I never did catch up with him by using telemetry, but weeks later, his carcass was found next to a pond where he had been killed by some other predator. The fifth loss was a sakret that was flown slightly overweight and was also run over while I was tracking him as he went fly-about, ignoring my calls for him to return. The telemetry signal went dead while he was out of sight about a mile away from me and I only found out several days later what had happened when his body was handed into a wildlife center and they called the number on the reward tag he carried. He had been found by the side of a road. I had flown that hawk for seven years and he was like a member of the family, and I still miss him today. Because all of those losses were preventable, I take the blame for them, as any falconer should. Only by assuming blame can the same thing be prevented from happening again. This also applies to hawks that die while in a falconer's care. One must face up to and learn from the lessons that are apparent in order to avoid repeating a bad experience.

Since telemetry has revolutionized falconry, hawks that are lost can now be tracked and relocated even if not recovered. However, telemetry is only as good as the operator who uses it. I once chased a hawk belonging to a friend, using his telemetry, only to have the receiver batteries die when we were miles from the nearest town. He had not changed them in two years and had no spares with him! Some falconers try to save a few dollars by buying the cheapest transmitters

Wrapping Up

or receivers available. A good telemetry set will cost around $1,000. If a hawk is flown for 10 years, that is $100 a year. That, to me at least, is a good investment. For a purchased hawk, each time it is recovered using telemetry, the purchase price of the hawk can be deducted from the price of the telemetry. My telemetry has paid for itself many times over. If properly cared for, receivers will last a long time, I am still using one I purchased secondhand in 1998! I owe it thousands of dollars for the hawks it has helped me recover.

The Future

Where falconry will be in the future is anyone's guess. I can envision a time in the not too distant future when we fly with our trained hawks, at least our longwings and eagles, as they pursue their quarry, in some form of microlight aircraft as my friend Scott Mason has already begun with paragliders in Nepal. Although not actually hawking while flying with his hawks he has shown that the possibility is there. In the U.S., the West really is still wide open and largely unexplored for falconers. Coyotes, cranes, geese and other quarry rarely utilized could provide thrilling sport for eagles and large longwings as they are followed in flight by the falconer in a microlight aircraft. I would like to see out of the hood flights with longwings receive greater attention. Hawking with longwings in the U.S. has focused almost exclusively on waiting-on flights but with so much open ground, out of the hood flights are entirely possible. We would have to work with the various authorities to make some quarry species available for their sporting properties alone but where such species, such as gulls and geese are common, this might be possible. Crows are already available as a quarry in most states and provide great flights where the ground is open enough. I would also like to see Harris' Hawks flown more at game birds. While quail, pheasants and occasionally partridge are being taken, few falconers take the time to teach their Harris' Hawks the techniques required to bring such species to bag on long distance, two and three stage flights.

In other countries, particularly the Arab states, where quarry is becoming scarce, some falconers are turning their attention to racing their longwings with prizes for the owner of the fastest hawk. New training techniques are used to get the hawks fit including the use of lures dragged behind radio controlled aircraft. While I feel sympathy for these falconers, trying to make the most of a bad situation, I hope falconry in the U.S. doesn't go too far down that road. We still have plenty of places to go hawking, access to wild taken hawks and any number of captive-bred hawks of various species. While we continue to enjoy this freedom we should make the most of it and not get caught up too much in alternative methods of satisfying our need and desire to work with birds of prey.

May I make a plea here to all practicing falconers and especially to those just coming into the sport to remember that we are merely the latest generation to practice falconry. The history we have should be cherished, the talented falconers that went before us honored and respected. In this day and age, some seem to think we are superior to those falconers who have gone before or even to those around us. But while we may have captive breeding and telemetry and deep freezers for hawk food, all of which make our life easier, the basic relationship between a hawk and a falconer is still the same as it was 4000 years ago when falconry began. I would like to think that falconers who come after us will look back on our generation with respect for what we accomplished, and I would hope that the falconers of today will treat those who went before us in a like manner.

Finally, for the sake of our children, some of whom will hopefully follow in our footsteps and for the sake of any future falconers entering the sport in other ways, I urge the practicing falconers of our time to teach and show respect for the hawks we fly, the quarry we pursue, and for other people both inside and outside the sport. Thus the falconer seen carrying a hawk on the fist while pursuing our ancient pastime will hopefully remain as respected as he has been since the sport's beginnings, many centuries ago.

Wrapping Up

The future of falconry. My sons Ethan and Ryan with their Lanner Falcons.

Falconry: A Guide for Beginners

Suggested Reading

Beebe, F.L., & Webster, Jr., H.M., <u>North American Falconry and Hunting Hawks</u>, Western Sporting, 2013, 9th edition, 8 ½" x 11", hard bound, dust wrapper, 2 Volumes, Slip Case, 832 pages, hundreds of images: color plates and illustrations. Contents: Front Matter: Acknowledgements, Dedication to Frank Lyman Beebe, Foreword by Jim Enderson, Introduction: So You Want to be a Falconer by Harold Melvin Webster, Jr.; Forty-eight Chapters in five Sections: Introduction to North American Falconry (11 Chapters), The Broadwings (5 Chapters), The Shortwings (6 Chapters), The Longwings (11 Chapters), Further Reading (15 Chapters); Six Appendices: The Hawks of Falconry, Anatomy of a Raptor, Glossary, Bibliography, References, Anglo-Indian Hood Chart with Patterns and Index.

Beebe, F.L., *A Falconry Manual*, Hancock House, 2008, 5 ½" x 8 ½," perfect bound, b/w photographs & sketches, 197 pages.

Blaine, G., <u>Falconry</u>, Coch-y-Bonduu Books, 2002, hard bound, dust wrapper, b/w photographs and illustrations.

Brewer, G., *Buteos and Bushytails*, GLB Publications, 1995, 8 ½" x 11," hard bound, gold gilt cover & spine, b/w photographs & sketches, 135 pages.

California Hawking Club, <u>Apprentice Study Guide</u>, Western Sporting, 2009, 8 ½" x 11," spiral bound, b/w photographs & sketches, 122 pages.

California Hawking Club, <u>Apprentice Manual</u>, Western Sporting, 2004, 8 ½" x 11," saddle stitched, b/w photographs & sketches, 48 pages.

Chindgren, S., <u>The Art of Hawking Sage Grouse</u>, House of Grouse Publishing, 2018, 12 ½" x 11," hard bound, dust wrapper, color photographs and artwork, 188 pages.

Suggested Reading

Clark, W.S. & Wheeler, B.K., *Hawks of North America*, (Peterson Field Guide), Houghton Mifflin Co., 2001, 5" x 7 ½," durable plasticated cloth cover, color plates showing species color morphs, distribution maps, color photographs & sketches throughout, 320 pages.

Clark, W.S. & Wheeler, B.K., *A Photographic Guide to the Hawks of North America*, Princeton University Press, 2003, 6 ½" x 9 ½," perfect bound, color plates, 190 pages.

Coulson, J. and T., *Harris' Hawk Revolution*, Parabuteo Publishing, 2012, hard bound, pictorial color cover, dust wrapper, color photographs, 20 chapters, literature cited, index, 672 pages.

Ford, E., *Falconry, Art and Practice*, Blandford Publishing, 1992, hard bound, 7 ½" x 10", color and black and white photographs plus artwork, 191 pages.

Derbyshire M., *Out of the Hood*, Coch-y-Bonduu Books, 2017, hard bound, dust wrapper, b/w photographs.

Fox, N., *Understanding the Bird of Prey*, Hancock House, 1995, 8 ½" x 11," hardbound, pictorial color cover, b/w photographs & sketches, color section, 375 pages.

Glasier, P., *As the Falcon Her Bells*, William Heinemann Ltd., 1963, 6' x 9", hard bound, dust wrapper, b/w photographs and illustrations.

Glasier, P., *Falconry and Hawking*, Batsford Publishing, 1998, 3rd edition, 8" x 10," hardbound, dust wrapper, b/w photographs & sketches, color section, 352 pages.

Hollinshead, M. 1993 *Hawking Ground Quarry*, Hancock House, 1993, 5 ½" x 8 ½," hard bound, cloth cover, color section, 167 pages.

Kimsey, B.A. & Hodge, J., *Falconry Equipment*, Kimsey & Hodge Publications, 2007, 4th printing, 8 ½" x 11," perfect bound, b/w sketches, 178 pages.

Loft, J., *A Merlin for Me*, 2006, 2nd edition, Privately Published, 6" x 8 ¾", hard bound, dust wrapper, b/w illustrations, 310 pages.

Falconry: A Guide for Beginners

Mavrogordato, J. G., *A Falcon in the Field*, Western Sporting, 2005, revised American edition, 7" x 10", hard bound, dust wrapper, color artwork throughout, 269 pages.

Mavrogordato, J. G., *A Hawk for the Bush*, Western Sporting, 2005, revised American edition, 7" x 10", hard bound, dust wrapper, color artwork throughout, 269 pages.

McDermott, M., *The Imprint Accipiter II, Including Tame Hacking*, Western Sporting, 2009, 2nd edition, 6" x 9," hard bound, gold gilt cover/spine, dust wrapper, color photographs throughout, 273 pages.

McElroy, H. 2008, *Desert Hawking IV*, Privately Published, 2008, 1st edition, 8 ¾" X 11", hardbound, 368 pages, 327 illustrations: color photographs, drawings and artwork.

McGranaghan, L., *The Red-tailed Hawk, A Complete Guide to Training and Hunting North America's Most Versatile Game Hawk*, Privately Published, 2007, 8 ½" x 11," soft bound, dust wrapper, b/w photographs & sketches, color section, 187 pages.

Michell, E.B., *The Art & Practice of Hawking*, 1900, Methlien & Co, London, Photogravures by GE Lodge & illustrations, 304 pages. (Subsequent editions printed: 1959, 1962, 1964, 1967, 1969, 1971, 1972, & 1975.)

Mullenix, M., *American Kestrels in Modern Falconry*, Western Sporting, 2004, 3rd expanded edition, 6" x 9," hard bound, dust wrapper, b/w photographs & sketches, hood patterns, 140 pages.

Nelson, J.W., *Hoods, Hooding and Hoodmaking*, Western Sporting, 2016, 8 ½" x 11," hard bound, 3 Major Sections: Hoods, Training to the Hood & Hoodmaking, 23 chapters, 100s of b/w photographs & sketches, 5 appendices, index, hood fitting chart & patterns, 592 pages.

Oakes, W., *The Falconer's Apprentice, A Guide to Training the Red-tailed Hawk*, EagleWing Publishing, 2001, 5 ¼" x 8," perfect bound, b/w photographs, 173 pages.

Suggested Reading

Oakes, W., *Beginners Circle, A Collection of American Falconry Magazine*, Articles from 1996 to 2003, EagleWing Publishing, 2006, perfect bound, 5 ¼" x 8," 170 pages.

Oliphant, L., *Developing the Modern Gamehawk*, The Four-week Window and Other Natural Approaches, Privately Published, 2015, 8 ½" x 10 ¾"," hard bound, 15 chapters, appendices, references, 164 pages.

Perkins, D., *Understanding Goshawks*, D.A.P. Consulting Inc., 2008, 8 ½" x 10 ¾", hard bound, color photographs, 179 pages.

Roy III, J., *Dirt Hawking, A Rabbit and Hare Hawker's Guide*, Hancock House, 2010, 5 ½" x 8 ½," hard bound, pictorial color cover, color section, 304 pages.

Roy III, J., *Duck Hawking, and the Art of Falconry*, Hancock House, 2004, 5 ½" x 8 ½," hard bound, pictorial color cover, color section, 320 pages.

Stevens, R., *Observations on Modern Falconry*, Hancock House , 6" x 9", hard bound, 114 pages.

Stevens, R., *The Taming of Genghis*, Hancock House, 6" x 9", hard bound, 129 pages.

Upton, R., Falconry, *Principles & Practice*, A&C Black, London, 1991, hard bound.

Turner, R., *Gamehawk*, Drawings by Haslen, A., Privately Published, 1991, 5 ¾" x 8 ¼", hard bound, dust wrapper, 144 pages.

Walker, A., *The Encyclopedia of Falconry*, The Derrydale Press, 1999, 8" x 10," hard bound, dust wrapper, b/w photographs & sketches, color section, 170 pages.

Twenty-one Contributing Authors, *The Complete Merlin, The Merlin and Red-headed Falcon in Falconry*, Western Sporting, 2018, 8 ½" x 11," hard bound, dust wrapper, color plates and b/w sketches by Ron D. Digby, 400 pages.

Falconry: A Guide for Beginners

Woodruff, B., *Trapping Essentials, An Illustrated Guide to Trapping Raptors*, Western Sporting, 2008, 7" x 10," perfect bound, b/w photographs & sketches, 197 pages.

Standard

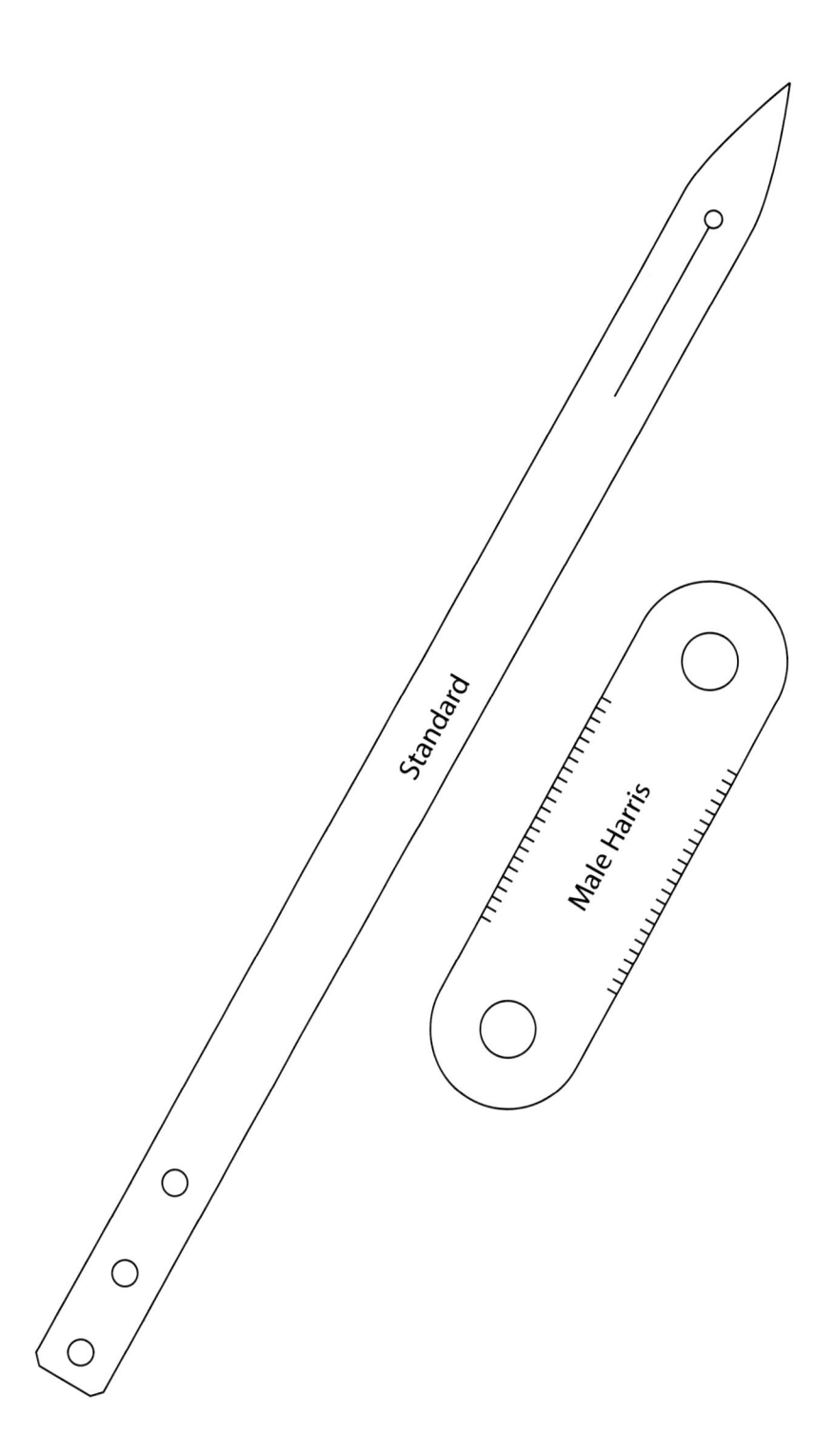

Male Harris

Large

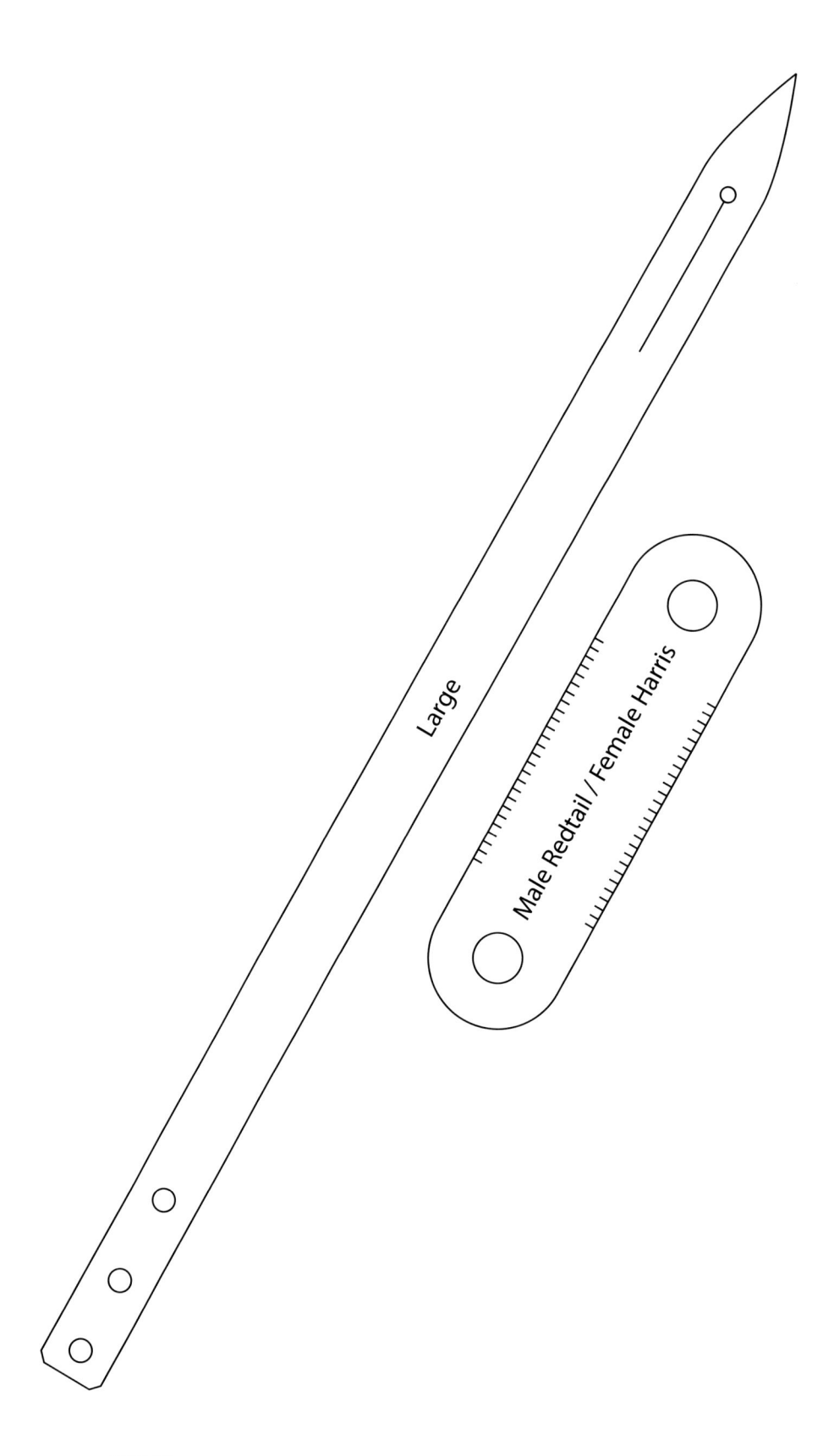

Male Redtail / Female Harris

Heavy Duty

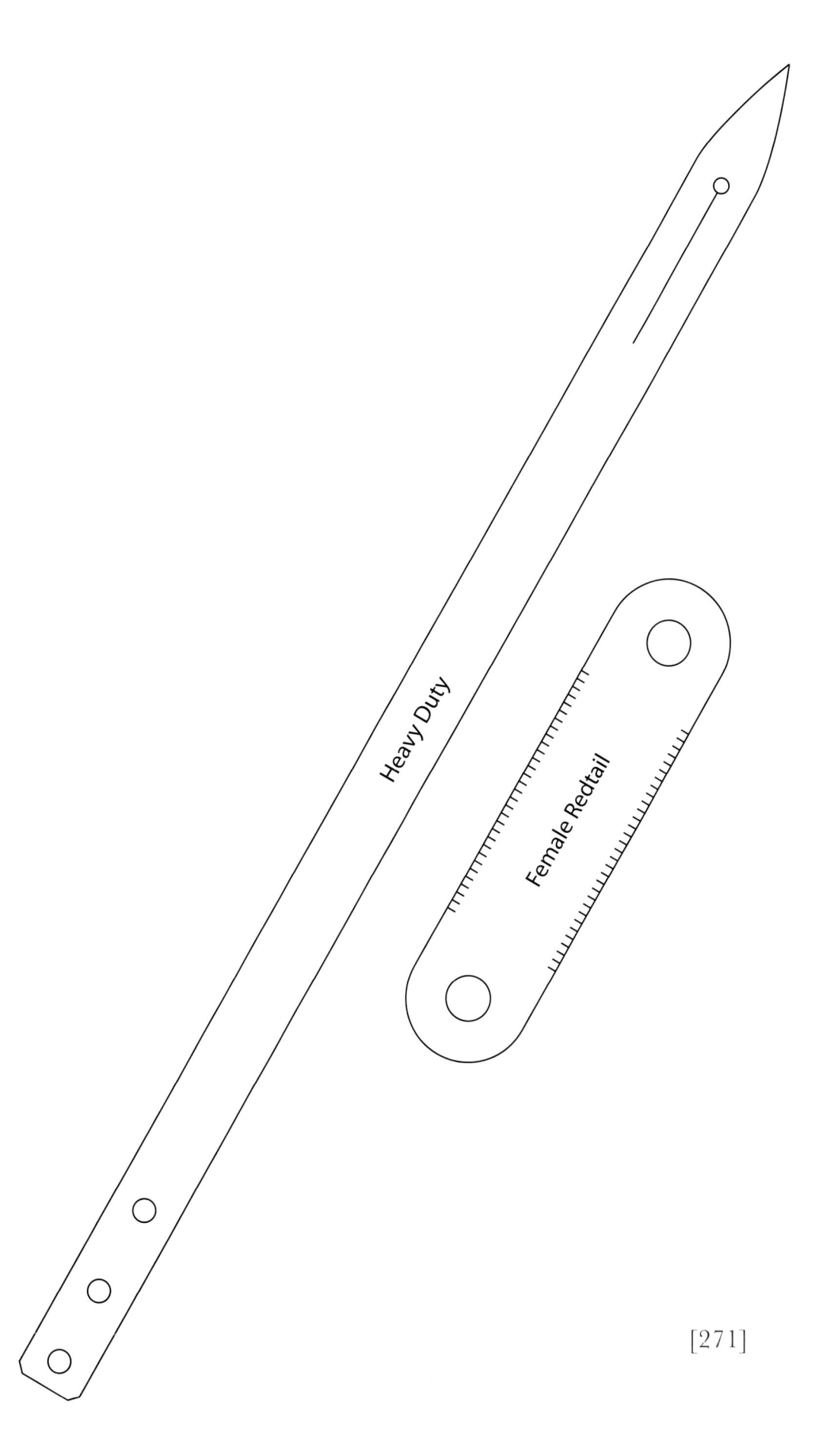

Female Redtail